Empire in Waves

SPORT IN WORLD HISTORY

Edited by Susan Brownell, Robert Edelman, Wayne Wilson, and Christopher Young

This University of California Press series explores the story of modern sport from its recognized beginnings in the nineteenth century to the current day. The books present to a wide readership the best new scholarship connecting sport with broad trends in global history. The series delves into sport's intriguing relationship with political and social power, while also capturing the enthusiasm for the subject that makes it so powerful.

Empire in Waves

A POLITICAL HISTORY OF SURFING

Scott Laderman

UNIVERSITY OF CALIFORNIA PRESS

BERKELEY LOS ANGELES LONDON

University of California Press, one of the most distinguished university presses in the United States, enriches lives around the world by advancing scholarship in the humanities, social sciences, and natural sciences. Its activities are supported by the UC Press Foundation and by philanthropic contributions from individuals and institutions. For more information, visit www.ucpress.edu.

University of California Press
Berkeley and Los Angeles, California

University of California Press, Ltd.
London, England

© 2014 by The Regents of the University of California

Library of Congress Cataloging-in-Publication Data

Laderman, Scott, 1971–
 Empire in waves : a political history of surfing / Scott Laderman.
  p. cm. — (Sport in the world ; 1)
 Includes bibliographical references and index.
 ISBN 978-0-520-27910-0 (hardcover : alk. paper) — ISBN 978-0-520-27911-7 (pbk. : alk. paper)
 1. Surfing—History. 2. Surfing—Political aspects. I. Title.
GV840.S8L33 2014
797.3′2—dc23

2013032583

Manufactured in the United States of America

23 22 21 20 19 18 17 16 15 14
10 9 8 7 6 5 4 3 2 1

For Izzy and Sam

CONTENTS

Acknowledgments

I had the privilege of growing up near the beach in California. I learned to surf in Santa Monica, where I was born, and spent countless hours chasing waves up and down the coast. After high school I moved north, enjoying a couple of years in Santa Cruz before leaving for the Bay Area, where I spent much of my free time surfing at Ocean Beach in San Francisco. I now live about as far from the ocean as one can live in the United States. Yet I still regularly surf. As ridiculous as it may sound, my adopted hometown of Duluth, Minnesota, enjoys probably the best waves in the Midwest. It may be colder, less consistent, and smaller than California, but I still find the pleasure and solace in Lake Superior that I found in my younger years in the Pacific. Surfing, in other words, has been important to me for the better part of my life. As has history. I first consciously began to conceptualize *Empire in Waves* in 1993, when, as a university student, I spent the summer as an editorial intern at Orange County–based *Surfer* magazine. It was a tough commute from L.A., particularly when waiting tables at night, but what an experience. I worked with great people, joined the editors for periodic surf breaks, and claimed my first publication—a brief article on a Pearl Jam benefit for Aaron Ahearn, a young surfer and sailor in the U.S. Navy who was disciplined for going AWOL and blowing the whistle on the Navy's practice of dumping garbage offshore. I was also, at that time, becoming increasingly active in human rights issues. I soon found myself presented with an intellectual conundrum. As an activist I knew a fair bit about Indonesia and its occupation of East Timor. As a surfer I knew a lot about Indonesia but nothing about the occupation of East Timor. Why? My attempt to answer that question represents the origins of this book.

Not many people have the opportunity to make a living by combining their personal and academic interests. I recognize my good fortune and the debt I owe to those many friends and colleagues who made it possible. I want to first thank John Hamlin, Eileen Zeitz, and the University Education Association for their seemingly inexhaustible energy and assistance in trying times. And I thank Sue Maher, dean of the College of Liberal Arts at the University of Minnesota, Duluth (UMD), for her moral and financial support. I am also indebted for research assistance to the Society for Historians of American Foreign Relations; the Graduate School, the McKnight Arts and Humanities Endowment, and the Imagine Fund of the University of Minnesota; and the Office of the Executive Vice Chancellor for Academic Affairs at UMD.

Research for this project has required the use of sources that are not the typical fare of historians, and numerous people helped me locate and access them in recent years. I am grateful to Barry Haun, Becky Church, Dick Metz, and Tom Pezman at the Surfing Heritage Foundation (now the Surfing Heritage and Culture Center) in San Clemente, California; Gary Sahagen at the International Surfing Museum in Huntington Beach, California; and Craig Baird at Surf World in Torquay, Victoria, Australia. Craig was also a generous host during my stay in Torquay, having me over for dinner and taking me out for a much-needed surf. Al Hunt has perhaps the world's largest collection of surfing magazines, and he generously provided me with access to his extensive archive. Al and his wife Andrea also invited me into their home in New South Wales, where they introduced me to Paul Scott. I thank all three of them, as well as Craig, for the kindness they showed this traveling American.

Both Craig and Al assisted me as I collected the illustrations for this book. So, too, did Verity Chambers, Cori Schumacher, Maria Cerda, Peter Simons, Stu Nettle at *Swellnet*, Luke Kennedy at *Tracks* magazine, Jeff Divine at the *Surfer's Journal*, Jeff Hall at A-Frame Media, Sunshine Carter in the UMD Library, and Dustin Thompson in the UMD Visualization and Digital Imaging Lab. They have my deep appreciation.

I visited several archives in Hawai'i. I am grateful for the assistance I received at the Bishop Museum from Charley Myers, Tia Reber, and Ju Sun Yi; at the Hawaii State Archives from Gina S. Vergara-Bautista and Luella Kurkjian; and at the University of Hawai'i at Manoa from Dore Minatodani, Jodie Mattos, and Sherman Seki. My friend Hoku Aikau was a wonderful host during my Hawaiian stay, as was Ed Coates, who lent me equipment and took me out for some small but fun waves near Waikiki. In California, Barbara Hall at the Margaret Herrick Library of the Academy of Motion Picture Arts and Sciences was, as always, tremendously helpful. So, too, was the Herrick Library's desk staff and, up north, that of the Pacific Film Archive at the University of California, Berkeley. At the National Archives II in College Park, Maryland, I was aided by Edward O. Barnes and David A. Pfeiffer. Cory Czajkowski helped me navigate the Pan Am papers at the University of Miami. Sue Hodson of the Huntington Library in San Marino, California, and Clint Pumphrey at Utah State University helped me from a long distance with their institutions' Jack London materials. Kristi Rudelius-Palmer and Mary Rumsey made possible my research in the Human Rights Library of the University of Minnesota, Twin Cities. And Kay Westergren, the interlibrary loan specialist at the University of Minnesota, Duluth, ably and amiably fielded my many requests.

Numerous scholars read or heard pieces of this book as conference or seminar papers or draft chapters. I thank Chris Endy, Sayuri Guthrie-Shimizu, Andy Johns, Paul Kramer, Dennis Merrill, Mark Rice, Brad Simpson, Mike Sunnafrank, and Glen Thompson for their insightful comments. Dion Georgiou and the participants in the Sport and Leisure History Seminar at the Institute for Historical Research in London provided excellent feedback and questions. So, too, did Diane Negra, Stephen Boyd, Jack Thompson, and several others at University College Dublin; Scott Lucas and Michele Aaron at the University of Birmingham; Kimberly Marsh and the participants in the Travel Cultures Seminar at the University of Oxford; and Tony Collins, Matthew Taylor, and their colleagues at the International Centre for Sports History and Culture at De Montfort University. In 2012, I had the good fortune to spend three weeks in Japan as a representative of the Organization of American Historians. Danielle McGuire, Priscilla Wald, and Sachiyo Shindo provided helpful criticism of my work. Rumi Yasutake provided me with a rich exchange on Alexander Hume Ford. And Yuka Tsuchiya, Yujin Yaguchi, Nao Nomura, and Hiroaki Matsusaka—among too many others to name here—were gracious hosts and the source of hours of stimulating conversation.

I thank the surfers who allowed me to formally interview them: Tom Carroll, Tom Curren, Mike Hynson, Dick Metz, Martin Potter, and Shaun Tomson. Like the others mentioned in these acknowledgments, they may not agree with everything (or anything) in this book, but their willingness to meet and speak with me attests to their commitment to a fuller understanding of the pastime to which they have devoted their lives. The same goes for those many people who have patiently responded to my queries and humored and assisted me during my research. I thank, among others (including some already named), Doug Booth, Greg Borne, Brittany Bounds, Clifton Evers, David Theo Goldberg, Alex Leonard, Jess Ponting, and Isaiah Helekunihi Walker.

I worked with a dream team at the University of California Press. Niels Hooper and Kim Hogeland could not have been better editors. Kate Warne, Pamela Polk, Jamie Thaman, and Michael Bohrer-Clancy expertly guided the manuscript through production. In addition to an anonymous referee, I thank Mark Bradley, Susan Brownell, Chris Endy, and Chris Young for their wonderful feedback as readers. The same goes for the representative of the press's faculty board. I am grateful to Chris Axelson for generously allowing me the gratis use of his photograph for the book's cover. And Carol Roberts once more created my index. There is a reason I keep asking her.

Finally, my family. My siblings-in-law, Robert and Paul Torres and Molly Carter-Torres, were always quick to lend me a car, put me up, and give me equipment and head out for a surf during my stays in California. My parents-in-law, Ernie and Karen Torres and Bernadette Torhan, showed me innumerable kindnesses as I was conducting research and writing. My mother, Jackie Laderman; brothers, Mark and Greg Laderman; and sister, Mary Ann Corbett, continue to be a deep wellspring of love and support. John Hatcher and I may not be related, but we might as well be. His friendship and humor, both in and out of the water, have brought me immense joy when it is needed most. He is also an incisive critic. And what can I say about Jill Torres, my partner for over twenty years. Words cannot begin to express how much she means to me. For always being there, and for bringing me my greatest work—Izzy and Sam, whom I love more than anything and to whom I dedicate this book—I remain eternally grateful.

A Political History of Surfing

RAFAEL LIMA CAME FOR THE WORK but returned for the waves. A thirty-year-old Cuban American journalist and screenwriter, Lima found El Salvador much to his liking. The surf at La Libertad, the coastal town roughly twenty miles from the capital, was "clean, fast, [and] uncrowded," he wrote in a photograph-studded piece for *Surfer* magazine. El Salvador provided "some of the best waves in Central America," including a "long, howling, rock-strewn, hollow point break" that, with a six-foot swell that "held up all morning," left him and his companions "[s]urfed out."[1] Accounts touting the discovery of waves at such and such a place are hardly unusual in the surfing literature. They are, in fact, the bread and butter of the genre. What distinguished Lima's travelogue from others, however, was both its timing and the nature of its author's employment. The year was 1982—deep into the Salvadoran regime's violent crackdown on peasants, union organizers, human rights activists, and other civil society elements—and Lima was returning to the country after a stint training some of the paramilitary forces carrying out much of the regime's repression.

The former martial arts editor of *Soldier of Fortune* magazine, Lima had, by the time of his excursion, already developed quite a résumé. He had spent time in Guatemala in the employ of an American company instructing that country's right-wing militias in "anti-insurgency and light weapons." He had then worked for "one of the largest landowners in El Salvador, training a small army to combat guerrillas on the huge cotton plantations."[2] Now he was "back to go surfing." True, he had surfed in Central America during his previous visits to the region, using "my Indians"—a term Lima repeatedly deploys—to maintain security while he sought temporary solace in the waves.[3] But this trip was different. This one was for pleasure.

The politics of Lima's account were predictable. El Salvador was "a country gone mad with bloodletting," he wrote, leaving little doubt as to who was responsible. The left-wing insurgents were the "hostile attackers," while those he trained to "defend and protect themselves" possessed "[f]aces lined with years of torment and hunger," "[f]aces that would rather farm and raise children than fight."[4] But Lima was no angel. There was a young "whore" he berated for her gold-toothed ugliness, telling her in English that "[t]his revolution is prettier than you are."[5] And his story dripped with the hypermasculine sensibilities of the Reagan era, employing militaristic language to describe the act of wave riding: "guiding a high-tech projectile at maximum cruising speed," "honing in on a long-distance target," "stringing staccato explosions of power with long-range speed bursts," "blasting his moving target with pinpoint accuracy."[6] Given the contentiousness of U.S. foreign policy during the Reagan era, it is not surprising that Lima's account evoked outraged responses. "[P]lease do not publish any more articles by soldiers of fortune who deal in death for the highest bidder and who happen to surf," a Californian wrote in one of several critical letters to *Surfer.*[7] Others found nothing to criticize. "There might be a lot of political unrest and foreign influence in the internal affairs here," conceded a surfer serving in the U.S. Army in Honduras, "but we are trying to modernize and stabilize the situation at hand."[8]

The case of Rafael Lima is certainly unusual. Most surfers were not involved in training the paramilitaries or death squads of Latin America. Most, in fact, paid them little heed. The Lima account does, however, starkly reveal the ways that surfers, as people and as tourists, inevitably maneuvered through an inherently political world. Surfing is of course ultimately about pleasure. People ride waves because it is fun. Gliding across the face of a moving mass of water, turning off the top of a folding lip, tucking into a barrel: these feel good, so much so that surfers often speak of the wave-riding experience as something akin to a spiritual quest. Yet pleasure, like "the personal" once highlighted by the women's movement, is political. We must thus come to appreciate surfing in political terms. Although surfing may involve a specific person riding a specific wave at a specific beach, those waves travel vast distances, just like the surfers who set out across the planet to ride them. Surfing, in other words, is a natural global phenomenon, and it enjoys a rich and complex global history. It is the goal of *Empire in Waves* to tease from this history some of the politics inherent to the enduring quest for aquatic pleasure.

．． ．

While surfing was a pastime enjoyed for centuries in ancient Hawaiʻi, it was nearly extinguished following Hawaiians' contact with the West. *Empire in Waves* begins, as does modern surfing, with an examination of this decline— as well as the early years of surfing's revival and globalization—in the context of American empire-building. In the nineteenth century, Congregationalist missionaries endeavored to remake much of Hawaiian society and culture as part of a general Western effort to "civilize" the barbarous residents of the island chain while, at the same time, dispossessing them of their native lands. Such was the missionaries' success in uplifting the "infant race" that, one contemporaneous observer noted, by the early 1890s it had become exceedingly difficult to "find a surf-board outside of our museums and private collections." The imperial project would shift, however, following Washington's annexation of the Hawaiian Islands just several years later. As chapter 1 demonstrates, surfing, in the first decades of the twentieth century, underwent a surge of popularity as boosters such as Alexander Hume Ford sought to transform Hawaiʻi into a "white man's state," turn Waikiki into a beckoning paradise for the growing number of Pacific tourists, and establish islands more broadly as a crucial outpost of American global power. No longer a disreputable pastime of licentious natives, surfing was used to sell Hawaiian tourism—and white settlement—in popular magazines and promotional literature, in the process strengthening the grip of the haole class over the native population with whom the sport originated.

If surfing had become thoroughly Americanized by the first few decades of the twentieth century—though always, as Isaiah Helekunihi Walker has shown, in the context of ongoing resistance from the Hawaiian people— Americans increasingly sought to make it global.[9] Ironically enough, it was two Hawaiian men, the legendary lifeguard George Freeth and the five-time Olympic medalist Duke Kahanamoku, who perhaps most famously helped plant the roots of global surf culture. But they were not alone. By the 1950s and 1960s, thriving communities of surfers could be found not only in the United States but in Australia, South Africa, New Zealand, France, and Great Britain. Surfing, moreover, entered the commercial and political mainstream. Hollywood developed a fascination with Southern California beach culture, churning out such motion pictures as the *Gidget* series and the popular comedies of Frankie Avalon and Annette Funicello, while those charged with crafting U.S. foreign policy gave the surfing lifestyle a bit part in official Cold War cultural diplomacy.

One of the hallmarks of surf culture in the post–World War II era has been its close relationship to Third World tourism. In this respect, surfing has mirrored U.S. foreign policy, as both were deeply concerned with the so-called peripheral states of the Cold War, and both placed primacy in the exploitation of those nations' resources. For the U.S. government, it was the oil, copper, rubber, and other minerals and commodities desired by American corporations; for surfers, it was the waves. Yet where Washington was concerned that revolutionary nationalism might interfere with America's grand strategy of global capitalism, surfers' concerns generally began and ended at the water's edge. For them, what happened on land—the national liberation movements of Africa, the counterinsurgency warfare of Central America, the state-sponsored repression of Southeast Asia—was of little serious concern. The waves were all that mattered.

If the Hollywood beach films of the 1950s and 1960s hinted at surfing's commercial ambitions, the growing surf exploration of the postwar era, such as that portrayed in Bruce Brown's *The Endless Summer* (1966), was at the heart of surf culture's more organic foundations. The advent of commercial jet travel in the 1950s, in particular, afforded surfers an opportunity to seek out new wave frontiers. A growing number of haoles brought to Hawai'i by their military service began to call the islands home, while Mexico and other Latin American countries became favored stomping grounds for American surf travelers. Chapter 2 focuses on the growth of global surf tourism from the 1940s through the 1970s, viewing such tourism as an unofficial form of cultural diplomacy. Accompanying these jaunts, I argue, was the construction of an exceedingly simplistic surfing imagination. For the surf travelers of the post–World War II period, the political universe of the Cold War was banished from surfing's popular grand narrative. Surfers preferred to see themselves as pioneers navigating a world of bountiful waves and always-smiling locals who lived in lands uncomplicated by imperial concerns.

Whether they liked it or not, however, surfers—mostly young Westerners who routinely traveled where few other foreign tourists bothered to visit—inevitably found themselves enmeshed in the practical realities of U.S. foreign policy. This is perhaps truer of no place more than Indonesia, the vast archipelago north of Australia considered the premier surfing destination on the planet. What had, in the 1950s, been a leading Third World proponent of nonalignment in the broader Cold War struggle became, by the late 1960s, a staunch American ally in Washington's ideological competition with China and the Soviet Union. It was in 1965 and 1966 that Indonesia's neutralist Sukarno government was essentially overthrown in a U.S.-backed coup that culminated in the deaths of hundreds of thousands of people. In the decades that followed, Indonesia stood out as a leading recipient of U.S. military aid and diplomatic support, whether in Jakarta's brutal and consistent repression of internal dissent or in its 1975 invasion and genocidal occupation of East Timor. As chapter 3 examines, it was shortly after the massacres of the mid-1960s that Indonesia began to capture the attention of American and Australian surfers, who discovered on its thousands of islands some of the finest waves in the world. With the cooperation of the Suharto regime, which boosted international surfing contests and even sponsored an outer-island junket for visiting foreigners, surfers helped promote tourism across the island chain. Surfing magazines regularly published features on Indonesian "surfaris," while filmmakers captured the nation's waves and people in a host of productions. In such features, whether print or filmic, the nation was represented not as a site of dictatorship and state repression—which was how too many Indonesians experienced life in their country—but as an exotic paradise with primitive locals who welcomed the West's interest in their homeland. *Empire in Waves* examines both this discursive erasure and surfers' collaboration with the Indonesian authorities, illustrating how the touristic impulse that is virtually intrinsic to the sport of surfing has inevitably been imbued with political meaning.

Just as Indonesian repression was written out of surfing's popular grand narrative, so, too, was South African apartheid. For over two decades after *The Endless Summer* featured what it called the "perfect waves" of South Africa's Cape St. Francis as the film's apotheosis of surf travel (with, it must be noted, nary a word about the country's notorious system of racial segregation), young Americans and Australians ventured to the apartheid state to enjoy its rich coastal bounty. Nearly all of these young tourists were white; surfers of color who traveled to South Africa, such as the Hawaiian professionals Dane Kealoha and Eddie Aikau, were denied entry into restaurants or hotels and were technically prohibited from surfing on many of the country's finest beaches, which were reserved exclusively for those with fairer complexions. In the 1980s, a number of professional surfers decided to adhere to the sporting boycott called for by the global antiapartheid movement by forgoing international surfing contests in South Africa. The boycott movement generated considerable debate in the surfing community. Among South Africa's white minority were some of the most accomplished surfers in the world, and the nation's beaches had become globally famous for the superior quality of their waves. Nevertheless, to the boycott's proponents, forgoing participation in the South African leg of the surfing world tour was a morally necessary step in opposing racial oppression. The boycott's opponents, however, viewed such actions as an ill-advised politicization of what they considered an apolitical sport. Chapter 4 examines this historical epoch—a three-decade saga that culminated in surfing's discovery that it was not in fact above international politics—situating the debate over apartheid in the surfing community within the broader context of modern sport and global affairs.

Recognizing the confluence of politics and economic policy, *Empire in Waves* likewise explores the development of commercial surf culture and its relationship to global neoliberalism. What began as small outfits founded by surfers looking for ways to subsidize their wave-riding lifestyle had become, by the 1980s and 1990s, billion-dollar corporations with a retail presence throughout the industrialized world. Clothing brands such as Quiksilver, Billabong, and Rip Curl were increasingly found not only in traditional surf communities but also in inland malls from Topeka to Kuala Lumpur. By the close of the twentieth century, surf culture had indeed gone global. With billions of dollars at stake, it is little surprise that "non-endemic" corporations would seek to tap the surf market, and, by the early twenty-first century, the "organics" faced growing competition from Nike, Target, and—perhaps most bizarrely of all—the Abercrombie & Fitch subsidiary Hollister. Yet unexplored by scholars has been the extent to which the manufacture and assembly of surfwear products has been enabled by the neoliberal trade policies pursued by the United States and its industrial allies. In particular, the so-called "race to the bottom" that has mixed a minimal standard of environmental regulation with an abundant supply of low-wage workers has been at the heart of American efforts to promote "free trade." Clothing and apparel manufacturers have benefited enormously from this situation.

There has thus emerged a paradox in modern surf culture. On the one hand, surfing valorizes exploration not only for the potential discovery of waves in unspoiled paradises but also for the fostering of cross-cultural contact between surfers from the industrialized West and the millions of villagers throughout the littoral Third World. Inherent in these encounters has been a romanticization of the poor as living simple and happy lives, free of any desire for modernity. On the other hand, the corporations that have become associated with global surf culture both rely on and perpetuate that impoverished condition, fueling the "race to the bottom" by exploiting the surplus of laborers or the owners' capital mobility when those same Third World villagers seek higher wages and better working conditions. Chapter 5 explores these unresolved tensions.

·   ·   ·

Empire in Waves is by no means exhaustive. It is not intended to be *the* history of surfing. Rather, the book employs a number of important developments in modern surf culture to explore a series of premises: surfing is not a mindless entertainment but a cultural force born of empire (at least in its modern phase), reliant on Western power, and invested in neoliberal capitalism. Acceptance of even that first premise is hardly a given. Mentions of surfing far more often elicit amused chortles involving "cool dudes" and "gnarly waves" than they do serious contemplation. But, I argue, surfing—however rooted it may be in the individual pursuit of pleasure—has been a pastime impossible to divorce from the political universe in which it originated, spread, and took root. If modern surfing was born of conquest—a reasonable argument, I suggest, in light of America's unlawful annexation of the Hawaiian Islands in 1898—its global diffusion certainly owed a great debt to the imperial management necessitated by twentieth-century American power. It was not long before surfing's pleasurable beach culture emerged as a staple in the globalization of American life, whether through early tourism in Hawai'i and Latin America, the military diffusion of the sport to Japan and other oceanic locales, the Third World "surfaris" of young American travelers, or the global export of Hollywood beach films in the 1950s and 1960s. At the same time, surfing's relationship to American power has been detached from its popular association with discovery and pleasure. Yet it was the colonization of Hawai'i by the United States that rendered surfing American. It was American foreign policy, which favored elite-led capitalism over revolutionary socialism, that made the world safe for discovery by generations of surfers. And it was the global economic system exemplified by the "Washington consensus" that enabled the low-wage manufacture of surf culture's sartorial accoutrements. *Empire in Waves* sets out to trace this international history.

ONE

How Surfing Became American

THE IMPERIAL ROOTS OF MODERN SURF CULTURE

WHEN NATHANIEL B. EMERSON, the outgoing president of the Hawaiian Mission Children's Society, stood before an assembly of the organization in July 1892, he was full of praise for his missionary predecessors who had worked tirelessly to uplift the "infant race" populating "that fragment" of the Polynesian islands he now called home. Having overseen the "birth of a [Christian] nation," it had devolved upon this earlier generation of missionaries, Emerson maintained, "to swathe the tender limbs of the newborn, to counsel as to the nutriment suited to its earliest needs, to direct its first tottering footsteps, to give it the alphabet of learning, to initiate for it such intellectual, moral[,] and religious tuition as becomes a candidate for admission into the fraternity of nations." This was, to be sure, "a task beset with difficulties, imposing large responsibilities, and demanding great earnestness, devotion, and practical wisdom." But, Emerson assured his audience, "success" had been "attained."[1] Christian civilization had taken root in the Hawaiian archipelago.

Emerson was speaking before the congregated guests not to celebrate this heavenly victory, however. His immediate concern was of a much more worldly nature. He took to the podium that July day to defend his missionary predecessors—many of them the fathers and mothers of those assembled in the room—from charges that they had engineered the demise of a number of "noble" Hawaiian sports. The "children of nature" whom the proselytizers saw as their charges had developed a number of pastimes "worthy of perpetuation," Emerson believed. The fitness of "surf riding" and other activities to "develope [sic] and invigorate the frame and to impart and maintain a virile courage and endurance" was one, the outgoing president insisted, that "should be cultivated in every race."[2] Emerson was certainly right about surfing's invigorating qualities. But, to Hawaiians, it was about much more. From the selection of a tree out of which a board might be shaped to the interactions of the wave riders and spectators, surfing, which involved all strata of society—young and old, commoners and royalty, men and women— represented a ritualized set of practices at the core of what it meant to be Hawaiian. How shamefully misguided, therefore, that certain critics had seen fit to blame the missionaries for the decline of surfing and other sports, Emerson continued. He, for one, would have none of it. His predecessors "exercised no direct or appreciable influence" in "the death and retirement of Hawaii's ancient sports and games," he assured the audience. On the contrary, "they were utterly powerless to arrest the tendency towards the substitution of imported and foreign games for the worthy sports and exercises indige-nous to the soil and race."[3] The Hawaiian people, that is, had collectively chosen to no longer indulge their traditional pursuits. It was their choice. Prohibitions had not been imposed on them.

But Emerson's tutorial—in essence, that Hawaiians simply lost interest in a number of cultural activities as the annual Makahiki festival was discon-tinued, the kapu system was abolished, foreign games were introduced, and people's focus increasingly turned to war making—is much too exculpatory and self-serving.[4] He and his missionary predecessors bore no responsibility for the destruction of traditional Hawaiian culture, he suggested. They were not invaders or exploiters. The fault lay with the Hawaiians themselves. The missionaries of the early nineteenth century, according to this narrative, were a "dispensation of light" that had "wing[ed] its way as a new *Lono* [a Hawaiian deity] across the waters." They filled a "vacuum in Hawaii's social and religious institutions" following the death of Kamehameha in 1819, and the people embraced the Western arrivals with "enthusiasm."[5] The seeds of Christianity were planted, and, as they sprouted, "the old life, its worship, festivals, public games, and festivities with all the abuses that gathered about them" began to dissipate.

Surfing was among the casualties, Emerson said regretfully. Or so it ap-peared. "The sport of surf riding possessed a grand fascination," he noted, "and for a time it seemed as if it had the vitality to hold its own as a national pastime. There are those living, perhaps some present [in the audience], who remember the time when almost the entire population of a village would at certain hours resort to the sea-side to indulge in, or to witness, this magnifi-cent accomplishment. We cannot but mourn its decline." So great had been the retreat from this noble tradition that, Emerson continued, "to-day it is hard to find a surf-board outside of our museums and private collections."[6] While Emerson's accounting was perhaps an exaggeration, it is nevertheless true that the number of practitioners of the sport had fallen tremendously by the last decade of the nineteenth century.

Yet Emerson's lamentation for surfing's diminished popularity seems misguided. The problem had not been wave riding per se, he suggested. Rather, it was that surfing had "felt the touch of the new civilization." For those perplexed by the meaning of this message, Emerson offered clarification. "[A]s the zest of this sport was enhanced by the fact that both sexes engaged in it, when this practice was found to be discountenanced by the new majority, it was felt that the interest in it had largely departed—and this game too went the way of its fellows."[7] Emerson, in essence, wanted it both ways. Surfing was a healthy pastime, but it was one whose scantily clad practitioners, both male and female, horrified many proponents of "the new civilization," particularly in that wave riding served not only as a pleasurable endeavor in its own right but also as a form of sexual courtship.[8] For those being tutored in the modest ways of the missionaries' Christian deity, surfing was certain to meet with divine disapproval. Its practitioners were much too licentious. Wave riders thus faced a stark choice: immediate gratification—though with eternal damnation—or the immeasurable bounties of a heavenly future. Put that way, surfing would not have appeared to stand a chance.

Except that it did. While the number of Hawaiian surfers dropped precipitously as the nineteenth century unfolded, wave riding, as historian Isaiah Helekunihi Walker reminds us, did in fact continue.[9] It is true that surfing was witnessed by haoles much less frequently as the decades passed.[10] Given the economic changes that upended Hawaiian customs and the physical decimation of the Hawaiian people following the 1778 arrival of Captain James Cook, this is understandable. After all, the sandalwood, whaling, and sugar industries fundamentally reshaped Hawaiian society and leisure practices—there was far less time for surfing—while a population in the islands that David Stannard conservatively estimated as 800,000 prior to contact had been reduced, largely through the introduction of foreign pathogens for which Hawaiians enjoyed no immunity, to approximately 135,000 by 1823.[11] By the 1890s, the number of Hawaiians stood at fewer than 40,000.[12] Even if one were to accept that Stannard's pre-contact estimate is too high, as Andrew Bushnell has argued, this still represents a staggering loss of life.[13] Under such circumstances it seems obvious that the number of surfers would have decreased. Those that continued to ride the waves were survivors of not only the biological onslaught introduced by white contact but also a radically different labor system and the concerted efforts of at least some white missionaries to demonize a pastime they associated with barbarism and sexual indecency.

In this the Hawaiian people shared experiences similar to those of American Indians. This is hardly surprising. Most of the Protestant missionaries who arrived in Hawai'i in 1820 came from the United States, a polity occupying a considerable landmass whose indigenous population required decades of military pacification. Accompanying this imperial expansion was, more often than not, Christian proselytization. Indian peoples were assumed by the white invaders to be racial inferiors. The Americans thus set out to racially uplift the savages in their midst. This meant an effort to eradicate those cultural traditions that were a presumed mark of indigenous barbarism and replace them with Christianity. When Indian people were not simply killed outright, the invaders, nearly always projecting an image of unquestioned benevolence, sought to eliminate the use of native languages, the practices of native spirituality, and many of the basic structures of native society. Frivolity was frowned upon while industriousness was expected. These pious white Christians were, they insisted, only doing God's work. It was true that the settler population found itself greatly enriched as Indian peoples were dispossessed of most of their native lands.[14] But this was just a coincidence. Or so the story goes.

In Hawai'i it was much the same. Hiram Bingham, probably the most prominent leader of the missionary movement in the first half of the nineteenth century, was, as someone reared in New England, a product of that American worldview. Indeed, his detailed account of his experiences with the Hawaiian people closely mirrors the North American imperial literature of the era. Recalling his memorable "first intercourse with the natives," for example, Bingham, sounding much like those who first made contact with the Indian peoples of North America, found that

the appearance of destitution, degradation, and barbarism, among the chattering, and almost naked[,] savages, whose heads and feet, and much of their sunburnt swarthy skins, were bare, was appalling. Some of our number, with gushing tears, turned away from the spectacle. Others with firmer nerve continued their gaze, but were ready to exclaim, "Can these be human beings! How dark and comfortless their state of mind and heart! How imminent the danger to the immortal soul, shrouded in this deep pagan gloom! Can such beings be civilized? Can they be Christianized? Can we throw ourselves upon these rude shores, and take up our abode, for life, among such a people, for the purpose of training them for heaven?"

These were questions of the gravest import. The answer to all of them, Bingham happily assured his readers, was an emphatic yes.[15]

When Bingham contemplated the "idolaters of reprobate mind" he encountered during his Polynesian crusade, he perceived a fertile crop of Hawaiians begging for religious conversion.[16] But this would be about much more than Sunday worship. It would mean accepting the norms of white civilization, including modest (albeit impractical) dress, the abolition of gambling, and Christian notions of sexual propriety. All of these handicapped surfing, a sport best enjoyed free of sartorial encumbrance on which both Hawaiian men and women wagered.[17] So, too, did the missionaries' emphasis on constant work as a means of self-improvement. Recreational pursuits such as wave riding—the "most popular of all . . . pastimes with all ranks and ages," according to a nineteenth-century historian of the islands—suffered.[18] So would Hawaiians subscribe to these Christian precepts? Bingham and his contemporaries found, in time, a surprisingly receptive audience. They were undoubtedly aided by the ongoing decimation of the Hawaiian people. "Natives," wrote Lilikala Kameʻeleihiwa, "perceived that missionaries might give them eternal life and, more immediately, save them from the impact of the foreign diseases that were sweeping the Pacific."[19] Acceptance of the Christian deity, in other words, promised rewards in both this life and the next. There was a practical benefit to conversion. Not surprisingly, many did accept the Christian faith. But the disavowal of cultural practices such as wave riding was an entirely different matter.

. . .

The Protestant missionaries of nineteenth-century Hawaiʻi never directly prohibited surfing. Such a prohibition was not necessary. In the missionaries' effort to impose an entirely new worldview on the Hawaiian people, it was made abundantly clear that surfing and other traditional pastimes would only hinder the heathens' moral progress. And moral progress *was* imperative, they believed. Arriving on the Big Island in 1820, Lucia Ruggles Holman, the wife of missionary-physician Thomas Holman, was promptly greeted and welcomed by the Hawaiian royal family, which offered her and her companions "cocoanuts, bananas, plantains, breadfruit, sweet-potatoes, tarrow[,] and 2 hogs."[20] Still, notes historian Patricia Grimshaw, the young woman found herself horrified by "volcanic Kailua, where the chief attraction for Hawaiians, the surf, held no joy for the Americans."[21] The local people, Holman wrote to her sister, were deplorable "beyond description," having "sunk to the lowest depths of sin and depravity." They "appear to glory in what should be their greatest shame," she insisted. "There is no sin, the commission of which, disgraces them—indeed, there is nothing that disgraces them but work." Hawai'i seemed to lack any redeeming qualities. Even the fruits and vegetables "taste heathenish," complained the young missionary. Perhaps, Holman said hopefully, the "pleasant sunshine of the Gospel" could turn things around.[22]

It was a tall order. Sheldon Dibble, writing two decades after Holman, was repulsed by the "oppression, destitution, and ignorance" that greeted he and his fellow Christian soldiers. The Hawaiians' "degrading practices, their social condition[,] and their catalogue of crimes" left him appalled. This included their sporting activities. The "evils" that resulted from "[p]laying on the surfboard" and other amusements were too legion to sufficiently describe. "Some lost their lives thereby, some were severely wounded, maimed and crippled; some were reduced to poverty, both by losses in gambling and by neglecting to cultivate the land; and the instances were not few in which they were reduced to utter starvation. But the greatest evil of all," Dibble suggested, "resulted from the constant intermingling, without any restraint, of persons of both sexes and of all ages, at all times of the day and at all hours of the night."[23]

These were decidedly colonialist views. The white missionaries of Hawai'i, like the armies of self-styled saviors that people imperial history, saw their charges in racially inferior terms, ascribing to them a barbarity that rings almost otherworldly to twenty-first-century ears. And wave riding was most certainly an element of that savagery. Surfing, wrote haoles in the Hawaiian-language newspapers they employed to achieve their social aims, was "immoral." It was "the reason," claimed an article in *Ke Kumu Hawaii*, "people become indolent and [was] the root of lasciviousness."[24] It made Hawaiian men "lazy," insisted another, as they "would spend all their time surfing."[25] And the same was said to be true more broadly. The residents of La'ie did not like attending the missionaries' religious services because they "would rather surf," one report indicated in 1835.[26] Another equated surfing with sin, instructing readers to "remember the words of the Lord when he said, 'Go and sin no more.'"[27] As Richard Armstrong's *Ka Nonanona* revealed, the message could be distilled to three words: "[s]urfing is wrong."[28]

No, it was not necessary for the missionaries to prohibit surfing. It was tightly enough "hemmed in by 'blue laws' against gambling and nudity, both of which had been nearly as important to the sport as riding itself," concluded historian Matt Warshaw.[29] When this assault on Hawaiian customs is combined with the Protestant emphasis on industriousness and the physical devastation of the Hawaiian population, it is little wonder that surfing entered a period of decline. As early as the second half of the 1830s, the transformation was already apparent. William S. W. Ruschenberger, a surgeon on a round-the-world voyage, commented at that time on the "change [that] has taken place in certain customs, which must have influenced the physical development of the islanders. I allude to the variety of athletic exercises, such as swimming, with or without the surf-board, dancing, wrestling, throwing the javalin [*sic*], &c., all of which games, being in opposition to the severe tenets of Calvinism, have been suppressed, without the substitution of other pursuits to fill up the time." Ruschenberger was dubious of the missionaries' denials of responsibility. "Would these games have been suppressed had the missionaries never arrived at the islands?" he asked.

> It is fair to presume that they would have continued in use. Can the missionaries be fairly charged with suppressing these games? I believe they deny having done so. But they write and publicly express their opinions, and state these sports to be expressly against the laws of God, and by a succession of reasoning, which may be readily traced, impress upon the minds of the chiefs and others, the idea that all who practice them, secure to themselves the displeasure of offended heaven. Then the chiefs, from a spontaneous benevolence, at once interrupt customs so hazardous to their vassals.[30]

While a significant number of Hawaiians continued to resist the assault on their cultural traditions, as scholars from Noenoe Silva to Isaiah Helekunihi Walker have ably demonstrated, the missionaries, by convincing some Hawaiians that surfing contributed to their moral turpitude, were able to achieve many of their desired objectives without the need to issue a blanket prohibition on wave riding.[31]

In light of this ideological offensive, it seems disingenuous for a number of missionaries to have absolved themselves of any responsibility for surfing's decline. To be sure, there were visiting whites, including missionaries, who celebrated the sport and hoped it would survive what Nathaniel Emerson, in his 1892 speech to the Hawaiian Mission Children's Society, innocuously called "the new civilization."[32] The German-born journalist Charles Nordhoff, for instance, extolled the wave riders of Hilo in 1873, maintaining that those Americans fortunate enough to be there on a "rough day" with "heavy surf" would be witness to "one of the finest sights in the world."[33] Among the islands' missionaries, there was none more enthusiastic than the Reverend Henry T. Cheever. Writing in 1851, Cheever unequivocally praised the "surf-players" he would see enjoying the waves along the Hawaiian coast. Their pastime, he opined, "is so attractive and full of wild excitement to Hawaiians, and withal so healthful, that I cannot but hope it will be many years before civilization shall look it out of countenance, or make it disreputable to indulge in this manly, though it be dangerous, exercise. Many a man from abroad who has witnessed this exhilarating play, has no doubt inly wished that he were free and able to share in it himself." Admitting publicly what he suspected others thought privately, Cheever confessed: "[f]or my part, I should like nothing better, if I could do it, than to get balanced on a board just before a great rushing wave, and so be hurried in half or quarter of a mile landward with the speed of a race-horse, all the time enveloped in foam and spray, but without letting the roller break and tumble over my head." As "[b]oth men and women, girls and boys," together found time to indulge in this enviable "diversion," however, Cheever was perhaps naïve in suggesting that civilization had not already "look[ed] it out of countenance" or otherwise "ma[d]e it disreputable."[34]

Certainly the missionary leader Hiram Bingham seemed to recognize as much, though without offering the hope for the sport's survival displayed by Reverend Cheever. "The adoption of our costume greatly diminishes [the Hawaiians'] practice of swimming and sporting in the surf," Bingham observed in his 1848 tome, "for it is less convenient to wear it in the water than the native girdle, and less decorous and safe to lay it entirely off on every occasion they find for a plunge or swim or surf-board race. Less time, moreover, is found for amusement by those who earn or make cloth-garments for themselves like the more civilized nations." Bingham acknowledged the declining number of Hawaiians participating in what he identified as "the favorite amusement of all classes," though he appeared adamant that the missionaries had nothing for which to apologize. "The decline or discontinuance of the use of the surf-board, as civilization advances," he wrote, "may be accounted for by the increase of modesty, industry[,] or religion, without supposing, as some have affected to believe, that missionaries caused oppressive enactments against it. These considerations are in part applicable to many other amusements. Indeed, the purchase of foreign vessels, at this time, required attention to the collecting and delivering of 450,000 lbs. of sandal-wood, which those who were waiting for it might naturally suppose would, for a time, supersede their amusements."[35] Given the central importance placed by missionary ideology on the sanctity of labor, it was only natural, that is, that the Hawaiian people—a people who, in Bingham's telling, unreservedly embraced Christian civilization—would emphasize industriousness over the "many . . . amusements" that were central to Hawaiian cultural life.[36]

As in North America, a fair number of those advocating the racial uplift of the indigenous Hawaiian population found themselves materially rewarded as they came to dominate the economic life of the islands. During the nineteenth century, land was divided and passed into haole hands.[37] With the physical decimation of the native population, tens of thousands of laborers were imported from the Philippines, Japan, and elsewhere in the Asia Pacific. Commodity agriculture—especially sugar—proved increasingly important, and the descendants of a number of missionaries came to control its trade. In time, the haole elite sought political power to match its dominance of the export-oriented economy. This meant undermining the sovereignty of the native kingdom. When Queen Lili'uokalani attempted in 1893 to restore the authority of the Hawaiian monarchy following the 1887 imposition of a constitution favored by powerful haole interests, her government, after the U.S. minister in the islands sent in a contingent of American troops, grudgingly "yield[ed] to the superior force of the United States of America" and the haole leaders that the American minister, John L. Stevens, was supporting. Lili'uokalani did so, she wrote at the time, "under . . . protest" and "until such time as the Government of the United States shall, upon the facts being presented to it, undo the action of its representative and reinstate me in the authority which I claim as the constitutional Sovereign of the Hawaiian Islands."[38]

That day would never arrive. In 1898, five years after the haole-led coup d'état that ultimately brought about the Republic of Hawai'i—a coup that even the United States president, Grover Cleveland, recognized as unlawful—Washington annexed the islands in the face of overwhelming opposition by the Hawaiian people.[39] The annexation was clearly unconstitutional. Customary international law required land to be annexed through a treaty. This presented a problem for the United States, however, because its constitution mandated that treaties be ratified by a two-thirds majority vote in the Senate. Such a majority was not possible. Congress thus bypassed this constitutional requirement by passing a joint resolution in favor of annexation. (Resolutions require only a simple majority.) The failure to secure a treaty, argues J. Kehaulani Kauanui, rendered the entire enterprise illegal.[40] Such legal shortcomings did not prevent the United States from working to consolidate its territorial land grab in the decades that followed, however. And as Hawai'i became American, so, too, did surfing.

ALEXANDER HUME FORD AND THE CONSOLIDATION OF THE PACIFIC EMPIRE

However much the number of surfers had fallen by the end of the nineteenth century, surfing began to once more flourish as the twentieth century unfolded. As with its decline, this was due, at least in part, to the immediate concerns of the American imperial project. Just as contact had physically decimated the native population while the missionary onslaught had sought the cultural transformation of those who survived, following Hawai'i's annexation by the United States in 1898, a number of Americans sought to profit from the islands' tropical climate by further opening up the territory to tourists as what one promotional booklet called "a marvelous out-of-door wonderland, a picnic ground from the earth."[41] Their objectives were obvious. For years tourism's economic potential had been apparent. In 1888, for instance, a Honolulu newspaper, noting the considerable sums expended by visitors, argued that inducing "people to come and see us is wise policy and promotive of our own material interests."[42] As the twentieth century dawned, surfing would prove instrumental in marketing the "out-of-door wonderland" image.[43] Robert C. Allen, who served for thirty-five years after World War II as the islands' most tireless and effective booster, identified the sport as the first of four "entities" that provided an isolated Hawai'i "with publicity far beyond any paid advertising could possibly have generated."[44] But even decades before Allen assumed his postwar leadership role, a middle-aged South Carolina–born journalist had seized upon the idea of using surfing to sell the archipelago as an exotic, though safely *American*, tropical retreat.

Alexander Hume Ford was an unlikely champion of the sport. Orphaned at an early age, Ford spent much of his early professional life as a writer in

New York and Chicago. After stints as a dramaturge and staff journalist, he became a roving freelance reporter. At roughly the same time that the United States was annexing Hawai'i, Ford was tramping across Siberia and eastern Europe as a foreign correspondent for a handful of American magazines. Before long, however, his career began to decline. Then, in 1907, at the age of thirty-nine, Ford arrived in Honolulu.[45] "It was the thrill of the surfboard that brought me to Hawaii," he later wrote. As a schoolboy he saw a picture in his geography book of "Hawaiian men and women . . . poised upon the crest of monster rollers," and, he said, he "longed" to join them.[46] Almost immediately upon his arrival he took to the waves. The reason was simple: "There is a thrill like none other in all the world as you stand upon [a wave's] crest," he gushed in the pages of *Collier's*.[47] Ford was in fact rather late in his discovery; others had already uncovered and touted the "pure joy" and "spiritual intoxication" to be found in the waves off Waikiki.[48] But Ford pushed it further than most. After nearly three months of daily four-hour sessions, the journalist could claim to "ride standing."[49] He quickly emerged as surfing's leading evangelist, corralling Hawaiian "beachboys" and visiting Americans alike into his cause—most notably among the latter, the celebrated author Jack London, whom Ford introduced to surfing in 1907. "Learn to ride a surfboard," Ford advised the readers of *St. Nicholas* magazine. "[I]t is the king of sports."[50]

The extant literature, both print and filmic, has too often treated the South Carolina transplant as just some apolitical eccentric who found surfing and got stoked; at the same time, it has considerably exaggerated his contribution to surfing's early-twentieth-century resurgence. Joseph Funderburg, for instance, maintained that Ford was "the mastermind who was responsible for the revival of surfing and one of the builders of the new Hawaii." Joel Smith believed it "tempting to think there might not have been a revival at all" if not for Ford. And for Ben Marcus, Ford was one of three haoles—Marcus included the mixed-blood Hawaiian waterman George Freeth in that category—"who led the rebirth" of the sport.[51] But contrary to these and other accounts, and as Isaiah Helekunihi Walker importantly reminds us, surfing was not an extinct pastime resurrected by the recently arrived haole.[52] It had in fact already been experiencing a renaissance among a new generation of mostly Hawaiian men.[53] Walker speculated that this was because "the surf offered escape and autonomy for Kanaka Maoli [Hawaiians] in an unsettling time."[54] The United States had recently annexed Hawai'i in the face of overwhelming Hawaiian opposition, and the islands'

FIGURE 1. Alexander Hume Ford saw in surfing a means to further his vision of a "white man's state." Ford (right) with Jack London (center) and Charmian London (under umbrella) in 1915 on the beach in Waikiki. Credit: Charmian Kittredge London, *Our Hawaii* (New York: Macmillan Company, 1917).

powerful haole elite was rendering the native population increasingly marginal as the annexationists consolidated their wealth, power, and privilege. Whatever the reason a number of young Hawaiians took to the ocean at the turn of the century, there is no doubt that Hawaiian surfers were already riding the waves of Waikiki when Ford (followed weeks later by Jack London, who admiringly referred to these Hawaiians as "black Mercury[s]" and "natural king[s]," members of the "kingly species" who have "mastered matter and the brutes and lorded it over creation") first entered the waters off O'ahu in 1907.[55]

If much of the literature has perhaps ascribed to Ford greater credit for surfing's revival than his contribution in fact merits—credit that Ford himself helped to foster—it has given almost no attention to the colonialist presumptions that drove the American transplant's missionary zeal.[56] These presumptions operated on at least two levels. On one, Ford adopted, as historian Gary Okihiro noted, the "familiar colonial trope of 'going native' and, for the sake of natives, enacting cultural and environmental rescue and preservation." This was a "racialized burden" he and other haoles carried in ensuring the triumph of civilization in the island chain.[57] On the second— and this has gone almost entirely overlooked in the surfing literature—Ford became a major proponent of not only consolidating America's imperial grasp of Hawai'i but of doing so in the interests of whites. Ford, as a South Carolinian, was a product of the Jim Crow South. There is no evidence that he viewed favorably the sort of racist violence popularized by the Ku Klux Klan, but it is incontestable that he embraced the racist suppositions of the post–Civil War era.

Ford's reporting was peppered with encomiums to the spread of white civilization, and it is hard not to imagine him viewing the Pacific islands as a laboratory in which could be realized his ideal white American society. Ford, to be sure, was hardly alone in embracing this mission.[58] A short book published by the American officials who overthrew the monarchy was clear about its authors' desire "to increase [the islands'] civilized population by accessions from without" and to "attract... desirable settlers."[59] Yet Ford rose above most of his contemporaries in being more vocal, persistent, and tireless than others. Indeed, by 1917 *Sunset* magazine was pronouncing him "Hawaii's best booster and the busiest man in the mid-Pacific."[60] And, crucially, Ford possessed the ideological convictions necessary for such a colonialist project. In his turn-of-the-century dispatches, Ford had already been praising the opening of Asia to American and British industrial influence, a region where, he predicted, "will be expended much restless energy of the Anglo-Saxon race"—so long, that is, as the "Anglo-Saxon push" did not "give way before the wily Slav" or "the agile, hardy Jap."[61] But even such nods to transatlantic racial solidarity would soon be ditched for a capitalist enthusiasm that was distinctly American in character. In a 1901 piece in *New England Magazine*, for instance, Ford proudly celebrated the displacement of European might by the power of American manufacturing and mechanized agriculture. From the country's "new colonial dependencies" ("our far off Philippines," for example) to Asia, Africa, Australia, and Europe, the "American idea is making a triumphant sweep the world over." The "vast and seemingly limitless resources" of the United States "make her prominently the land of promise for all time," Ford proclaimed. And "when to this is added the intelligent, almost divinely inspired population we possess," he wondered, "can such a country produce any other than a race of master workmen?"[62]

In Hawai'i Ford saw both promise and peril. Shortly before his arrival in 1907 he had rediscovered the "actual practical possibility" of "Christian socialism" at the American Colony in Jerusalem. The Holy Land inspired the South Carolinian. He revered the selflessness, fraternity, and perseverance of the Americans in the Middle East, and he marveled at their willingness and ability to demonstrate American beneficence.[63] The United States, Ford believed, was an inherent force for good. This had implications for Hawai'i, which Ford wished to see populated by waves of white Americans who might marshal the territory into statehood. Peopling the islands with his fair-skinned compatriots would become, for the restless mainlander, a personal crusade of the utmost moral necessity. The onetime South Carolinian not only took to the nation's press but even set out across the United States itself in an effort to encourage such settlement.

Ford came to his view of the islands early. As a passenger transiting through O'ahu on his way to Asia a few years before his 1907 relocation, Ford was on the ground long enough to conclude that the Hawaiian people were "happy" but "childlike" and lazy. "[T]he native Hawaiian shirks work if he can on any day of the week," he maintained.[64] Ford especially viewed with concern the many Asians who had made the islands their home. Having accompanied a delegation of two-dozen congressmen on an official visit in 1907, Ford was adamant that the territory "be redeemed from the Oriental, fortified and Americanized as it should be." This he saw as a form of humanitarianism. In Ford's mind, "attracting white American settlers" was synonymous with "aid[ing] the islanders." Colonization thus became a selfless "campaign for the welfare and protection of the islands."[65] Opponents of this American project were, in such an ideological framework, naturally enemies of humanity. Even in these early moments, then, Ford's disdain for Hawaiian nationalists, and his belief that they ought merely to stand by as American civilization proceeded unabated, was evident.[66] He was anything but generous, for instance, in speaking of the deposed queen Lili'uokalani, "leader of the 'outs'" and a hypocrite who surrounded herself with "Haoli-haters (despisers of the whites)."[67] If he could muster only one positive comment about the former monarch, it was a hint of pleasure at her capitulation: she seemed finally to recognize that "she is for all time but a citizen of the land over which she once ruled."[68]

Ford also criticized the Hawaiian representation in Congress, lamenting the fact that "[i]t is not possible at present for Hawaii to send a white delegate to Washington." Passage of the Hawaiian Organic Act of 1900, which restored the voting rights of many indigenous islanders, had seen to that. The best that Ford could say of Jonah Kuhio Kalaniana'ole, the territory's representative in Congress (as well as a surfer and recent heir to the Hawaiian throne), was that as "a native he does not stand in the way" of white progress. This was attributable, Ford suggested, to the "particularly fortunate" fact that Kuhio was accompanied in Washington by a Merchants Association–paid secretary, George B. McClellan, "an American-born worker who, as the equal of any in the national capital, is respected by all his coworkers with whom he labors shoulder to shoulder for the Americanization of our island territory."[69] Ford's concern was not solely with Hawaiian nationalists, however. He especially feared the racial threat presented by the influx of Asians. "The most recent official reports from Hawaii," Ford wrote in *Collier's* in 1909, "indicate that over fifty-one percent of its population is Japanese and that the little brown people there are outracing, births over deaths, all other nationalities in the islands combined. Perhaps seventy-five per cent of the population of Hawaii is of Oriental extraction." It seemed terrifying that, barring a change in demographic trends, "another generation may see Hawaii a State of the United States, with yellow Senators sitting in our Capital [*sic*] at Washington." Of course, Ford reassured his readers, the "hope of the people is otherwise, and a campaign, with limitless capital behind it, is now in progress to repeople the islands with white men."[70]

Ford was tireless in championing that cause. This was, of course, a cause that was hardly unique to Hawai'i. It found expression in Sun Belt development more broadly. Ford's boosterism in many ways echoed that of his American counterparts in the Southwest, such as those generations of individuals who sought to create in sun-drenched Southern California a model white society centered on leisure and pleasure.[71] Yet Hawai'i had its own special set of challenges. Convincing "the white population so badly needed" to "pour in" was, Ford recognized, an arduous task. Already the sugar industry had "populated the islands with one hundred and fifty thousand Orientals" as "field hands," he pointed out. If the "consensus of opinion" was that "sugar was the millionaire's crop," then "pineapples, coffee, rubber[,] and perhaps sisal" were "the crops that could best be raised by homesteaders." The problem faced by the 1907 congressional delegation Ford accompanied—and, by implication, the United States more broadly—was "how to help the coffee industry so that the thousands of homesteads offered to American citizens for settlement in Hawaii may be taken up and utilized to a profit by the white man."[72]

The islands, after all, were no easy sell. The Hawai'i of the early twentieth century was not the Hawai'i of the post–World War II era. The promotion of tourism thus came to play a useful role in encouraging the arrival of that "white population so badly needed" in the American territory. The logic was impeccable. "[A]s California and Oregon and Washington have learned," a representative of the Marshfield [Oregon] Chamber of Commerce told his hosts during an official visit to Honolulu in 1911, "the tourist of today is the taxpayer and resident of tomorrow."[73] Or, as the Hawai'i Tourist Bureau stressed while "induc[ing]" travelers to visit us," "we cannot emphasize too strongly the fact that Hawaii is not only a wonderland to visit but[,] far more important, an ideal country in which to establish a residence."[74] Tourism, in other words, would be an important first step in enticing white settlement.

And surfing, with which Ford became obsessed, might go some distance in encouraging this effort. Having learned to "ride standing" just months earlier, in 1908 the former South Carolinian founded the Outrigger Canoe Club on the beaches of Waikiki. The club, which quickly began to "flourish," soon emerged as an important social venue for the islands' haole elite, with its membership rolls populated by judges, political leaders, and many of Hawai'i's leading businessmen.[75] Ford was its first elected president; the annexationist Sanford B. Dole was its second.[76] There is a good deal of uncertainty about precisely how the Outrigger came about.[77] There is less doubt, however, about why it was created. The "main object" of the club was "to give an added and permanent attraction to Hawaii and make Waikiki always the Home of the Surfer, with perhaps an annual Surfboard and Outrigger Canoe Carnival which will do much to spread abroad the attractions of Hawaii, the only islands in the world where men and boys ride upright upon the crests of the waves."[78] Or, as Ford wrote in 1910, the club began when "several malihinis, or newcomers, . . . recognized the picturesque charm to the tourist of surf-board riding, an art that was rapidly dying out owing to the fact that Waikiki beach was becoming closed to the small boy of limited means."[79] Given the steady construction of beachfront hotels and residences, the Outrigger would ensure coastal access to people of "limited means." This ability of locals to reach the water would encourage the practice of surfing, which in turn, Ford believed, would attract free-spending tourists to Hawai'i. And he was right. The tourists did show up, though Ford would later come to rue his success. Surfing, he wrote in 1931, had been "one of the greatest assets toward bringing the confounded tourists to our over hospitable shores," where they were becoming a "nuisance" and a "calamity," though an "inevitable" one.[80] But this frustration was years away. In 1908 the future looked bright.

There was, moreover, an additional and more immediate reason for the Outrigger's founding. With the planned visit to Hawai'i of Theodore Roosevelt's Great White Fleet in the summer of 1908, the club, it was believed, could provide an excellent showcase for what was uniquely Hawaiian. This meant the Pacific islands' most popular water sports. "What better way to demonstrate the charm and culture of old Hawai'i than for the Navy men to experience first hand [*sic*] the regal sports of surfing and outrigger canoeing!" one history of the club proclaimed. The Outrigger thus organized two major efforts in anticipation of the visit. It "placed dozens of surfboards and some forty outrigger canoes at the disposal of the Navy men," and it sponsored a "water carnival" for the visiting personnel—an event that was, by all accounts, a tremendous success. The carnival featured a "surfboard contest" between approximately twenty surfers, the most impressive of whom seemed to be Harold Hustace, whose wave-riding skills prompted cheers from the beach.[81] There was also an organized regatta that, together with the "most thrilling event," the surfing competition, drew an estimated four to five thousand spectators. This was a remarkable turnout; one press report called it "probably the largest crowd that has ever gathered at the swimming beach."[82] The success of the planned activities undoubtedly pleased two of the Outrigger's charter members, territorial secretary (and Theodore Roosevelt appointee) A. L. C. "Jack" Atkinson and Hawaii Promotion Committee member Hart P. Wood. Both men had assumed leading roles in the fledgling club, allowing their offices to host its first organizational meetings. In the wake of the July events, the future looked promising. Yet these developments were notable not only for the details of what transpired but also for what they collectively represented: an early confluence of the histories of surfing, tourism, and the military.[83] Indeed, Ford believed surfing to be favorably linked to American military power. The water sports pursued at the Outrigger Canoe Club, he later ghostwrote for the U.S. secretary of the interior, had made "the boys of Honolulu grow up into great[,] strong[,] athletic[,] and daring men" who proved "most valuable" to the United States in the First World War.[84]

From the beginning, the promotion of surfing was closely bound to issues of race. Despite Ford's occasional nod to "the native" in some of his early writing, he appeared determined to render the pastime white. There was, of course, a certain irony in this desire, as the countless hours Ford and his colleagues spent surfing off Waikiki inevitably left them with varying shades of suntanned skin. Surfing, in this way, transgressed perhaps the most fundamental signifier of racial identity: color. Assertions of whiteness thus became less a matter of pigmentation than of faith, one in which whiteness was posited rather than marked. This had implications for the organization of

Hawaiian surf culture. Haole surfers in the years following annexation were not the imperialist missionaries of the nineteenth century. They were not seeking to simply supplant native culture with their own. On the contrary, they appropriated one of the most beloved pastimes of indigenous Hawaiians, and, in "going native," they were often left with darkened skin. Yet these haoles still insisted on the maintenance of racial boundaries. The Outrigger Canoe Club, which formed the center of the white surfing community, maintained such boundaries both in its organization and in its membership. As late as 1930, Ford was pushing for the Outrigger to be overseen by "a white caretaker," while an "Oriental group"—from whom, much to Ford's consternation, "the old spirit of work ha[d] left"—attended to the club's more menial duties.[85] And for years the Outrigger effectively discouraged the Hawaiian people from its membership rolls. "The Outrigger Canoe Club is practically an organization for the haole (white person)," Ford nonchalantly remarked of its de facto segregation.[86]

He exhibited less nonchalance in celebrating the aquatic ascendance of his white compatriots. White mastery of surfing, Ford claimed, was grounded in the dynamics of race. "[I]t is the white children only who have successfully mastered the Hawaiian sports," he wrote in 1908. The Chinese in Hawai'i had not done so. Nor had the Portuguese. "The Japanese seemed never able to acquire the difficult knack." It was only "the small white boy" who "very quickly became more adept than the native himself."[87] The proof, he suggested, was in the competitions. Hawaiian surfers of course disagreed. Precluded from joining Ford's club, frustrated by the encroachment of haole surfers in the waters off Waikiki, and "disgusted" with the racism of Outrigger members, Hawaiians officially formed the Hui Nalu (Club of the Waves), which had been loosely organized since 1905, as a surfing and swimming association in 1911.[88] The Hui Nalu contained numerous well-known surfers, from champion swimmer Duke Kahanamoku and his brothers to Jonah Kuhio Kalaniana'ole, the prince who served after 1902 as the territory's delegate to Congress. It also contained some women, though not in the numbers suggested by their historical prominence in wave-riding accounts.

Surfing competitions became a means through which Hawaiians and the haole elite contested each others' superiority. Ford, for his part, was unambiguous in his boasting. "[A]t the recent surfing carnivals in honor of the visits of the American battleship and later of the cruiser fleets," Ford wrote for a national audience in 1909, "practically every prize offered for those most expert in Hawaiian water sports were won by white boys and girls, who have only recently mastered the art that was for so long believed to be possible of acquirement only by the native-born, dark-skinned Hawaiian."[89] He seemed especially proud that "a white boy now fourteen years of age" had won "the medal given to the most expert surfboarder" for the third time. "The white man and boy are doing much in Hawaii to develop the art of surf-riding. Games and feats never dreamed of by the native are being tried," he boasted.[90] Indeed, by 1912, "the native" had disappeared from Waikiki altogether, Ford remarkably claimed. It was "white men and boys" who "kept [surfing] alive."[91] As even those with the most casual knowledge of twentieth-century surfing history will recognize, Ford was patently wrong about the disappearance of Hawaiian surfers. But his statement is instructive. The Outrigger founder was, in essence, attempting to create his own reality. Not only did Hawaiian surfers still exist but, by nearly all accounts, they excelled over whites. Matt Warshaw called Ford's boasts "ridiculous," noting that Hawaiians "usually didn't bother to enter surfing competitions" or were not invited.[92] And when they did, Isaiah Walker wrote, they emerged "victorious."[93]

Yet Ford's objectives were less empirical than political. When he found surfing and the incomparable thrill it represented, Ford found a lure for drawing white immigrants to Hawaiʻi. He took to the national press to sing the sport's praises, writing articles for *Collier's, St. Nicholas, Travel*, and *Paradise of the Pacific*.[94] He worked with the film production company Pathé to create a surfing motion picture.[95] He even founded his own monthly publication, the *Mid-Pacific Magazine*, which ran for twenty-five years. *Mid-Pacific*'s inaugural issue in January 1911 was dominated by images of surfing on its front and back covers, and its first article, replete with numerous photographs, was entitled "Riding the Surfboard."

It might seem startling that that first article appeared under the byline of the Hawaiian surfer and swimmer Duke Kahanamoku.[96] But that inaugural issue also contained a stark reminder of Ford's racialist and colonialist vision—an acknowledgment, as it were, of the extent to which surfing and the American empire had become entwined. Ford included a posthumous article by the congressman Abraham L. Brick extolling "our outpost in the Pacific." Strategically and commercially, Brick wrote, the Hawaiian Islands "are destined to become *the* isles of the ocean," and it was incumbent upon Americans to ensure that they "eventually come into the union a white man's state."[97]

This colonization of the islands consumed Ford, and, as noted earlier, he worked relentlessly to promote white settlement. By 1908, a year after his arrival on Oʻahu, Ford had been appointed secretary of the Transportation

FIGURE 2. Ford used his *Mid-Pacific Magazine* to promote Hawai'i as the center of a U.S.-led Pacific stretching from Asia and Australia to the Americas. Surfing, as prominently featured on the cover of its inaugural issue, could, he believed, help lure those white settlers he thought necessary to cement American rule in the islands. Credit: Courtesy of the Hawaiian Collection, Hamilton Library, University of Hawai'i at Manoa.

Committee by the territorial governor, Walter F. Frear. It was a wise choice, as Ford would in no time be recognized as Hawai'i's greatest booster. As secretary of the committee, he was charged with traveling to the mainland to advance the Pacific territory's interests. His views of his mission, as well as the fervor with which he embraced them, were made abundantly clear during his journeys. Writing to Frear in January 1909, Ford displayed no ambiguity about the future he envisioned for the islands. "We used to send train loads of people out to look at lands in the good old days & established some very successful colonies," he noted from Chicago in excitedly reporting the Homeseekers Association's interest in Hawai'i.[98] Why should the twentieth century be any different?

Months later Ford penned a sequence of enthusiastic articles for *Van Norden Magazine* intended to entice white migration. "Hawaii is to-day the land of opportunity for the quick, active, courageous white man, and everyone from President Taft down wishes to see it conquered for and by Anglo-Saxon Americans," he proclaimed.[99] In a piece entitled "Hawaii Calls for the Small Farmer," Ford insisted that the "richest land in all the world . . . must be Americanized." With the erection of "monster fortifications" for the U.S. military and the Panama Canal under construction—a canal that would only enhance the "strategic and commercial importance" of the Pacific islands—it was the duty of every "loyal citizen" who "understands something about the fundamentals of farming" to cooperate in America's colonial endeavor. Ford approvingly quoted Charles W. Fairbanks, the second-term vice president to Theodore Roosevelt: "I would like to see this American territory occupied by those whose blood is the blood that ran through the veins of our ancestors." He then proceeded to lay out how profitable Hawai'i could be for the small farmer and invited him to accomplish the "patriotic result" of white dominance under eventual Hawaiian statehood.[100] "Here is the business center where Occident and Orient meet," Ford had written a couple of months earlier. "[I]t is for the white man in America to say whether or not the opportunities, but beginning to open up, shall ripen and fall into his hands, or into those of the alien."[101]

Forget Frederick Jackson Turner's 1893 lamentation for the closing of the frontier. As far as Ford was concerned, the frontier had presented itself again. In the wake of his courtship of the Homeseekers Association in Chicago and with white immigrants slowly trickling in to the islands, Ford recognized that his cause would benefit from additional visual enticements. "I wish Hawaii had some slides it could send for use in lectures in Chicago and working up interest in Hawaii for the white man," he wrote to Governor Frear. Yet even without the slides, the "white man" appeared sold on the vision—or so at least Ford claimed. There was enthusiasm "[e]verywhere along the coast," he reported of his travels, with people along the western seaboard, just like "the transportation companies," wanting "to come in & help."[102] But Ford was onto something. Visual representations of Hawai'i—images that spoke to the exotic splendor unique to the island chain—could go some distance in selling the Hawaiian dream. And nothing spoke more fully to what was uniquely Hawaiian than the indigenous sport of surfing.

Ford had already laid an important foundation in this regard with his opening of the Outrigger Canoe Club in 1908.[103] His inauguration of *Mid-Pacific Magazine* in 1911 should also be understood in this context. It was not for nothing that in 1910 one newspaper account identified Ford as an "arch promoter of surf riding exhibitions and other things for the good of Hawaii."[104] To be sure, he was not the first booster to employ surfing in marketing the islands. An 1898 pamphlet on Hawai'i produced by the Canadian-Pacific Railway and the Canadian-Australian S.S. Line featured a photograph of a "native . . . with surf board." The "recent acquisition of the Hawaiian Islands by the United States," the pamphlet enticed would-be visitors, meant the opening "to the pleasure and health-seeking tourist [of] a delightful semi-tropical country of virgin beauty and unrivalled attractiveness—a new world to Americans and Europeans, in which the resources of modern civilization contribute materially to an easy and pleasurable exploration."[105] Surfing also appeared the following year in the *History of the Hawaiian Islands and Hints to Travelers Visiting the Hawaiian Islands* published by the Hawaiian Gazette Company.[106] By 1915, surfing had made the cover of Ferdinand Schnack's *Aloha Guide*, the "standard handbook" of Honolulu and the islands "endorsed" by the Chamber of Commerce and the Hawaii Promotion Committee.[107] In *Aloha from Honolulu*, another 1915 piece of promotional literature, surfing—the "most popular of Hawaiian pastimes"—claimed a full-page photograph.[108] Postcards abounded, and the archives are replete with materials from the first few decades of the twentieth century that feature wave riding as one of the islands' principal draws.[109] Nevertheless, probably no individual at the time more fully developed Hawaiian tourism—and used surfing as a marketing tool—than did Alexander Hume Ford.

Perhaps the most ambitious effort in this regard was Ford's creation in 1911 of the Hands-Around-the-Pacific Club, which was rechristened the Pan

FIGURES 3A AND 3B. With its exoticism and implication of masculine derring-do, it is not hard to imagine how surfing could serve as a popular draw in selling Hawaiian tourism and settlement, such as in these early-twentieth-century promotional pamphlets. The surfer in the pamphlet on the left is Duke Kahanamoku. Credit: Courtesy of the Hawaiian Collection, Hamilton Library, University of Hawaiʻi at Manoa.

Pacific Union in 1917. Endowing his new movement with immediate respectability, the club's initial honorary officers included the prime ministers of Australia and New Zealand, the governor of Hawaiʻi, and the governor-general of the Philippines.[110] Under whatever name it used, the organization was "essentially an outgrowth of the tourist-promotion activities" in which Ford was deeply enmeshed in the first two decades of the twentieth century.[111] Indeed, the club's formation followed Ford's unsuccessful 1907 at-

tempt to create, with joint Hawaiian and Australian leadership, a Pan-Pacific Tourist and Information Bureau, and it coincided with his participation in 1911 as a founding board member of the Pan-Pacific Congress, a Honolulu-based multilateral organization created to promote Pacific-area tourism, immigration, and development. Surfing was instrumental to these endeavors. When the congress sponsored the Mid-Pacific Carnival in 1913, its official poster, in a stark departure from the religious conservatism of the nineteenth century, proudly featured a scantily clad Hawaiian poised on the nose of a surfboard. The following year's poster continued with the surfing theme while tapping into the burgeoning culture of celebrity; it presented Duke Kahanamoku, the "champion swimmer of the world," casually sliding

FIGURE 4. The Pan-Pacific Congress, which Ford helped launch, was a Honolulu-based multilateral organization that sought to promote tourism, immigration, and development. For the organizers of its Mid-Pacific Carnivals, there was no more attractive means of promoting the magic of Hawai'i and the progressive vision of the organization than through illustrations of men riding waves. Credit: Postcard for the Mid-Pacific Carnival, February 19–24, 1917, Folder: 9-4-60 Haw. Promotion-Comm. Pan Pac. Congress, Box 662, Central Classified Files, 1907–1951, Office of the Territories, Record Group 126, National Archives II, College Park, Maryland.

down the face of a Hawaiian wave. And surfing would again be used in subsequent years.

Ford's ambitions were grand. Having already worked to promote white domination of Hawaiʻi, his more global activities seemed to reflect his belief that whites had global obligations. Like Albert P. Taylor, who directed the Hawaii Promotion Committee and sought to create a Pacific American Union to ensure the "maintenance of American supremacy in the Pacific," Ford viewed his responsibilities in global terms.[112] His was, he assumed, an inherently benevolent vision. "I have learned that where race prejudice has been overcome, race preference remains, and it will never be otherwise, and should not be," Ford reminisced in his later years. "Race preference will not preclude interracial friendship, interracial understanding. I have found everywhere in Asia that the Nordic is always a powerful, dynamic machine, ever leading, ever envied, ever misunderstood, ever unwelcome, but always bringing to the static Asiatic better things and better government than he has ever known. The Nordic has, in my Nordic opinion, a tremendous mission of leadership to fulfill, an obligation to the entire world, which he cannot escape."[113] Ford, as one such Nordic specimen, did not seek to escape his racial obligations.

THE HAWAIIAN GLOBALIZATION OF SURFING

At roughly the same time that Ford was enacting his vision of white global leadership, surfing began, with Ford's assistance, to slowly creep beyond the warm Hawaiian shores. Just as it was Hawaiians who spearheaded surfing's turn-of-the-century resurgence—a resurgence that has since been attributed to Alexander Hume Ford—it was Hawaiians who served as the most notable diplomats for their ancestral sport. Two young men who had distinguished themselves at Waikiki, George Freeth and Duke Kahanamoku, were particularly important in this respect, setting in motion the transformation of surfing from a uniquely Hawaiian cultural activity into a pastime enjoyed by millions of people on every continent. Of these two early emissaries, Freeth remains the least well known. This is surprising, as it was Freeth, a mixed-blood Hawaiian regarded as perhaps the most skilled wave rider of his generation, who firmly planted the seeds of what would become California's renowned surf culture.[114] In 1907, he left Hawaiʻi for the Golden State with letters in hand from Ford, Jack London, and the Hawaii Promotion

Committee. His objective, wrote the *Pacific Commercial Advertiser*, was to "give exhibitions of Hawaiian water sports to the people of that section."[115] Within months of his arrival, the media bestowed upon Freeth a national reputation through the work of London, the celebrated author who took to the pages of *Woman's Home Companion* that fall to excitedly relate his experiences months earlier in Waikiki. There, London watched Freeth "tearing in on the back of [a wave], standing upright on his board, carelessly poised, a young god bronzed with sunburn."[116] London appreciated not only the young Hawaiian's wave-riding skills but also his generosity in providing the celebrated author with a number of pointers when he himself took to the surf. Freeth's reputation only grew when London's article was reprinted the following year in England's *Pall Mall Magazine* and then, in 1911, as a chapter in London's travelogue *The Cruise of the Snark*.

The aquatic skills that had so enamored London, Ford, and the Hawaii Promotion Committee were the same skills Freeth brought with him to California, where he found work for two of the major developers of the period, Abbot Kinney and Henry Huntington. Kinney was the force behind the faux Italian development of Venice, just south of Santa Monica, while Huntington poured his energies into creating what he envisioned as "the great resort of [the] region" in nearby Redondo Beach.[117] Both Kinney and Huntington paid Freeth—dubbed "the Hawaiian Wonder" while under Huntington's employ—to give surfing exhibitions to the thousands of curious residents flocking aboard Huntington's Pacific Electric Railway to the sandy shores of Santa Monica Bay.[118] There, one contemporaneous account reported, "[m]any people daily gather to watch the Hawaiians in the surf . . . showing their skill in aquatic exercises."[119] Such dexterity in the waves, demonstrating how the ocean was a space that could be enjoyed rather than simply feared (as had until then been the case), marked the beginning of Southern California's beach culture.

Duke Kahanamoku, who graced the 1914 Mid-Pacific Carnival poster mentioned earlier, is by far the better known of surfing's early ambassadors. A five-time Olympic swimming medalist, the inspiration for the Duke's chain of restaurants in Hawai'i and California, and a man who has been immortalized in statuary from Australia to the American Midwest, Kahanamoku took surfing Down Under, offering beachside demonstrations in Sydney in 1914 and 1915 (as well as in New Zealand weeks later) that helped set in motion the creation of what is probably the world's most vibrant national surf culture.[120] Though subjected early to "wisecracks" by white American mainlanders about being "a Red Indian without feathers," Kahanamoku demonstrated the seriousness with which he would have to be taken when, in August 1911, he shaved multiple seconds off the existing records in the 50-, 100-, and 220-yard swimming races.[121] He would go on to win a handful of medals, including three golds, at the 1912 Olympics in Stockholm, the 1920 Olympics in Antwerp, the 1924 Olympics in Paris, and the 1932 Olympics in Los Angeles, in the process upending many of the white-supremacist beliefs of the era.[122]

Still, as with Freeth, surfing remained Kahanamoku's greatest passion. His 1914 and 1915 demonstrations in Australia, while not in fact the first instances of board riding in that country, nevertheless marked what Grady Timmons called "the real beginning of the sport Down Under."[123] When Kahanamoku first took to the Australian waves in late December 1914, the *Sun* newspaper could not help but be taken by the "thrilling spectacle." To the *Sydney Morning Herald*, it was a "magnificent display." The *Sunday Times* was perhaps most effusive. "Nothing more remarkable in the way of a natatorial exhibition has ever been seen locally," the paper declared without equivocation.[124] People flocked to the beach to witness Kahanamoku's "wonderful water feats." The crowd that gathered for one exhibition "was the biggest that has ever congregated at Dee Why since the inland aboriginals came down to spear fish in the lagoon and dance corroborees round their shell-fish naps on Long Reef"; the estimated four thousand spectators gave Kahanamoku an ovation.[125] While by no means solely responsible for the rise of Australian surfing, the Hawaiian went some distance in popularizing it. His wave-riding skills were in fact quickly exploited as a marketing spectacle: an advertisement for two carnivals sponsored by the Queensland Amateur Swimming Association proudly featured Kahanamoku poised on his board.[126]

Kahanamoku's surf riding was met with similar enthusiasm in New Zealand. At New Brighton, a coastal community outside the South Island city of Christchurch, the Hawaiian was welcomed by a "great gathering of people, the pier and beach being lined with spectators, and the champion got a great reception." Unfortunately for those present, Kahanamoku had to limit his exhibition to bodysurfing instead of "standing on the board," as "the calm day had flattened the sea."[127] Conditions in Wellington were more advantageous. There, recorded the *New Zealand Times*, an "unprecedented crowd" appeared at Lyall Bay "in anticipation of seeing the world's champion swimmer . . . perform some of his famous feats on the surf-board. It was estimated that over 5000 were present, and the beach was black with people." The Wellingtonians were not disappointed, "loudly applaud[ing]" Kahanamoku's unusual aquatic "feat."[128] Another display a week later left the "hundreds of onlookers" who had gathered to watch Kahanamoku "astounded . . . with his exhibition of surf-board riding."[129] "There are numbers of high-class surf-shooters in Honolulu, and some white people among them," Kahanamoku told an Australian journalist, "but, as with every other game, a few can do better than the great majority. It was with the few I delighted to be."[130] In Australia and New Zealand, he in fact stood alone.

The young Hawaiian, who also gave surfing demonstrations on both American coasts and would go on to tout surfing's exhilaration and health-giving qualities to America's youth, received considerable press coverage during his wave-riding displays.[131] More than anything, however, Kahanamoku, like his contemporary George Freeth, allowed his body to serve as his media. While operating within the racial constraints of a brown-skinned athlete in a white-dominated world, Kahanamoku demonstrated what it meant to be a surfer at a time when a common vernacular for the pastime did not exist.[132] Some media would speak of "surf-board swimming." Others would refer to "surf bathing" or "surf shooting." Whatever the term, Kahanamoku and Freeth demonstrated, through their skills in the water, that their ancestral pastime not only had survived the missionary onslaught of the nineteenth century but, spearheaded by these same supposed racial inferiors, would again thrive in the twentieth.

Though not at first. It would not be until after World War II that surfing really began to enjoy explosive international growth. Given the crippling nature of the Great Depression, the slow global expansion of the sport during the interwar period is hardly surprising. Still, in Hawai'i, people continued to find joy in the waves. This was true during World War I, when the letterhead of the Hawaii Promotion Committee, which was dominated by an image of surfers at Waikiki, happily pronounced that the islands were "Out of the War Zone," and it remained true in the years that followed.

By the latter half of the 1920s, wrote Jane Desmond, "surfing was an established part of tourist iconography and tourist itineraries," and the covers of national magazines began to feature smiling surfers screaming down waves.[133] Visitors who witnessed these water-bound athletes along the Hawaiian shores exclaimed it "hard to find a more graceful or exhilarating sight."[134] Even British artists and small-town New England newspapers saw fit to address this "most fascinating" and "picturesque phase of the island life."[135]

HONOLULU, HAWAIIAN ISLANDS, U. S. A.   January 9,1917.

Honorable Franklin C. Lane,
    Secretary Department of Interior,
    Washington, D.C.

Dear Sir:

        I am sending you under separate cover copy of the
Pacific Commercial Advertiser of Sunday, January 7th. containing the
story of a plan for the formation of a Pacific America Union, based on
the organization of the Pan American Union, the latter having its own
building at Washington, in which work having particular reference to
the upbuilding of Commerce and travel relations between the United
States and the republics of Central and South America is done.

        The plan of the Pacific America Union embraces
Hawaii, the Philippines, American Samoa, Guam and Alaska, and is
designed to build up great commercial, social and travel interest in
the units of Pacific America than at present exists.   I have been at
work on this plan for the past five or six months and did not make
ir public until assured by confident authorities that it was logical,
feasible and practicable.

        I have asked Prince Kalanianaole, Delegate from
Hawaii at Washington, to take the initiative with the plan before Congress if found practicable in this session of Congress.   You, as a
member of the Congressional party which visited Hawaii will appreciate
the value of such a plan, and I trust you will have opportunity to
read the story of the plan as it appears in the Advertiser.

        May I express the hope that I shall hear from
you on this subject, and with Aloha, I remain

                    Very truly yours,

                        SECRETARY

FIGURE 5.   How central was surfing to the marketing of Hawai'i? The letterhead used by the Hawaii
Promotion Committee during the World War I era is illustrative. Credit: A. P. Taylor to Franklin C.
Lane, January 9, 1917, Folder: 9-4-60 Haw. Promotion-Comm. Pan Pac. Congress, Box 662, Central
Classified Files, 1907–1951, Office of the Territories, Record Group 126, National Archives II, College
Park, Maryland.

By the mid- to late 1930s, tens of thousands of people were traveling to Hawai'i every year.[136] Indeed, the territory was increasingly viewed by Washington as a refuge from the Second World War. "I am sure you must be having exceptional success with the tourist business in Hawaii when so many other places are closed at the present time. [. . .] May [the war] never come to ou[r] beloved Hawaii," one official told the executive secretary of the Hawaii Tourist Bureau in late 1939.[137] The personal views of the official—the acting director of the Interior Department's Division of Territories and Island Possessions—were likely representative of many mainlanders at the time. "In this tragic and war-torn world I would like to come back to Hawaii immediately and hole in somewhere on the Kona coast away from wars and rumors of wars," she confided. But it was not just about escape, argues Jane Desmond. The "uncertain modernity of the 1930s" and the emergent "nostalgia for a pre-industrial past" made Hawai'i appealing to "elite white mainlanders [who] could experience" a "more authentic life." After all, the promotional literature suggested, the "paradisical Hawaiian . . . knew how to relax, how to live in gracious harmony with the environment, [and] seemed to have an abundance of pleasure in a time of scarcity." Americans responded to this "alternative vision."[138] Tourists "keep coming . . . in numbers," the Hawaii Tourist Bureau announced just days before the Japanese attack on Pearl Harbor.[139] Once there, they were encouraged to rent a surfboard, ride the waves in an outrigger canoe, or take a surfing lesson.[140]

Yet the Japanese attack quickly put an end to such visions of pleasant isolation. If the Japanese assault outraged the United States, it was also a reminder that Hawai'i was not necessarily the pacific refuge that many Americans believed it to be. What had been tourist sanctuaries prior to America's entry into the war quickly became militarized institutions serving the American war machine. The Royal Hawaiian Hotel on the shores of Waikiki, for instance, began functioning as "a haven for U.S. Navy submarine personnel between forays on enemy shipping"—it was leased to the navy for five years as a rest and recreation center for the Pacific Fleet—while "entanglements of barbed wire" lined the beach.[141] Tourism and war quickly became conjoined—or reconjoined, as the case may be—as the islands served the "wartime needs of hundreds of thousands of fighting men seeking relaxation between Pacific battles."[142] And Hawai'i was not alone. California, which in the prewar years was a distant surfing outpost, underwent a similar militarization.

Wave riders in the Golden State numbered in the mere dozens—Matt Warshaw estimated about two hundred—during the 1930s.[143] In part this was for structural reasons. The stretch of coast from San Diego to Santa Barbara that is today peppered with multimillion-dollar homes, parking lots, and fast-food restaurants was, prior to the Second World War, a sparsely populated strip of often difficult-to-access beaches. Most Americans did not own automobiles, and lifeguards were relatively scarce. And for people of color, the coast was virtually off-limits. Whether through prejudicial municipal codes, segregated housing patterns, or threats of white violence, the beach was—unlike in Hawaiʻi—a space reserved almost exclusively for whites. Those white surfers who did venture to the water would spend their days in some combination of surfing, fishing, and diving, especially for the abalone and lobster that were abundant along the Pacific coast. Yet it would not be long before California, and especially Southern California, began to undergo major change. With the Japanese attack on Pearl Harbor, the West Coast became an important region for American wartime preparedness. Industry began cranking out military hardware as Japanese Americans found themselves tossed into isolated concentration camps. Uncle Sam wanted young men in uniform, and rationing and scarcity became the home-front norm. The long coastal strip, meanwhile, was transformed from a welcoming space into a site of potential attack. Indeed, a number of beaches along the California coast that are today popular surf spots—Malibu, San Onofre, and others—were deemed off-limits to the public for security reasons. To try to surf in such places was to flirt with treason. Wave riding could suddenly be illegal.[144]

Within a few years, however, the restrictions imposed by World War II would be replaced by the flowering of modern surf culture. The end of the war in 1945 heralded momentous developments. Most obviously, materials and technologies developed during the war enabled advances in surfboard design. While solid wood boards that required nearly superhuman strength to carry were increasingly being replaced by hollow boards in the 1930s, war technologies were enabling even newer designs that drew on balsa, marine plywood, fiberglass, polyester resin, and polyurethane foam.[145] These lighter boards opened up the sport to countless newcomers. So, too, did the development of wetsuits—another beneficiary of wartime technology, and one that was reciprocated when O'Neill began manufacturing "custom-tailored thermal barrier diving and surfing suits for [the] U.S. Navy."[146] The American security establishment benefited from surfing in other ways, too. Agents of the Office of Strategic Services, the wartime intelligence agency that preceded the CIA, used paddleboards, which they rode as surfboards, as reconnaissance vehicles.[147] And it was announced in 1953 that an "underwater surfboard" had been developed with "potential value as a compact submarine for the [U.S.] Navy's daring frogmen who swim in close to the enemy's shores and ships."[148]

But perhaps the most obvious explanation for surf culture's explosive postwar growth was economic. With the massive expansion of the middle class in the 1950s there emerged a large demographic of American consumers who sought pleasure and leisure at the beach. Nearly all of them were white. For a number of these new beachgoers, especially after *Gidget* hit the big screen in 1959, surfing became a favorite, if still subcultural, pastime. The beaches of California—not to mention Hawai'i, Australia, South Africa, and elsewhere across the planet—soon resembled an endless sea of bronzed skin. It was, depending on one's perspective, either a propitious beginning or a dismal end.

TWO

A World Made Safe for Discovery

TRAVEL, CULTURAL DIPLOMACY, AND THE POLITICS
OF SURF EXPLORATION

PETER TROY WAS A LEGENDARY EXPLORER. His name may not reso-
nate outside portions of the littoral world, but, to surfers who came of age in
the 1960s and 1970s, it is every bit as weighty as those of Columbus, Cook,
and Magellan. A thin, blond-haired Australian, Troy emerged as a highly
regarded surfer when still in his teens, winning the Victorian novice surfing
title in 1955. He might have remained a mere local figure had it not been for
the postwar globalization of surf culture. In 1956, Troy's Torquay Surf Life
Saving Club hosted the International Surf Life Saving Carnival to coincide
with that year's Olympic Games in Melbourne. The carnival included teams
from Australia, New Zealand, Ceylon (Sri Lanka), South Africa, England,
and the United States, and Troy, as the local titleholder, was asked to give a
surfing demonstration. An estimated fifty thousand spectators were on hand
to see the young Victorian work his way across the waves on his sixteen-foot
hollow board. But it was the American contingent, riding shorter, lighter, and
more maneuverable equipment—their "Malibu" boards were approximately
nine feet long—that made the biggest splash. These American board designs
inspired Australian replication, and the result was equipment capable of
tackling breaks, such as Bells Beach, that had previously been considered
unrideable.

This heralded a new era in the history of Australian surfing. The sport
metamorphosed from an activity undertaken by lifesavers patrolling a particular beach to one in which individual surfers set out along the coast in
search of the best possible waves. For some of these surfers, the local beaches
were soon not enough. Working at the time as an accountant for Price
Waterhouse in Melbourne, Troy's global yearnings—the seeds of which, he
said, had been planted by the Americans in 1956—only intensified. "I had

no desire to be an accountant but I wasn't sure how to leave my job," he recalled. "When I saw my first *Surfer* magazine, I saw a glimmer of hope. . . . I realized that here was another way of life."[1]

Troy was twenty-four years old in 1963 when he left Australia, surfboard in hand, to become what Brendan McAloon called "surfing's first vagabond."[2] Over the course of three years, he tackled Europe's Atlantic Seaboard, surfed the warm waters of Hawai'i, helped popularize his beloved sport in Brazil—now a competitive surfing powerhouse—and explored the African coast. He did so by air, boat, foot, road, and rail. He toasted the children of European diplomats, sweated through a South African gold mine, rode in stuffed freight cars with Peruvian peasants, and consumed his fill of cheap wine in Franco's Madrid. *Surfer* christened him "one of the most effective roving ambassadors for the sport."[3] And the travel bug never left him. Troy would be back at it years later, discovering, in 1975, the world-class right-hander at Indonesia's Lagundri Bay with two of his Australian compatriots. By the time he died in 2008, he had visited well over 140 countries.[4] Troy's travels are now the stuff of legend. In that long-ago era before blogs and YouTube, he wrote occasional dispatches for the monthly surfing press. This not only made him something of a minor celebrity but also situated him as an exemplar of Cold War surf culture.

. . .

Surfing had come a long way from its near extinction decades before in that cluster of small Pacific islands in which people rode waves while standing. A Hawaiian tradition that had almost disappeared by the turn of the twentieth century had become, by 1945, a minor global pastime; then, in the decades following the Second World War, surfing emerged not only as a sport enjoyed by millions of enthusiasts worldwide but, significantly, as a form of cultural encounter that might go some distance in bridging national or political divides. A variety of factors contributed to surfing's phenomenal growth. Foremost among these was the sport's embrace by the American culture industries. In films ranging from *Gidget* (1959) to the "beach party" pictures of Frankie Avalon and Annette Funicello, Hollywood appropriated surfing and its youthful, seemingly carefree lifestyle while designating Southern California the presumptive center of the surfing universe. Television likewise took to the sport. Gidget made her small-screen debut in 1965 with a young Sally Field in the series' title role, while ABC's *Wide World of*

Sports, recognizing surfing's striking visual qualities, had begun regularly pumping contests into American living rooms in 1962. Surf music became a popular genre, with performers such as the Beach Boys, Dick Dale, and Jan and Dean emerging as best-selling performers. Surfing even entered the world of American letters. Eugene Burdick published *The Ninth Wave* in 1956—Burdick would shortly thereafter coauthor the influential Cold War novels *The Ugly American* and *Fail-Safe*—and Tom Wolfe, that paragon of New Journalism, released his collection of essays *The Pump House Gang* in 1968.[5]

Surfing—or at least some version of it—had entered the commercial mainstream. Yet the surf culture popularized in the 1960s was essentially a moneymaking artifice. For every *Bikini Beach* (1964) or *Beach Blanket Bingo* (1965) that purported to reveal the ways of the surfer, there was a shoestring-budget documentary—a traditional "surf flick"—relegated to high school and civic center auditoriums up and down the coast. This more organic community would itself soon reach the mainstream, but not before establishing a foundational element of contemporary surf culture: the primacy of travel to the modern surfing experience. Surfers, like waves, move across and along the oceans. If the first half of the twentieth century was marked by the revitalization and growth of Hawaiian surf culture and its first tentative steps into the wider world, the second half was characterized by widespread global interaction, with surfers ready participants in the rise of Cold War travel cultures. The expansion of the white middle class in the 1950s opened up new horizons for those afflicted with wanderlust. Places that were once only reached following weeks-long transoceanic voyages could, with the growth and increasing affordability of commercial air travel, welcome wide-eyed tourists after flights lasting mere hours.

For no destination was this truer than Hawai'i, where the tourism industry exploded in the fourteen years between the war's end in 1945 and the establishment of statehood in 1959. But it was not just about pleasure travel. The growth of Hawaiian tourism coincided with the escalation of the Cold War, and Hawai'i, which was already situated at the heart of American power in the Pacific, became even more militarized as Cold War tensions increased.[6] If not for this militarization, however, surf history might have unfolded quite differently. The armed forces brought several major figures in the development of modern surf culture to Hawai'i, including Bruce Brown, whose *The Endless Summer* (1966) made him surfing's most influential documentary filmmaker, and John Severson, the founder of *Surfer* magazine.

Both Brown and Severson further exposed the rich Hawaiian surf to California's wave-obsessed youth.[7] Yet even for those without military ties, Hawai'i had become surfing's mecca. It was the place mainlanders went to assert their wave-riding chops. By the 1960s, a surfer could not be said to have reached surfing's heights unless he (or, far less frequently, she) had successfully ridden O'ahu's North Shore.

And yet, for a number of surfers, the distant trip to Hawai'i was not enough. Surfing was increasingly about the search, the journey, the discovery. In this vein, a number of young men (and it *was* almost exclusively men) set out to chart something of the littoral world. Their voyages were not the "Grand Tours" of previous centuries. Yes, they revolved around pleasure. And yes, they dripped with the trappings of empire. But those undertaking the journeys were not generally members of the landed elite, their itineraries were fluid, and the object of their gaze was not the patrimony of the West. These were young men looking for waves, most often in relatively untouristed destinations, and they relished their cultural exchanges along the way. The discoveries were undoubtedly important to them, but "the search"—as the wetsuit and apparel maker Rip Curl later designated an influential advertising campaign—was just as significant. These were essentially backpackers with boards, seeking out those quieter parts of the planet where they might be alone—or close to it—with the locals and the ocean. And like their backpacker counterparts, wandering surfers were, as Peter Troy put it, "always trying to enter the life of [those] locals."[8]

Troy's early travels are illustrative. He began his global jaunt in 1963 by ship, making his way across the Indian Ocean and through the Mediterranean on his way to the British motherland. It might seem natural that a white Australian would begin his excursion in Europe, though Troy was there not to imbibe the art and architecture of Florence or the café culture of Paris. It is not that "culture" did not interest the Australian. It did. After passing through the Red Sea, for instance, he ventured inland to explore the antiquities of Egypt, and he wrote home about the magnificent paintings he saw in European cities such as Seville.[9] But Troy was traveling the world to surf, and the principal culture he sought was not the high culture of the Grand Tour but the subculture of modern surfing. He began his European adventure in the Channel Islands, finding surprisingly good waves in Jersey. While there, he saved an Italian waiter from a near drowning, which earned him notice in the English press, and he took surfboard orders from the locals and offered wave-riding lessons.[10] From the United Kingdom he left for France, where he entered an international contest just hours after disembarking in Biarritz. Despite his exhaustion, he won. Troy, a recently arrived and still traveling Australian, was pronounced the European surfing champion.[11]

The young Victorian then made his way to Spain and Portugal. He rode small waves in San Sebastián with traveling companion Rennie Ellis, a fellow Australian and an agent for Severson's *Surfer* magazine, and he scored solid surf at the Portuguese beach of Guincho.[12] The locals were impressed. "Amazed spectators stared at us from the beach," Ellis reported in Australia's *Surfing World*. "Afterwards a local approached us and in halting English and raptured tones he told us that until then he had thought Christ was the only person who could walk on the water."[13] The Spanish and Portuguese— both at that time living under right-wing dictatorships—struck Troy for different reasons. In Spain "the people generally were lethargic, apparently not politically minded, poor[,] and mostly unkempt in appearance." But the Portuguese "were very anti-communist (and didn't dare speak their own views on politics and government to a fellow countryman in fear that he may be a secret agent of a rival party—we heard of many so-called stories to back these accusations), hard working, industrious[,] and of a general western world standard."[14] There was little doubt which country he viewed more favorably. But Troy intended to see far more than the European Atlantic. Together with Ellis, he volunteered aboard an Indonesian-made ketch that took the two Australians to the Americas.

Along the way the yacht would stop in Morocco, Madeira, the Canary Islands (where Troy found "the best surfing conditions outside Biarritz"), and several places in the Caribbean.[15] When Troy reached Florida, he was quickly adopted by Miami's "surfing fraternity"—a term he applied to his fellow surfers worldwide—which showed him around the city and introduced him to the Florida waves.[16] Desperate to make it to California, he found work as a driver, delivering a vehicle across the United States to Los Angeles, from where he immediately boarded a flight to Hawai'i. He did so, he wrote to his parents, "with visions in my mind of the lei clad Hawaiian girls in costume and the balmy weather of this romantic island group blessed with the best climate of any place in the world and the venue for the International and World Surfing Championships at Makaha—my dream of a lifetime almost now in reality—in fact, no turning back even if I wanted to."[17]

Troy was not able to compete at Makaha; the start of the contest was moved up because of favorable wave conditions, and Troy arrived too late.

He did, however, get to surf the warm Hawaiian waters, though a couple of unfortunate wipeouts at Pipeline and Sunset Beach left him with a badly lacerated face and coral abrasions on the shoulder, back, right foot, and elbow.[18] From Hawai'i he would be going to Peru, but Troy first took a return detour to California—a state whose wealth and technology amazed him. The day the Australian spent viewing the ostentatious lifestyle of Los Angeles's rich and famous was "one of the most eye[-]opening days I have yet had the fortune to live."[19] But California was intended as a mere stopover. Traveling through Mexico by automobile and train, Troy departed from Mexico City with a friend for Lima. In the Peruvian capital, he proceeded to the coastal district of Miraflores, the heart of the Peruvian surf community, which had a long history. As far back as 3000 BCE, indigenous fishermen in Peru were riding waves on bundled reeds now called *caballitos* (little horses). However, the country's modern surfing history dates only to the 1920s, when a number of Peruvians took to riding homemade boards on the beaches of Barranco, a popular community along the Lima coast. Then, in 1939, Carlos Dogny, a wealthy sugarcane heir, returned from a trip to Hawai'i, where he had learned to surf, bringing with him a board he was given by Duke Kahanamoku. At Miraflores in 1942, Dogny founded Club Waikiki.[20]

Club Waikiki served as the center of the Peruvian surf community. It was here that Troy discovered the contingency of surf culture: what was sometimes considered a disreputable activity in Australia or the United States could be a marker of wealth and privilege in portions of the Third World. The club was invitation only and restricted to two hundred members, each of whom paid a substantial entrance fee (approximately $1,200 in 1964) followed by monthly dues. The beachfront grounds were extravagant. They contained a squash court, two pelota courts, a shuffleboard court, workout facilities, a heated pool, dining facilities with jacket- and bow-tie-clad waiters serving four-course meals, a bar, a marble dance floor, and staff to wax and carry one's surfboard to and from the water. Troy found this arrangement difficult to take. A "native laborer" would have to work twenty-five hours to earn the cost of his lunch, he wrote, as "per head of population" Peru had, according to Troy, "the second lowest standard of living in the civilized world." "[T]o eat at the Club Waikiki with a hundred hungry Indians looking down on you" from the hilltop above required "some mental adjustment," he confessed. Still, "[w]hen in Peru do as the idle, wealthy, aristocratic Peruvians do!" he wrote home.[21] And he did. His existence was certainly not as ostentatious as that of one member, a thirty-two-year-old bachelor who owned three Jaguars and a helicopter, the latter of which he would use to go surfing during the lunch hour.[22] But neither was it modest. In Peru, surfing was an elite sport. Troy did not bat an eye, for instance, when, with the 1965 World Surfing Championships held in Lima, the president of the country received a delegation of visiting competitors at the Government Palace.[23]

If Club Waikiki awoke Troy to the elitism of Peruvian surf culture, Rio de Janeiro introduced him to the frenetic surf energy of Latin America's largest nation. He arrived in Brazil in late May 1964, just weeks after the Brazilian armed forces overthrew, with American support, the democratically elected government of João Goulart. Troy had come far from his white-collar Australian roots. "[D]ressed in jeans, tattered shirt, locally made riding boots [...], long blonde [sic] hair, unshaven, suntanned, humping a bed-roll and cloth hammock and food sack, I cut quite a figure," he wrote his parents from the bush.[24] Troy unwittingly became a minor celebrity after riding the waves of Rio's world-famous coast. He appeared on the front page of Brazilian newspapers, was interviewed for Brazilian television, and was consulted by the Brazilian lifesaving services. Troy undertook his Latin American travels at a time when military rule was becoming firmly ensconced across the continent. Just two years after the Cuban Missile Crisis, Latin America in 1964 was deeply enmeshed in the Cold War. In Brazil, Troy expressed no interest in politics—at least he did not comment on the military regime in his letters home—but in Paraguay, where he traveled briefly after leaving São Paulo, Troy was impressed. The country was then living under the Alfredo Stroessner dictatorship. Stroessner came to power in 1954 following a military coup d'état, and he ruled the corrupt (and, for much of the time, U.S.-backed) Paraguayan state—one of the worst human rights violators in South America—until 1989. Troy recognized that Stroessner was a "dictator," though he considered him a "popular" one, and "the country has made remarkable progress" under his rule, he told his parents in August 1964. The evidence cited by Troy illustrates the extent to which tourists hailing from the industrialized West often conflate material trappings that remind them of home with "progress" in the nations they are visiting. There were, Troy wrote of Paraguay under Stroessner, "machined fence posts, town indicators, mile signs[,] and direction indicators."[25]

As the jaunt in landlocked Paraguay suggests, Troy spent more and more time away from the ocean. What was originally conceived as a surfing-centered voyage became a hitchhiking odyssey across vast swaths of the

Latin American, European, and African interiors. There were occasional opportunities to surf, but Troy's interests broadened with each passing mile. Still, there was no doubting the significance of his globe-trotting to the international surfing community. Peter Troy was, one of the Australians who discovered Lagundri Bay with him opined, "the grand-daddy of surf exploration," spending years on the road with a backpack, some instruments with which to write, and a dwindling reserve of funds.[26] However, he was nowhere near as successful in popularizing surf exploration as were a couple of Southern California teenagers in the mid-1960s. Robert August and Mike Hynson are, to surfing enthusiasts today, household names. This is not because the two photogenic teens—one a blond-haired regularfoot, the other a dark-haired goofyfooter—racked up any championship trophies; neither of them, in fact, was a professional competitive surfer. Rather, August and Hynson just happened to be asked by a budding twenty-something filmmaker whether they wanted to appear in his new movie.

Bruce Brown had already made a series of popular films for surfing audiences in the late 1950s and early 1960s, among them the cleverly titled *Slippery When Wet* and *Barefoot Adventure*. All August and Hynson would have to do for Brown's newest project, *The Endless Summer*, was to travel, smile, and surf. They would not even have to talk; Brown would provide the picture's narration. August and Hynson readily agreed, and the result was Brown's artful chronicle of the two surfers chasing the summer, with its warm water and consistent waves, from California to Africa and points between. Shot in 1963, *The Endless Summer* traveled the traditional surf-film circuit of civic center and high school auditoriums in California, Hawai'i, Australia, and South Africa over the two years that followed. But Brown was convinced his documentary could appeal to a broader audience. With *Gidget* and the Annette Funicello/Frankie Avalon beach-party movies having achieved wide commercial success, surfing's popular appeal at that time was unmistakable. No major distributor would touch the untested documentary, however. Brown thus decided to rent a venue "about as far as one can get from the ocean and surfing," a press release for the film noted, so as to screen it to an audience of surf-culture neophytes.[27] By any measure, Wichita, Kansas, fit the bill. "[O]pening a surfing film in Wichita is like distributing Playboy Magazine in a monastery," Brown opined. "In Wichita, most of the natives think surf is a new brand of detergent . . . or something."[28] In spite of what would seem, by all reasonable predictions, to have been a uniformly disinterested audience of landlocked Midwesterners, *The*

Endless Summer proved a runaway success. Opening opposite *My Fair Lady* and *The Great Race*, the documentary "slaughtered them both during its two-week [Kansas] run," reported the *Hollywood Citizen News*.[29] Brown then took the film to New York City, where it showed to enthusiastic audiences for a remarkable forty-seven weeks.[30] Shot on a budget of $50,000, *The Endless Summer* would ultimately gross an estimated $30 million worldwide, rendering it one of the most successful documentary films of all time.[31]

Its cultural impact was profound. The *Washington Post* would dub it a "classic" account of "the sport's golden age."[32] Members of the National Screen Council, which in January 1967 awarded *The Endless Summer* its Boxoffice Blue Ribbon Award—"unusual for a documentary," the group noted—were ecstatic. "You could be 85 and never have put a toe in the water and still think this is great," chimed one. "Who would have thought I would sit enthralled for 91 minutes by a documentary about surfing!" said another.[33] Brown came in for extraordinary praise. To *Time* magazine he was the "Bergman of the Boards"; the *New York Times* christened him the "Fellini of the Foam."[34] So historically significant is *The Endless Summer* that in 2002 the Library of Congress selected the picture for inclusion on its exclusive National Film Registry. The movie's signature poster, featuring the silhouettes of Brown, August, and Hynson "backlit by the sun," has been "immortalized," noted the *Washington Post*, in the Museum of Modern Art in New York City.[35] *The Endless Summer* theme music, composed and performed by the Sandals, helped define the surf music genre. As a global project, the film awakened thousands of surfers to the possibilities of exploration in Africa, the South Pacific, and other exotic locales, and it introduced countless people worldwide to California's more genuine surfing "subculture" (as opposed to the caricature that appeared in Hollywood's teenage surf movies).[36] Yet in ways that have not been explored by scholars, *The Endless Summer* also illustrates how, during the height of the Cold War, the United States came to view surfing as an ideological weapon in its anti-Communist crusade, for in May 1967 it was announced that the documentary would appear, under State Department sponsorship, at the biennial Moscow Film Festival.[37]

It is not difficult to envision the film's appeal to those tasked with American cultural diplomacy. In its story of two young Californians who meet the locals while looking for surf in Senegal, Ghana, South Africa, Australia, New Zealand, Tahiti, and Hawai'i, Brown's picture is entertaining, funny, and visually striking. But it is much more than that. Through its protagonists' carefree travel, *The Endless Summer* highlighted the freedom afforded

Americans—unlike most of those living in the Soviet bloc—to explore and discover the nations of the world. In the stars' quest for nothing more than good waves and fun, the film illustrated the pleasurable lifestyle promised by the capitalist system that made such leisure possible. And in the visiting surfers' interactions with the locals—as embarrassingly racist as some of these interactions may appear to audiences today—*The Endless Summer* painted a portrait of the United States as a benevolent and sympathetic power at a time when, given the escalation of the war in Vietnam, the U.S. image was suffering in much of the Third World. Such people-to-people encounters, for which global tourism played a leading role, were an important Cold War weapon at the heart of America's soft overseas propaganda.[38]

For reasons more nepotistic than meritorious, *The Endless Summer* was withdrawn from the Moscow festival just weeks before it was to get under way. The Soviets told Washington that it needed to whittle down the number of films it intended to present, including just one commercial documentary. The United States had planned to show two: *The Endless Summer* and *The Young Americans* (1967), a patriotic account of high school- and college-age American choral singers performing in venues across the United States. Marc Spiegel, the Russian-speaking executive of the Motion Picture Association of America (MPAA) who traveled to Moscow to consult with the Soviets, recommended *The Endless Summer*.[39] But Columbia Pictures, whose founders' scion made *The Young Americans* and which served as the film's distributor, "prefer[red]" its own documentary, MPAA chief and U.S. delegation organizer Jack Valenti notified Spiegel.[40] The MPAA, of course, represented the big American studios, while *The Endless Summer* was made by Bruce Brown Films and distributed by the small art-film company Cinema V. It was no contest. *The Young Americans* received the official nod.

Much to the frustration of the American contingent, in the end it, too, failed to show in Moscow. Its scheduled presentation was abruptly canceled by the Soviets without official explanation. Informally the authorities stated that the film was considered "American propaganda" by "high-level" Soviet viewers.[41] This incensed Valenti, who had been assigned by the State Department to oversee American activities at the festival. "If the portrayal of young, wholesome Americans as they tour the United States giving concerts, climaxed by appearances in patriotic settings in Washington, is propaganda, then this was 'propaganda,' and about as good as could be found," Valenti wrote to Washington. "But it was, first of all, an excellent motion picture."[42] While Valenti believed *The Young Americans*' cancellation was ultimately a coup for the United States—the "meaning of the cancellation was not lost on Festival delegations or the world press, and thus the indirect effect was to benefit the United States," he concluded—the MPAA chief was in fact being shortsighted. The censorship may have redounded to Washington internationally, but it had no discernible effect on the Soviet citizenry, who viewed the festival films by the hundreds of thousands.[43] The most effective propaganda, of course, is that which does not appear as such. If the principal reason for the American film industry's investment in Moscow was "90% political," as Valenti wrote to Secretary of State William Rogers, he failed to fully appreciate that the showing of Bruce Brown's film, with its implicitly positive representations of the United States as a confident and courageous nation of economic abundance, would almost certainly have resonated with the Soviet people, as it had with countless Americans.[44] *The Endless Summer*, from this perspective, would have been a more inspired choice in 1967.

Those tasked with American cultural diplomacy gave surfing another chance not long afterward. The year was 1970, the place was Japan, and the setting was the first world's fair ever to be held in Asia: the Japan World Exposition, or Expo '70, in Osaka. Running for six months, the exposition was spread over 815 acres and featured the participation of seventy-seven countries, more than two dozen Japanese and foreign corporations, several U.S. and Canadian local governments, and three multilateral organizations. It drew an estimated 64 million visitors.[45] The general purpose of Expo '70, like the purpose of all world's fairs, was to showcase various nations' geographies, economies, cultures, and societies. Yet such exhibitions, regardless of their innocuous facades, are always political.[46] In 1970, deep into the Cold War, there was no question that the United States was competing with the Soviet Union over which country would mount the most impressive national display. "Whether we like it or not," wrote the chief of the American delegation to the director of the U.S. Information Agency (USIA), "we really are being thrown into a competition with the Russians over here."[47] American officials thus took their cultural work very seriously.

The United States Pavilion, with 100,000 square feet of enclosed floor space spread over a six-acre site, embodied the vision of architect Yasuo Uesaka. Its exhibits—organized by the USIA—were designed by the joint venture team of Davis, Brody, Chermayeff, Geismar, de Harak Associates and divided into seven categories: Folk Art, Ten Photographers, American Painting, Sports, Space Exploration, Architecture, and New Arts.[48] American officials assumed the highlight would be the space exhibit, which featured several spacecraft and a moon rock brought to earth by the Apollo 11 astronauts; the Soviets were also planning a space exhibit at Expo '70, so the moon rock afforded the Americans—who alone had undertaken manned lunar landings—an opportunity to demonstrate their national superiority. Yet competing for popularity was the exhibit devoted to sport. This is hardly surprising. Only war is more effective—and even that is debatable—in exciting people's passions. It was there, within the sports exhibit, that, so far as I am aware, surfing for the first time became an official object of U.S. cultural diplomacy.

By 1970, surfing was already firmly established in Japan. As was true of a number of places around the world, it arrived as an indirect by-product of American military power. Japanese fishermen had ridden *ita-go*, which were a primitive form of bodyboards, since at least the second decade of the twentieth century (and perhaps as early as the twelfth century), and there may have been people stand-up surfing on Honshu as early as the late 1920s. But it was, by all accounts, American servicemen stationed in Japan after World War II who planted the seeds of the sport's modern growth and popularity. They brought surfboards with them to Japan, where they shared their equipment and pointers with a number of curious locals. These locals began building their own boards and forming clubs and, by 1964, the clubs were competing against one another. In 1965, the Nippon Surfing Association was founded.[49] Word of Japan was getting out. *Surfer* reported sailors' accounts of "perfectly formed" waves in 1962 and ran an eight-page spread on Bruce Brown's Japanese travels for *The Endless Summer* in 1964.[50] *Petersen's Surfing Yearbook* followed up with a short piece in 1966, and *Surfer* published a ten-page feature on the country in 1968.[51] As they had with baseball, Japanese indigenized the aquatic pastime, developing a vibrant surf culture that, by the early twenty-first century, encompassed an estimated 750,000 surfers, seven surfing magazines, some nine hundred surf shops, and a professional surfing association.[52] Women were particularly well represented. Japan, wrote Michael Scott Moore in 2010, "may have a higher proportion of female surfers than any nation in the world."[53]

Despite its growing popularity at the time of Expo '70—*Surfer* had predicted in 1968 that within a few years the sport would be as popular in Japan as it was in Hawai'i and the United States—U.S. officials appeared oblivious to the existence of a Japanese surfing community when organizing their pavilion. They thought the sport, which they identified as "typically Ameri-

FIGURE 6. In an indication of the role surfing might play in U.S. cultural diplomacy, the United States created a sports exhibit for Expo '70 in Osaka, the first World's Fair to be held in Asia, that proudly featured surfing as a "typically American" pastime. Here, surfboards were mounted along the "sloping side" of the exhibit platform in what almost seemed like the rising face of a wave. Credit: Photograph of Expo '70, Folder: General—Exhibit Photos, Box 2, Entry #A1 1054-B: Files of the Design Office, 1967–1972, Office of the Director/ Osaka World Exhibition Office, Record Group 306, National Archives II, College Park, Maryland.

can," would be of interest to the Japanese public simply because of its "uniqueness, gad[g]etry, and polish."[54] Whatever their motivation, organizers gave surfing a prominent role in the sports exhibit. The centerpiece of the surfing material was a futuristic display of thirteen boards—five by Weber Surfboards (Dewey Weber), five by Rick Surfboards (Rick Stoner), and three by Wave Riding Vehicles (Bob White)—mounted over the metallic "sloping side" of the exhibit platform in a crude mimicry of a wave.[55]

There also appeared in rear-view projection a continual loop of fast-action motion pictures that contained surfing footage donated by Bruce Brown Films.[56] And photography of Hawaiian surfing was featured on the massive Man in Sport Transparency Wall created with the assistance of *Sports Illustrated*.[57] The American organizers were hoping to impart the growing significance of surfing across the United States, with boards representing the East Coast, the West Coast, and Hawai'i. They did research on the mechanics and history of surfboard design and compiled a list of well-known shapers, ultimately commissioning the work of a select few.[58]

And, it appears, the organizers succeeded in their diplomatic objectives. The reception to the American Pavilion was overwhelmingly favorable. The media, one U.S. official noted, was "almost embarrassingly lauditory [*sic*]." This was just as true of the sports exhibit as it was of the overall pavilion.[59] The sports materials, which included a good deal of baseball memorabilia—a sure hit in Japan—were, according to different press accounts, "authentic," "outstanding," and "excellent."[60] One journalist applauded U.S. commissioner general Howard Chernoff's confidence in sport's popularity, noting that it was "paying off in press attention" to the surfboards and several other items.[61] There were, nevertheless, occasionally discordant notes, most of them from visiting Americans. The wife of a naval aviator stationed in Atsugi lamented the presence of Leonard Freed's photographs illustrating some of the complexities of American society, with its racial injustice and poverty; the images filled her with "complete disappointment, embarrassment, and anger."[62] A mother from a suburb of Cleveland—a self-described "irritated and disgusted member of your silent majority"—complained to President Nixon that "some Japanese families (not VIPs) with children strapped to their backs" were allowed through the pavilion's VIP entrance while she and a group of American sailors were denied this privilege; if the sailors "had stayed home, burned their draft cards, grown their hair long, and blown up a college building, they would have been treated with more respect by the American government," she fumed.[63] And an Air Force colonel who visited Expo '70 while on leave complained, as did others, about the "ill kempt, long haired, dirty clothed, hippie[-]type singers" performing for those waiting to enter the pavilion.[64] As Chernoff reported to Washington, the Americans registering complaints were generally upset "because we wouldn't let them jump the long lines, or because they felt we didn't exhibit what they would have exhibited." They ignored "the fact that ninety-six percent of our audience is Japanese and it's to them, rather than the Americans, that we are aiming the exhibits," he said.[65]

The Japanese, conversely, "don't write too often," Chernoff told the USIA, and when they did it was "usually . . . because they were unable to find one of our six water fountains or because the lines were a bit long and exhausting."[66] There were, to be sure, Japanese displeased with the American participation in the fair, such as the students who organized as the Joint Struggle to Crush Expo and the Japan-U.S. Security Treaty.[67] But most Japanese appeared to respond favorably to the American pavilion, and opportunities to strengthen U.S.-Japanese ties abounded. One of these came from Tamio Katori. Katori was a surfer from Kanagawa Prefecture who made Maiami Beach, near Chigasaki, his local break. He visited the American exhibits and was deeply impressed with the surfboards displayed there. Katori wrote to U.S. officials, asking whether he could purchase the boards for his surfing club once the fair ended. To demonstrate the seriousness he attached to the request, he also telephoned the Americans and sought them out during a second visit. Katori wished to further spread surfing in Japan, and the boards, he told the Americans, would not only popularize the sport but also contribute to what he called "the goodwill between both countries."[68] Three of the thirteen boards had been lent by Bob White and would need to be returned to the Virginia Beach shaper, but the remaining ten had been purchased by the USIA. For the United States, concurring with Katori's request would be an effective means of disposing of a bulky exhibit while contributing to the globalization of this now most American of pleasurable pastimes and fostering transpacific amity. It was a no-brainer. The boards were sold.

The surfing display at Expo '70 may be a minor footnote in the larger history of U.S. cultural diplomacy, but it illustrates one of the ways that surfing increasingly intersected with American global power. It also starkly illuminates the extent to which surfing, like Hawai'i, had become naturalized as somehow American. Those U.S. military personnel who rode waves in Japan after 1945 were participants in the same twentieth-century globalization that saw such disparate phenomena as the export of Hollywood beach films and the creation of Osaka's surfing exhibit. But this was not an exclusively American globalization. Surfing offered an increasingly global culture. The Third World "surfaris" of young wave-riding enthusiasts who built an international fraternity helped to ensure as much. Australian waterman Peter Troy may have been the first serious explorer—or at least the first to attract a great deal of attention—but he was hardly alone. The American duo Kevin Naughton and Craig Peterson, for instance, fascinated thousands of young Westerners with their *Surfer* magazine dispatches throughout the 1970s.[69] Indeed, travel became, by that decade, an essential component of modern surf culture. "Just to clear something up," the editors of *Surfing* magazine once wrote, "we're not telling you to 'travel.' That's a given. We surf; it's assumed we're all infected with the *wanderlust*. The allure of new waves and cultures comes with the territory, much like chronic tardiness and public displays of bro-shaking. We know you crave the road; we all do."[70]

FIGURE 7. "Charlie don't surf!" While that may or may not have been true—the U.S. military in fact reported that Vietnamese revolutionaries were using wooden surfboards to surreptitiously move along the Vietnamese coast—there can be no doubt that *Apocalypse Now* (1979) perhaps immortally associated surfing with the Vietnam War. It was addressed even more extensively in *Apocalypse Now Redux* (2001), Francis Ford Coppola's extended version of the 1979 original. In this scene, Captain Benjamin Willard (Martin Sheen) steals an arriving surfboard from a helicopter crew while hustling surfing legend Lance Johnson (Sam Bottoms) away from the napalm-loving officer Lt. Col. Bill Kilgore (Robert Duvall). Credit: *Apocalypse Now Redux* © Zoetrope Corporation.

That road broadened with every passing year. As late as the early 1960s, Hawai'i had been the ultimate object of surfing desire. Then came *The Endless Summer* and its vision of cultural encounter. Mexico began to beckon, as did Peru and South Africa. Countries that had not previously graced tourist itineraries suddenly found themselves flooded with board-toting visitors. Surfers are "always the first to sniff out an untrammeled destination," wrote the *New York Times*.[71] If there was a coast, surfers came. They blazed trails around the world, vastly expanding or even opening the tourism profiles of nations from Morocco to Mauritius. As "countercultural rebels" (more on this in chapter 5), they were what Joseph Heath and Andrew Potter called "the 'shock troops' of mass tourism."[72] Yet no area of the world attracted more attention in the 1970s than Southeast Asia, with its warm water, cheap accommodations, and jungle-fringed beaches.

Southeast Asia had, of course, been much on the minds of young surfers throughout the second half of the 1960s. With the United States enmeshed in a brutal counterrevolution in Vietnam, millions of young men in the United States and Australia—the world's twin centers of global surf

FIGURE 8. Surfing during the Vietnam War was not just a figment of Hollywood's imagination. It was in fact a notable feature of the U.S. military's rest-and-recuperation circuit.
The military even sponsored surfing contests. In this photograph, several competitors exit
the water at a contest in Chu Lai in September 1966. Credit: Photograph of Captain Rod-
ney Bothelo, Elli Vade Bon Cowur, Robert D. Brinkley, Tim A. Crowder, and Steven C.
Richardson, September 26, 1966, ARC ID 532396, Record Group 127, Still Picture Records
Section, Special Media Archives Services Division, National Archives II, College Park,
Maryland.

culture—found themselves confronting the possibility of military conscrip-
tion. Filmgoers today can tell you all about surfing and the Vietnam War.
After all, they have seen *Apocalypse Now* (1979). In the film, Lt. Col. Bill
Kilgore, memorably played by Robert Duvall, calls for the destruction of a
coastal Vietnamese village so that he and his men can surf a nearby break.
They do so amid enemy fire. "If I say it's safe to surf this beach, captain, it's
safe to surf this beach," Duvall shouts at a doubting member of his unit.
It was during this sequence, probably the film's best remembered, that the
famous lines "Charlie don't surf" and "I love the smell of napalm in the morning" were uttered.

Francis Ford Coppola, who made *Apocalypse Now*, used the scene to illustrate the absurdity of the war, and most filmgoers probably assumed that the

idea of surfing in Vietnam during those blood-soaked years was a figment of Hollywood's imagination. But it wasn't. Young servicemen were surfing there as early as 1966.[73] Indeed, in September of that year the military sponsored a surfing contest in Chu Lai, which was won by Pvt. First Class Robert D. Brinkley of Newport Beach, California.[74]

Surfing in fact became so popular in Vietnam that the China Beach Surf Club, with eighty-two members, sought to create a competition circuit, while a U.S. military team was invited to compete at the 1966 world championships in San Diego.[75] Surfing was a great morale booster amid the death and destruction in Vietnam, and it became a staple of the rest and recuperation experience.[76] By 1969, the American armed forces, which had published a guidebook to Vietnam in the early 1960s that made military service there sound like a working holiday, was even operating a surf shop in Danang.[77] And it was not just the Americans. In 1967, the U.S. military reported that Vietnamese insurgents were using wooden surfboards to surreptitiously travel to an offshore island in Go Cong Province.[78] Did Charlie in fact surf? It is tempting to imagine a guerrilla finding respite on a quick wave or two upon returning to the Vietnamese mainland. But truth be told, we cannot say. What we do know, however, is that, like the Office of Strategic Services agents mentioned in chapter 1, the revolutionaries saw the way that modern surfing equipment could be marshaled for national security ends.

It is no accident that surfing, of all pastimes, made its way into *Apocalypse Now*. The film may be a modern adaptation of Joseph Conrad's *Heart of Darkness*, but it *is* an adaptation, and the man who adapted it was John Milius. Milius is most recognizable to Americans today as a right-wing screenwriter and director—among other films, he made *Red Dawn* in 1984—but surfers know him as one of their own.[79] The year before *Apocalypse Now* appeared, *Big Wednesday* (1978), which Milius cowrote and directed, was released to poor box-office receipts and reviews. It has since, however, become something of a cult favorite.[80] *Big Wednesday* is the story of three young surfers growing up in seemingly carefree Southern California in the 1960s. But it is not, despite initial appearances, all parties, pranks, and wave riding in Malibu. At the center of the film lurks the Vietnam War. Two of the protagonists—played by Jan-Michael Vincent and Gary Busey—feign physical or psychological afflictions to avoid the draft. The third, played by William Katt, volunteers to go to Vietnam. The war, and Katt's military service, tear the three men apart. Surfing reunites them.

FIGURE 9. Before he memorably wrote surfing into *Apocalypse Now* (1979), John Milius cowrote and directed *Big Wednesday* (1978), his now beloved story of a 1960s Southern California surf culture that found itself disrupted by the Vietnam War. Portions of the movie were to be filmed in El Salvador, but—much to the crew's frustration—the waves did not agree. It remained flat. The crew thus found plenty of time to relax, seemingly oblivious to the violence devastating the country around them. Photograph by Dan Merkel. Credit: © Merkel/A-Frame.

And so, in its own way, did the Latin American Cold War. Portions of *Big Wednesday* were filmed in violence-wracked El Salvador in the late 1970s. At that time, right-wing death squads and military forces aided by the United States were detaining, killing, and "disappearing" human rights activists, labor organizers, and peasant leaders. Indeed, "[m]urder and torture became especially commonplace" from 1977 to 1979, writes historian Stephen Rabe.[81] But the *Big Wednesday* crew need not have worried. They were safe.

The Australian publication *Tracks* reported that they were having a grand time at "a ritzy hotel in the resort town of Sunzal" while "terrorist attacks"—presumably a reference to the brewing left-wing insurgency resisting the military dictatorship—were exploding around them.[82] The production went swimmingly. (Not long afterward, as the Central American wars were devastating communities from Guatemala to Nicaragua, *Surfer* advised its readership, "For those into tubes and bullets, now is the time to go to El Salvador," where "[a]ll the local surfers are gone and the Americans are staying home."[83] The appeal was obvious to the James Wood character in Oliver Stone's *Salvador* [1986], who affectionately described La Libertad, where he planned to seek occasional refuge from photographing the war, as "the best surfing beach in the world.")

Big Wednesday was, for John Milius, a labor of love. As a screenwriter who grew up surfing Malibu in the 1960s, it is little wonder that Milius's sport has, through *Apocalypse Now*, become so memorably associated with the Vietnam War. Yet if the late 1960s and 1970s were characterized by surfing discoveries in Southeast Asia, Vietnam was hardly the country at the top of anyone's list. That would have been Indonesia, the wave-rich archipelago that underwent one of the most violent episodes in modern history at the same time that the war in Vietnam was raging nearby. The United States was deeply involved in that violence, too. If surfers today recall the era as something of a golden age for surf exploration, there is little appreciation for the broader context in which this worldwide travel unfolded. Put differently, surfing's relationship to American power has too often seemed divorced from its more popular association with discovery and pleasure. That was just as true of El Salvador as it was of Indonesia. Indonesia, in fact, became ground zero for the construction of discovery narratives at a time when surfing was beginning to secure its truly global reach. It is thus to that Southeast Asian archipelago, and its years of both horror and delight, that we now turn.

THREE

Paradise Found

THE DISCOVERY OF INDONESIA
AND THE SURFING IMAGINATION

FIRST CAME CONFUSION; then came the terror. On September 30, 1965, a small and seemingly disorganized group of Indonesian military officers kidnapped and killed six generals of the Indonesian armed forces. Among the deceased was the army commander, Lieutenant General Achmad Yani. The September 30 Movement, as the group was called, claimed that it was forestalling a U.S.-backed right-wing coup against Sukarno, the nationalist and nonaligned Indonesian president.[1] Amid the turmoil, Major General Suharto, the commander of the army's Strategic Reserve Command, assumed overall authority of the armed forces and crushed the insurgent movement. But Suharto chose not to stop there. Pronouncing the Indonesian Communist Party (PKI) entirely responsible for the affair, he proceeded to target it for extermination. Those tasked with wiping out the PKI—the military and its ideological brethren in various Muslim associations, youth groups, and anti-Communist organizations—initiated a massive campaign of organized violence.[2] For the victims, innocence was no defense. The perpetrators targeted not only the PKI leadership but also the party's unarmed members and sympathizers. The result was a "boiling bloodbath," an "orgy of flashing knives and coughing guns" whose outcome, *Time* magazine opined, represented the "best news" the West had received "for years in Asia."[3]

Within a year, the Indonesian Communist Party—the world's third largest—had been extinguished. So, too, had hundreds of thousands of lives. The violence was often intensely personal. Indonesian troops in most places initiated the slaughter.[4] Villagers would then frequently kill their neighbors. The deaths were generally delivered at close range, with civilian militias using bamboo spears, machetes, or army-supplied weapons.[5] Whatever its nature, the butchery was unstinting. "In many cases whole families were killed," Amnesty International reported, as "it was often said by the perpetrators that the liquidation of entire families would serve to eliminate the communist menace for all time."[6] The atrocities, moreover, were "accompanied by gruesome rituals," noted Robert Cribb: "the piling of corpses onto rafts, the nailing of genitalia of male communists to shop fronts, the blooding of witnesses[,] and so on."[7] In "several places," in fact, "the killers held feasts with their bound victims present. After the meal each guest was invited to decapitate a prisoner." It was apparently the goal of the perpetrators to "involve as many as possible in the killings."[8]

When the massacres finally drew to a close, as many as a million people lay dead and another half a million imprisoned, the "vast majority of them" without charge or trial.[9] Tens of thousands of these survivors would remain confined for years. "In terms of the numbers killed," the Central Intelligence Agency concluded in 1968, "the anti-PKI massacres in Indonesia rank as one of the worst mass murders of the 20th century."[10] Still, none of this concerned Washington. On the contrary, American support for the violence was unwavering, even "enthusiastic."[11] Suharto, it was clear, was a man with whom the United States could work. This would be apparent a decade later when the U.S.-backed regime commenced its invasion and genocidal occupation of East Timor. The 1975 aggression, as with the decision to destroy the Indonesian Communist Party ten years earlier, was undertaken with full American assent.

CONSTRUCTING INDONESIA

Indonesia became, in the last few decades of the twentieth century, the premier surfing destination on the planet. Situated just north of Australia, its decade of initial discovery—roughly 1970 through 1980—is the stuff of surfing lore. It was, for those who lived it, a golden age of the wave-riding past. But golden ages are complicated things. This one, like others, required that crucial details be written out. Virtually no accounts of Indonesian surfing history mention the widespread massacres of the mid-1960s or the authoritarianism and expansionism that followed. This is perhaps not surprising. Western media, and especially that of the United States, largely turned a blind eye to the Indonesian atrocities, emanating, as the violence did, from forces favored by Washington.[12] But these years of terror—the genocides, the aggression, and the widespread political repression—are central to the modern Indonesian experience, and to ignore them is to ignore the broader context in which surfing's discovery of the archipelago unfolded.

Surfing history, like surfing itself, has too often existed in an ideological bubble. Quests for pleasure of course foreground these accounts, and stories of exploration are at the heart of the sport's grand narrative. Pleasure and exploration are, to be sure, well represented in the case of Indonesia. What is missing is the other stuff: the decades of mass carnage and the steady complicity of the West. Those have essentially been erased—or, rather, never written, at least as far as surfing is concerned. Why? It is not that a cloak of mystery somehow blanketed the Indonesian record. On the contrary, from the first years of the Suharto era, that record had been addressed—sometimes extensively, often problematically—in the leading tourist literature. Recognition of the massacres of the mid-1960s, for instance, took very little time at all. As early as 1967, the guidebook series Fodor's was already writing of the "[t]housands of Communists and Communist sympathizers . . . killed in the nationwide anti-Communist purge."[13] By the time Bill Dalton, a contributor to the Australian surfing publication *Tracks*, published the first edition of his groundbreaking *Indonesia Handbook* in 1977, he was referring to "one of the most massive retaliatory bloodbaths in modern world history," with "the mass political murdering of perhaps one million people who were shot, knived, strangled, hacked to death."[14] Lonely Planet was slower to produce its own stand-alone guidebook to the archipelago, but, when it did so in 1986, the publishing house devoted an entire section of its historical synopsis—a section that spanned three pages—to what its heading called the "Slaughter of the Communists."[15] The invasion and occupation of East Timor claimed a couple more.[16]

In other words, awareness that Indonesia was an authoritarian state with a horrific human rights record—from the massacres of the 1960s and the "40–60,000 political prisoners" identified by Bill Dalton to the elimination and suppression of opposition and the denial of what Dalton called the "right of self-government" to East Timor—clearly existed.[17] It is undoubtedly true that the attention the Indonesian record received was insufficient, especially in the American mass media, and one could, and should, quibble with how it was framed.[18] This might explain the ignorance of millions of people from Muncie to Miami. But Australians tended to pay closer attention to Indonesia than did Americans, and surfers paid much closer attention than nearly anyone else. So what explains the absence of these issues in the surfing imagination? What accounts for the failure to wrestle with the question of whether traveling through Indonesia—and thus effectively subsidizing a regime engaged in widespread political repression—was morally responsible?

In considerable part, this was a logical outcome of modern surf culture. Most surfers venturing to the archipelago during the Suharto era were acting consistently with the ethos of their sport. There existed at that time a broadly shared sense that surfing was more than just an athletic endeavor; it provided a means of attaining spiritual transcendence. And as a spiritual pursuit, more earthly matters of politics or social injustice were verboten. Leonard Lueras, a journalist and best-selling author with more than thirty books on the Asia-Pacific region to his name, including a popular guidebook to Indonesia, captured the essence of many surfers' worldview better than anyone. Except for those "rare occasion[s]" when surfers themselves were directly affected, "[p]olitically," Lueras wrote approvingly, "surfing has managed to remain relatively pure and blind to the world's greatest social problems."[19] This association of surfing's purity with its detachment from an inevitably politicized world was, and is, significant. For globally wandering surfers to consider the political realities of the places they visited was to risk polluting the transcendence of the wave-riding experience. It is not that surfers were impervious to the revolutionary ferment of the 1960s and 1970s; in fact, they did occasionally speak out.[20] Their views, however, were usually quite limited. Surfers expressed deep concerns about the environment, for example, which was of course crucial to the enjoyment of their sport. But there was also a sense that surfing was itself a form of political engagement. "By simply surfing we are supporting the revolution," the acclaimed Australian wave rider Nat Young pronounced in 1970.[21] There was no need, then, to concern oneself with the lived political realities of those they encountered. Surfers, in essence, willed their own ignorance.

In this sense, their touristic priorities coincided with those of the Indonesian regime. Within several years of the bloodbath that enabled Suharto's ascension to power, Indonesia—and especially Bali—was already being constructed as a beckoning tourist paradise. This was not the first time it had been represented as such. Dutch authorities had earlier worked to replace popular notions of Bali as a land of fierce resistance to colonial conquest with colorful images of exotic splendor. "Eager to have the world forget its ruthless conquest of the island," wrote historian Adrian Vickers, the Dutch government in the 1920s and 1930s had begun "to promote Bali as a tourist destination." It was not a difficult sell. "More than any other tropical island,"

Vickers argued, Bali had become "the most exotic of exotic locations, a fantasy of all the splendors of the Orient and the beauties of the Pacific."[22] Thirty to forty years later, this provided excellent raw material for the new military regime. Apart from its ideological benefits—the masking of an authoritarian state with a land characterized by tropical bliss—tourism would serve the Indonesian authorities as a "vital source of foreign exchange."[23] It thus became an important national priority.[24]

Howard Jones, the former U.S. ambassador to the country, took a leading role in helping facilitate Bali's development. With the decimation of the PKI and the effective marginalization of Sukarno, the military authorities sought to secure immediate and massive foreign investment. Most of this investment was focused on extractive industries.[25] But tourism also received the new regime's attention. It was in this context that Jones was asked to serve as an intermediary between Indonesia and neighboring Singapore at a time when Lee Kuan Yew's government, which undertook a technical mission to Bali in April and May of 1968, believed that the growth of Indonesian tourism would deliver significant benefits to the fledgling Singaporean state.[26] In particular, increased global interest in Bali would be an effective means of placing nearby Singapore on what that country's finance minister called "the main stream" of a "rapidly growing Pacific area tourist trade."[27] Cognizant of tourism's potential, the Suharto regime, like its predecessor under Sukarno, began the important work of massaging Bali into a pleasurable global destination. The result of these efforts was quickly apparent. As early as November 1968, the U.S. embassy in Jakarta was reporting the "definite interest" of "a number of foreign airlines" in serving the Balinese market once the island's international airport was "fully operative."[28] While the physical development of Bali would in fact continue for decades, by the early 1970s the regime's discursive work was already showing success. Foreigners had begun to arrive. True, they were not the sort of free-spending tourists the government had initially desired. They were mostly hippies and surfers. Still, the mythmaking had succeeded. The "nucleus of tourist development" was in formation.[29]

Within the short span of three or four years—at a time when intrepid surfers embraced Third World travel as an essential element of surf culture, seriously exploring Africa, Asia, Latin America, and points between—Bali had emerged as perhaps the world's premier destination for thousands of young men (and it was almost entirely men) seeking world-class waves, warm water, and a hospitable travel environment. For many, this last criterion meant not only friendly locals but lodging, food, and transportation costs amenable to a community whose commitment to work was often subordinate to its commitment to surf. Indonesia, with its thousands of sun-drenched tropical islands, fit the bill. "Indonesian children," according to Matt Warshaw, "have long ridden waves on small wooden bellyboards, and America-born hotelier Robert Koke introduced stand-up surfing to the country in the 1930s at Bali's Kuta Beach. But surfing didn't really take root here until the late '60s, when visiting Australian and American flight attendants began testing the breaks around Kuta."[30] By 1973, as the number of visitors was rapidly increasing, the Australian periodical *Tracks* began asking whether "[p]aradise" had indeed been "[f]ound." The magazine, which extolled "some of the best surf discovered outside Hawaii" amid "cheap accommodation, beautiful tropical surroundings, an interesting culture, psychedelic mushrooms[,] and cheap grass," unequivocally answered its own question in the affirmative. It "seems that every second person is heading" to the archipelago, *Tracks* reported unsurprisingly.[31] Gerry Lopez, the legendary Hawaiian tube rider, explained why. "We discovered the biggest candy store for surf that could ever be," he recalled, "and we were completely and utterly just blown away by not only the quality but the consistency of the surf and the lack of people."[32] Bali thus became, by the mid-1970s, the "hottest new spot for the global surf traveler." It was, Warshaw wrote, "the surf world's new dream destination."[33]

Print journalists were hardly alone in celebrating the Indonesian discovery. Filmmakers did the same. In late 1971, several young surfers traveled around Bali and Java with photographer Albert Falzon in search of waves.[34] What they found was a beautiful left-hand pointbreak below the Hindu temple at Uluwatu.[35] The California-based magazine *Surfer* would, shortly afterward, declare that Uluwatu "may be the finest wave in the world."[36] Falzon's footage of the surf and the "primitive Asian culture" he discovered in Bali was released in *Morning of the Earth* (1972), a filmic "fantasy of surfers living in three unspoiled lands & playing in natures [*sic*] oceans," according to an on-screen narrative that opened the production.[37] Today, *Morning of the Earth* is perhaps the second most celebrated motion picture in surf history.[38] When it appeared in the early 1970s, it was very much a reflection of its era. The film dances psychedelically through Australia, Indonesia, and Hawaii; often looking like something out of an acid trip, the smell of burning dope practically wafts from the screen. Falzon, a cofounder of *Tracks*, the proudly independent magazine that for years shunned the glossiness of mainstream surf periodicals for the more earthy feel of matte newsprint, viewed surfing as a form of countercultural rebellion. The surfers in his film live simply and communally. Their aquatic passion is not merely a pursuit of pleasure; it is a unique form of communion with the natural world.

In traveling to Indonesia, then, Falzon's surfers discovered, to be sure, outstanding waves. Yet the filmmaker's interest was not only the surf. He also treated the Balinese people as an extension of nature. A small village through which a surfer walks is surrounded by lush vegetation. A local man paddling his boat is fully a product of the sea. So, too, are the fishermen gracing Bali's beaches, as is a prau sailing across the sunset that appears near the close of the film's Indonesian sequence. Earlier, the surfers share a smoke with several local men. One unself-consciously stands naked before two Balinese; in nature, the film reminds its audience, naked is natural. This exotic view was not unique to *Morning of the Earth*; the surf media was full of such representations. Surfers, in fact, began to sound a lot like anthropologists. "The native people" of Bali, one American visitor recorded in *Surfer*, "are small in stature" and "very attractive . . . as a whole." The "bush people went partially undressed, but there was a hint of social awareness and a tendency not to want to be photographed topless." Other parts of the island, meanwhile, were "rumored to have full-on primitives, like warriors and cannibals."[39] Nowhere in Falzon or *Surfer*'s vision of Indonesia was the reality of the country's repressive political environment, a reality that was in fact an "integral" component of Balinese history, one leading historian wrote. Complicating the portrait in *Morning of the Earth* and a bevy of related films and publications, there was a "dark side" to the Balinese "paradise," Geoffrey Robinson found, a "paradise" that had historically been characterized by "violence and conflict."[40]

Just several years before Falzon filmed his motion picture, in the mass violence that erupted following the September 1965 incident on Java, an estimated eighty thousand Balinese had been killed, a figure that amounts to roughly 5 percent of the island's people. The "populations of whole villages were executed," Robinson wrote, "the victims either shot with automatic weapons or hacked to death with knives and machetes. Some of the killers were said to have drunk the blood of their victims or to have gloated over the numbers of people they had put to death."[41] It was a time, wrote Adrian Vickers, when "the rivers literally ran with blood and the graveyards overflowed."[42] Such behavior obviously "did not fit well with the widely accepted view that Bali was an earthly paradise, whose artistic and deeply religious people lived in harmony with nature and with one another," Robinson added.[43] Or, as an official guidebook to Bali put it in 1970, a place where the people were "gentle and smiling," waiting to greet visitors to their "enchanting island," where "the traveler . . . is still the explorer, discovering untouched places and witnessing exotic rituals which have not diminished with the changing times."[44] In light of the horrific violence, one might have expected a popular reconsideration of the paradisial view. Nothing of the sort emerged in the surfing imagination, however. On the contrary, Bali (and Indonesia more broadly) remained in the early Suharto years a tropical fantasy world of brown-skinned, primitive locals—an Eden before the fall that, surf publications and films suggested, was begging for discovery and exploitation. Such a view was, however, little more than a "historical fiction," concluded Robinson, "a product of political calculation and conservative political objectives" that was given a "boost" by "a multimillion-dollar tourist industry that . . . found in Balinese 'tradition' a highly profitable scheme."[45]

When, in the mid-1970s, the first hints emerged that this new paradise had been despoiled, its innocence lost, the cause was not an overdue recognition of Indonesia's recent political violence and ongoing state repression. Rather, it was, more than anything, the inevitable arrival of the surfing hordes. Bali's celebration as a "[t]imeless [l]and," as *Tracks* characterized it in 1974, was regrettably coming to an end.[46] There were, to be sure, practical problems on the island. The food gave visitors the runs. The mosquitoes, while not numerous, were said to carry malaria. The coast was teeming with sharks, sea snakes, and sea lice. But the biggest problem was the growing number of surfers. There was a time, filmmaker Yuri Farrant reminisced in 1975, when "whole villages would gather to cheer a surfer riding waves, and watch him ride in wonder for hours." But "[i]t isn't like that now. The place isn't like that at all." Today, Farrant then complained, the Balinese people "are beginning to fight for your money. The peddlers won't leave you alone. It's worse than Tijuana."[47] The waves, moreover, had become packed. "It's crowded," he groused. "Kuta Beach . . . is almost unbearably crowded with surfers, and at Uluwatu, it's not uncommon to have 20 riders out and 20 more on the beach."[48]

Australian Steve Shamison agreed with Farrant's declensionist view. Before traveling to Bali, he had been told by his "stoked friends" how "far out it was." "They told me how cheap it was, how good the surf was, and how beautiful the people are," Shamison wrote in 1974. But the thirteen weeks he spent "in paradise" left him wondering whether that was still true. Apart from the dangerous surf—even experienced Hawaiian professionals were suffering grievous injuries—"food poisoning and intestinal infection are very common," he discovered, and "coral cuts" do not actually heal but "ulcerate." "It's bad," he concluded. And then there were the Balinese. "The local people are beautiful but their vibe is changing fast—very fast. And you can't blame them. They're tired of being yelled at because of language problems (ours, not theirs). Most are still stoked to help you and to make your stay pleasant but too many people are splitting without paying their bills. Before Bali became a scene, money didn't mean that much, but lately you can see dollar signs in their eyes." Moreover, the affordability of the island, which made it so accessible to scores of wandering surfers, was rapidly becoming a thing of the past. In November 1974, Shamison complained, "the price of everything everywhere here was DOUBLED by special proclamation of the Governor." Together with the increasingly crowded waves—Uluwatu "is becoming as common as the North Shore [of Oʻahu] in the surfing lexicon," Shamison rued, while the beachbreak at Kuta was "becoming so crowded" that "now even IT'S turning dangerous"—it seemed an unavoidable question whether this Indonesian "paradise" had lost its exalted stature.[49]

Part of the problem, grumbled American surfwear entrepreneur Duke Boyd, was that Bali was merely "a milk run for the Aussies," who had made Uluwatu "well known" through that country's surf media. Moreover, he noted, the island's waves had already been featured in at least four motion pictures.[50] In fact, so many Australians were traveling to Bali—an island that was to them much like Hawaiʻi was to Americans—that by 1977 the airline Qantas had taken to advertising in *Tracks* and was offering surfers package trips, including round-trip airfare, accommodations for thirty-four nights, "real" meals, and the use of a motorbike with which to get around.[51] Given Bali's rapid tourist development, it was "basically bullshit" to argue that places such as Uluwatu represented a secret still waiting to be discovered, maintained Boyd.[52] Yet there was hope. Bali was one of only thousands of islands in the archipelago. Yuri Farrant related how he "heard stories about a guy who had sailed to other islands in the region and who described a wave that started at 30 plus [feet], wound for 200 yards, the takeoff was at 15 [feet], and the wave kept winding on for an unbelievably long way. Perfect."[53] Jeff Divine heard similar tales. When visiting Bali, where by the mid- to late 1970s a sort of humdrum normalcy had taken much of the excitement out of surf tourism, a friend told him of "an island where there's a gaping left tube, better than Uluwatu, and where tigers stalk the beaches." It was "a place where the king of the island wears army fatigues, dark sunglasses, and charges you to surf his point-break waves."[54] There were discoveries, that is, awaiting those who chose to explore. Indonesia was in fact full of them, one Australian exclaimed. The country was "[o]ne of the few places in the world where there's any adventuring left!"[55] So explore, surfers did.

Michael Fay, in the summer of 1973, was among the first to publicly relate his other-island experience. Surviving the city of Jakarta's "sea of poverty and despair that makes a mockery of Indonesia's tourist face"—a rare sober note on some of the Indonesian realities that generally went overlooked in the surfing imagination—Fay and a companion found sanctuary on the southern Javanese coast in a "really beautiful bay . . . with high mountains all around and 4–6 foot swells moving into a gently curving series of bays and headlands." There they spent "pleasant days surfing glassy mornings, gazing at never before ridden points [sic] waves breaking on a stone bottom like Lennox [a surf break in Australia] and eating amazing fish meals." For a "nominal charge" they stayed in an "isolated losmen" situated "in a fairy tale setting a couple of kilos back from the coast, through winding jungle trail and rainforest." On each side of the losmen was a "stoney stream complete with steaming geyser—natural hot water." These were, Fay wrote somewhat understatedly, "[m]ellow times long to be remembered." And others could experience similar pleasure, Fay suggested, for the southern coasts of the Indonesian islands were a "surfin' land"—and "most of it" went "unridden."[56]

If Michael Fay was somewhat subdued in revealing the "[m]ellow times" he enjoyed outside of Bali, the American surfer and photographer Erik Aeder was positively giddy. In 1979, Aeder divulged his experience with a perfect right-hand reefbreak at an undisclosed location somewhere in the Indonesian archipelago.[57] Access was difficult. To get to the break, Aeder and his friend, Mark Oswin, had to travel to Indonesia by jet before flying a small, twelve-seat plane nearer to their destination; take an eight-hour boat ride to an offshore island; catch a lift on a coconut truck to a river in the interior; and then be paddled down the river and through a cave by a hired local fisherman. It took two days. But, they agreed, it was worth the hassle. After "pass[ing] slowly through the cavity, ducking and pushing the hanging pinnacles until we emerged into flat water at the mouth of the river[,] . . . all my imaginings solidified as a set swept across the reef outside," Aeder gushed. "I nearly fell out of the boat in excitement."[58] Aeder and Oswin were not in fact the first to surf Lagundri Bay; it had been ridden in 1975 by Peter Troy and two fellow Australians.[59] But Aeder's account, which was published in

FIGURE 10. Photographs of perfect waves and empty lineups are like pornography to surfers. Indonesia offered plenty of porn. This image, of an unnamed Lagundri Bay, appeared in *Surfer* magazine in 1979, during the golden age of Indonesian surf exploration. Photograph by Erik Aeder. Note: The image has been digitally altered to remove a crease. Credit: © *Surfer*.

Surfer, helped cement the mystique and allure of Indonesian travel. It is not difficult to discern why. Featuring gorgeous photographs of empty waves peeling into a spectacular tropical bay—the surfing equivalent of pornography—the magazine suggested that "countless adventures wait on untouched shores" for those willing to undertake them.

Speaking of this "land forgotten by time," Aeder's piece pointed to the thirteen thousand islands "scattered endlessly" across "the Indonesian chain," "[e]ach and every one of them" with "the formations of perfect reef point breaks. The gods of the sea[,] which the ancients held in fearful awe, brood from their mystic haunts to send waves of splendor to these magic shores." For those intrepid souls with the means to make the journey, Indonesia was a "storybook land of waves [that] becomes real to the seeker."⁶⁰

Apart from the dreamlike sense of exploration that *Surfer* imparted to its readers, Aeder's article is significant for its projection of a serene and universal pacifism onto the national population, a view evoked in virtually every account to appear in the extensive corpus of surfing films and publications from the 1970s through the present. While the American's 1979 report posited a bloody past—that is, "[b]efore the missionaries came . . . and tamed this violent society"—*Surfer* maintained that Indonesians were, without qualification, "a peaceful people."[61] That many Indonesians were "peaceful" was undoubtedly true. The same could be said of every society. Yet in broadly attributing such pacifism to an entire people (or, more accurately, a collection of peoples who make up the state of Indonesia), the magazine exacerbated the tendency of wave seekers to excise from the surfing imagination the U.S.-backed repression (and expansionist aggression) that had become a feature of Indonesian political life. *Surfer* offered nary a word about the orgy of violence that had consumed Indonesia in the 1960s. Nor, for that matter, was there even a hint of the ongoing violence that the Suharto regime was visiting on large numbers of people in the 1970s. This erasure of Indonesian realities—ones that, as both American citizens and tourists, Aeder and his compatriots were subsidizing twice over—was crucial.[62] The surfing imagination was not only ignorant of Indonesian repression and its facilitation by Jakarta's Western allies; it in fact demanded such ignorance, for to acknowledge the larger realities would have been to dispel surfers of the allure of exotic discovery in a timeless present in which they could play modern-day explorers in a corrupted political world.

SURFING THROUGH GENOCIDE

And in the 1970s, these larger realities were horrific. Rather than simply a "storybook land of waves" beyond "the hand of time," as *Surfer* envisioned it, Indonesia was, to at least one human rights organization, an "Asian gulag."[63] "With regard to numbers, time-scale, methods used by the government[,] and the history of mass killings and massive arrests, political imprisonment in Indonesia is without parallel today," Amnesty International concluded in 1977. The organization maintained that there were at least 55,000 political prisoners spread throughout the archipelago, though the "correct figure" was probably "as many as 100,000."[64] Torture, moreover, was disturbingly common. One former political prisoner who left the country in 1975—a young woman who had been "severely and sexually tortured" following her arrest in 1968—described the atrocities she saw visited upon other inmates: "the brutal treatment of a village headman who died under electrical torture, a woman who had boiling water poured over her head[,] and another woman whose nipples were cut off."[65] In 1976, Amnesty International asserted that a "pattern of brutal treatment of prisoners continues, especially during inter-rogation (which goes on even for those arrested 10 years ago), and also in those detention centers where torture is permitted by the local military commanders."[66] Testimony about one such commander, CPM Lieutenant Sulaiman, was presented before Congress in 1975. A letter written by a pris-oner in East Java and smuggled out of the country accused Sulaiman of be-ing a "psychopath." Among other things, political prisoners who "do not keep his rules are severely reprimanded, intimidated[,] and cruelly treated. They are kicked, trampled on, ordered to crawl on their hands and knees, beaten with his heavy army belt, and put into solitary confinement."[67] As of 1978, reported Amnesty International, the human rights situation in Indo-nesia remained "one of the most serious in the world."[68]

Indeed, the Indonesian authorities initiated a spasm of mass violence in the 1970s that faintly echoed the atrocities of the mid-1960s. This time, how-ever, their objects were not Indonesian. In 1975, the people of East Timor were targeted by the Suharto regime. The island of Timor is in the southern arc of the Indonesian archipelago, approximately four hundred miles north-west of Darwin, Australia. The western half of the island is part of Indone-sia; the eastern half was, until 1975, a Portuguese colony. "[W]ith friendly people, beautiful mountains, coral reefs, good Chinese food, [and] good wine," Timor "has it all," wrote future guidebook author Bill Dalton in *Tracks* in 1974.[69] But what may have seemed true to Dalton in 1974 quickly changed by 1975. Not long after his article appeared, much of the island be-gan its descent into hell. Indonesia, which obtained independence from the Netherlands in 1949, had never ruled East Timor. But as Portugal's global empire started to crumble in the mid-1970s, Jakarta sensed an opportunity. For months in 1975 the regime sought to provoke a casus belli for its planned intervention. It justified its provocations by falsely claiming that most Ti-morese wished to seek integration with Indonesia.[70]

Then, in early December—less than two weeks after East Timor declared its independence following months of Indonesian military harassment, a brief civil war, and the departure of the Portuguese authorities—Indonesia invaded and occupied the fledgling state. "[V]irtually all" of the military equipment used in the December invasion was provided by Washington.[71] "The soldiers who landed started killing everyone they could find," the one-time colony's former bishop recalled. "There were many dead bodies in the streets. All we could see were the soldiers killing, killing, killing."[72] FRETI-LIN, East Timor's governing party, immediately sought international assistance. "The Indonesian forces are killing indiscriminately," it broadcast from the capital, Dili, on December 7. "Women and children are being shot in the streets. We are all going to be killed. I repeat, we are all going to be killed. . . . This is an appeal for international help. Please do something to stop this invasion."[73] FRETILIN's plea fell on deaf ears. No one acted to stop the invasion. In fact, just the opposite occurred. Only hours before the December 7 broadcast, President Gerald Ford and his secretary of state, Henry Kissinger, met with Suharto in Jakarta. In the course of their meeting they gave the Indonesian regime a green light for its planned invasion. "We want your understanding if we deem it necessary to take rapid or drastic action," Suharto asked of his guests. Ford was accommodating. "We will understand and will not press you on the issue," he responded. "We understand the problem you have and the intentions you have." Kissinger asked only for attention to the delicacy of the invasion's timing. "[I]t would be better if it were done after we returned" to Washington, Kissinger informed the Indonesian president.[74]

Suharto graciously acceded to Kissinger's request. He was not so gracious to the Timorese. In the first year of the quarter-century occupation that followed—the Indonesians did not agree to withdraw from the territory until 1999—as many as sixty thousand Timorese may have lost their lives, according to Catholic Church sources.[75] But deaths were hardly the whole story. The repression also reordered Timorese society. Indonesia began an "encirclement" campaign in 1977 that attempted to "uproot much of the Timorese population and move it into designated hamlets." By 1979, at roughly the same time that *Surfer* was declaring Indonesians to be "a peaceful people," nearly half the population of the former Portuguese colony, or approximately three hundred thousand women, men, and children, had been displaced from their homes and placed in these military-controlled camps. There they lived in terrible squalor, at times succumbing to the ravages of their miserable existence.[76] Estimates differ, but by 1980 the number of fatalities would total at least one hundred thousand, and perhaps as many as twice that number, while the inclusion of atrocities and the deleterious conditions imposed by Indonesia after 1980 would render a figure "substantially higher."[77] Amnesty International reported in 1985 that, based on "[e]stimates from a wide range of sources," the number of deaths through the mid-1980s could have been as high as two hundred thousand.[78] Whatever the precise figure, the overall death toll in East Timor under the twenty-four-year Indonesian occupation was "proportionately comparable" to the atrocities in Cambodia under the Khmer Rouge, suggested Ben Kiernan.[79] In 1979, the UK-based but Indonesia-focused human rights organization TAPOL characterized this record as one of "genocide."[80] Scholars have generally agreed.[81]

Both the United States and Australia provided instrumental support for the Indonesian campaign. Among other reasons, Washington backed the Indonesian invasion and occupation because of Indonesia's strategic importance to the Americans and the desire not to complicate the bilateral relationship. As Henry Kissinger impressed upon Gerald Ford shortly before the invasion,

> Indonesia, the fifth most populous nation in the world, is more than three times the size of any other Southeast Asian country and includes within its border about half the region's total population. It is potentially one of the richest. Its geographic location and resources are of major strategic importance in the region. Flanking the Southeast Asian mainland, Indonesia controls the sea passages between the Pacific and Indian Oceans, including Japan's life line to Middle East oil; its own oil fields provides [sic] a significant portion of Japan's oil consumption and a small but increasing part of our own oil imports. Its other major resources—rubber, tin, and tropical products—are also of some significance to the United States.

Moreover, Kissinger continued, Indonesia under Suharto had carved out for itself "a somewhat unique diplomatic position as an anti-Communist but non-aligned country capable of carrying on a dialogue with both radical 'third world' states and the west while cautiously pursuing policies generally compatible with the latter."[82] In other words, Indonesia was important to the Americans; East Timor was not.

Matters of law and morality thus proved of little concern. Washington's priorities were clear and consistent. The Timorese would have to suffer. From the green light given by Ford and Kissinger to the "critical" provision of additional weaponry in 1977 to the diplomatic assurance that the United Nations prove, in the words of the U.S. ambassador to the organization at the time, "utterly ineffective" in undoing Indonesian aggression, American support was "fundamental to the Indonesian invasion and occupation," concluded East Timor's Commission for Reception, Truth and Reconciliation in 2005.[83] While not as determinative as the United States, Australia also rejected the sanctity of international law by acquiescing in Indonesian policy. "[S]uccessive Australian governments not only failed to respect the right of the East Timorese people to self-determination," the commission wrote, "but actively contributed to the violation of that right."[84] Prime Minister Gough Whitlam, for instance, met with Suharto in Central Java in September 1974, telling the Indonesian president that "Portuguese Timor should become part of Indonesia," though this should happen, he added, "in accordance with the properly expressed wishes" of the colony's inhabitants. This was important "for the domestic audience in Australia," an audience that, wrote Brad Simpson, "strongly supported meaningful self-determination."[85] In spite of the fact that the wishes of the Timorese people were not respected— a people that were overwhelmingly hostile to the Indonesian occupation— subsequent Australian governments consistently "appeas[ed]" the Suharto regime, even to the point of extending a "muted response" to the deaths of Australian nationals by the Indonesian forces in 1975.[86]

Australians and Americans were the two largest groups of surfers popularizing the Indonesian dreamscape, but the surfing imagination paid these realities no heed. The draw of the waves was too powerful. Peter Neely's oft-used *Indo Surf and Lingo: Hardcore Surf Explorer's Guide to Indonesian Surf Spots and Indonesian Language*, for instance, was utterly silent about the atrocities unfolding in East Timor, instead advising readers to "[t]alk to your local Indonesian Consulate" about a permit to enter the area. Timor was, after all, an island "with already proven . . . surf potential." In fact, Neely counseled, if "you have the time to explore, the possibilities are almost endless."[87] This appeal to explore the archipelago found its full expression at the dawn of the 1980s. The process of discovering outstanding waves was, two Americans wrote in 1979, "perhaps the single most exciting, gut-twisting, greening-with-envy sub-genre of the surf world which has come down the line in years."[88] And Indonesia, more than anywhere else, seemed perfectly suited for these sorts of missions. It was a "surfer's playground in paradise," regular visitor Dick Hoole opined, a "playground" whose thousands of islands, "many with magic coastlines, provide the richest surf potential on this planet." Bali, which had so enraptured some of the earliest surfers to visit Indonesia, was for many, by the late 1970s, merely "the launching pad for some of the most adventurous and rewarding modern-day surfaris." The other islands beckoned. "Your own fantasy island awaits you," Hoole promised the readers of *Tracks*.[89]

As the 1970s slipped into the 1980s, the desire of Western surfers to further explore the archipelago conveniently coincided with the regime's desire to open up islands beyond Bali to international tourism development. Its reasons were principally economic. Doing so would not only deliver financial benefits to the government—foreign exchange, increased investment, and improvements to infrastructure, for example—but also encourage modernization in villages across the country. Yet there was another benefit that might accrue to the regime, one that was certainly recognized by Jakarta. Developing tourism could assist the authorities in providing a positive view of Indonesia to a critical global audience. Surfers, in this context, would essentially serve as cultural ambassadors and grassroots propagandists. Their stories of a heavenly bounty of perfect waves overseen by "a peaceful people"—stories related in surfing magazines, newspaper articles, and within loose networks of friends and acquaintances—might overwhelm the more nightmarish visions of a corrupt "Asian gulag" familiar to human rights activists, development specialists, and the international political community. Notoriously frugal surfers may not have been the Indonesian regime's ideal tourists in the first years of Suharto's New Order, but by 1980 they were being actively courted by the authorities. "Indonesia Needs You!" a *Tracks* headline blared in August of that year. Next to the headline was an illustration of a pointing Indonesian military official in a clear mimicry of the iconic British posters of Lord Kitchener, the secretary of state for war, during World War I.[90]

Tracks outlined how "Indonesia's army generals" saw "you, the surfer, as part of the answer to their problems."[91] Officials, including Brigadier General Dading Kalbuadi, had taken notice of surfing's potential a couple of months earlier during the OM Bali Pro Am, the first international professional surfing contest held in Indonesia (and one that featured Indonesian as well as foreign competitors), and they began to envision surfers as agents of economic development across the island chain. The participation of Dading Kalbuadi was particularly notable, for he had overseen Indonesian covert operations against East Timor in 1975 before serving as commander of the Indonesian forces in the former Portuguese colony until 1978. At that point he transferred to the Bali-based Udayana territorial command, which included East Timor.[92] Dading, in his capacity as a military official in Timor,

FIGURE 11. Illustrating its article with a Lord Kitchener look-alike, *Tracks* reported in 1980 that Indonesian military officials had taken a keen interest in using surf tourism to promote village-level modernization throughout the archipelago. Note: The image has been digitally altered by placing the headline of the article underneath the drawing. Credit: Illustration courtesy of *Tracks*.

had not only been complicit in the widespread atrocities against the Timorese but had also been implicated in the killing by the Indonesian armed forces of five journalists based in Australia in the town of Balibo in October 1975.[93] Less than five years later, he was being feted at an international competition with heavy Australian participation. Dading, together with the governor of Bali and the Indonesian minister of youth, attended the contest's opening ceremony at Kuta, at which a military brass band led a procession of surfers onto the beach while armed soldiers with batons and German shepherds "herd[ed] the crowds into order." The Indonesian officials made a number of speeches before a group of foreign competitors staged a surfing exhibition for their hosts in the beachbreak waves fronting the contest pavilion. The army had reportedly promised a parachute display during the opening ceremony, but for some reason it failed to materialize.[94] Even without the parachutes, the contest's foreign participants were impressed. Australian surfer Jim Banks, for instance, praised how "well organized" the event appeared. "They really did a lot of work on it," he said. "[T]hey had the government in there, the army, everyone."[95] ("[T]he mind boggles at the role of the Government in this contest," journalist Kirk Willcox wrote the following year.[96]) For the Indonesian authorities, it was a public relations coup. "After the flak that Indonesia has received over East Timor," *Australian Surfing World* noted, "they were no doubt very pleased to get some good publicity going."[97] Notably, Dading's complicity in the genocidal violence in East Timor went unaddressed by the surf media; he was identified simply as "Chief of the Army of Udayana."[98]

The August article in *Tracks* on outer-island development did not offer a critical exposé of how the Indonesian authorities were seeking to use surfers; it was, rather, a discursion on how surfers and the regime could engage in a mutually beneficial relationship by encouraging tourism beyond Bali. This was a remarkable evolution. Whereas in the early 1970s the Indonesian authorities were concerned about the "pernicious influence" low-budget travelers "might exercise on . . . [Balinese] youth," toward the end of the decade, notes Michel Picard, the "hippie travelers," which would appear to include surfers, were being viewed "more positively" as a "supplementary market to that of deluxe tourism."[99] Surfers, in particular, were held in high esteem. "Surfing is not regarded as another corrupting cultural invasion," *Tracks* reported, "but as a positive influence. Officials appear to have made a distinction between 'hippies' who seem to drift without purpose and 'surfers' who they see as hardcore sportsmen and adventurers. In a nation where the ocean is a place to be feared as the home of demons, the surfer who treks huge distances to challenge this force is seen in an heroic light."[100] Surfers, as such, could begin to conceive of themselves not as gluttonous pleasure seekers interested only in finding waves but as economic missionaries delivering village-level modernization across the Indonesian archipelago.

There were, to be sure, some "problems." It was possible to "paint a rosy picture for the future of surfing in Indonesia and its improvement as a playground for Australians looking for waves," *Tracks* suggested. But surfers would still have to overcome certain hurdles. One of these was the threatened "intru[sion]" into unbridled touristic pleasure of "the delicate political situation that exists between the two countries." The surf media did not identify the nature or basis of this delicacy, but with the exception of the one-line statement in *Australian Surfing World* noted earlier, the ambiguous comment in *Tracks* was the closest the media ever came—at least in the materials I have examined in several archives in the United States and Australia—to acknowledging the political repression in Indonesia or the regime's brutal occupation of East Timor. But diplomatic strains were only part of the problem; there were also practical concerns. "Most breaks" were "still inaccessible," local transportation was "crude," "modern conveniences" were "nonexistent," and the "language barrier" was "mitigating against . . . rapid development of new surfing regions." Still, in spite of these difficulties—difficulties that, for many surfers, would only add to the thrill of exploration and sweeten the moment of discovery—*Tracks'* enthusiasm was evident: "Decentralization of the [surf] industry brings benefits to local village communities," it asserted. "A large proportion of village people gained little from Indonesia's general rise in prosperity, and some may have seen their welfare actually decline. Surfers can boost their economy." Claiming that surfers had already contributed to a rise in living standards for "the village at Uluwatu," the magazine argued that by "visiting other islands" they were "likely to make the same contribution."[101]

The Indonesian authorities apparently concurred. Lieutenant General Achmad Tirtosudiro, the regime's director general of tourism, spearheaded the official campaign. In order to "show his government's enthusiasm," as well as to "learn more about the sport," Achmad, during the 1980 OM Bali Pro Am, invited the contest organizers and a number of competitors to dinner at the Bali Hyatt Hotel. There he "spoke of the many islands to the east of Bali and invited surfers to disperse to these areas and explore their potential," *Tracks* reported. To encourage such exploration, the Indonesian government, upon the suggestion of filmmaker Alan Rich, sponsored a junket featuring Rich and seven surfers—six foreigners and Balinese standout Ketut Menda—to the island of Lombok, which is less than twenty-five miles from Bali across the so-called Wallace Line.[102] "[W]aves had been reported there but it had never been looked over properly," Rich recalled. Indeed, when he tried before leaving to "get info" about the island in Kuta, there was "virtually none." "Project Lombok," an excursion into a much less touristed part of Indonesia, thus commenced.[103]

On the whole, the group received—to the extent that local conditions allowed—the "red carpet treatment" during its travels.[104] The regime flew the surfers to Lombok, where they were greeted at the airport's VIP entrance by tourism representatives before being shuttled to the Sasaka Beach Hotel.

One participant who had previously stayed on Bali in a "dollar-a-day hovel" was particularly startled by the "high class" treatment he received when he was unexpectedly served breakfast in bed. The trip's most memorable moments occurred outdoors, however. Exploring the island was "[j]ust unreal," Rich wrote, as the surfers spent time "[w]alking through empty beaches" like "freaks in a fairytale." And the waves were "cooking."[105] The "gang cleaned up heavily with the discovery of several points in the [Uluwatu] category," *Surfer* revealed.[106] The authorities must have been pleased; the surfers discovered waves, the government received positive press, and the potential outside of Bali was made public. In the years that followed, the effort to encourage surfing across the archipelago continued, receiving a crucial boost from some influential global allies. *Tracks*, for instance, openly assisted the decentralization campaign. In light of the Indonesian regime's desire "to open up more and more now inaccessible spots, of which there are thousands, as long as surfers are keen to get to them," the magazine began doing its readers "a favor" by locating a number of widely dispersed breaks that had not previously been identified in the global surf media.[107]

While the Lombok trip in 1980 was the first time the regime had gone so far as to sponsor a surfing junket in an effort to decentralize surf tourism, it was not the first time surfers and the government had actively collaborated. In the late 1970s, for instance, the former U.S. surfing champion Rick Rasmussen, who used Indonesia as a manufacturing center for a clothing company he owned, revealed that he had arranged for the Indonesian government "and a sponsor from Singapore" to "set up surfing camps" around the archipelago "for the young boys there."[108] The government had in fact taken an interest in promoting surfing among local youths, participating in the annual contest of the Bali Surfing Club, for instance.[109] Rasmussen had also arranged for interviews with the Indonesian press, including the leading magazine *Tempo*, in an effort to promote the idea and "help gain more sponsors."[110] An arrest (he was eventually acquitted) on drug charges in Bali apparently put an end to the project. But the idea of surf camps—though primarily for foreigners, not Indonesians—was just taking off.

Not long before Rasmussen's Balinese ordeal, *Surfer* noted in 1978 another such budding relationship in a piece featuring the Indonesia that lay "[b]eyond Bali." Graced with photographs of long, seemingly perfect lefts, the magazine told of a "remote peninsula on the southeast tip of one among 6,000 inhabited islands" in the Indonesian archipelago. "Here man has yet to intrude upon nature," Tony Brinkworth wrote, conjuring up images of a timeless and fantastical golden age. Brinkworth reported the existence of an unnamed primitive camp located in a game reserve available to surfers for a fee of twenty-five dollars per day. "[T]his unmolested game reserve has a primeval quality about it," he suggested, "as though it were not today, but a thousand . . . years ago. Customs and beliefs have maintained themselves through the centuries in the scarcely populated interior jungle, almost solely inhabited by tigers and numerous species of birds and monkeys." Unlike increasingly visited Bali, at the surf camp at Grajagan (the name of the break on Java where the camp was located, though it went unnamed by *Surfer*) there were "no crowds, bad vibes[,] or ill-mannered people." What made this "little paradise" possible, Brinkworth noted, was the work of Michael Boyum, "an American surfer who's been living in Bali for the past six years" and the "founder, coach, and manager of the Bali Surf Club." Boyum, the magazine disclosed, "persuad[ed] the Indonesian tourist organization and government to support his surf camp on the island." In return for this concession, the cooperating "government officials each receive a monthly salary" to supplement their "official" wages.[111] The American was meanwhile rewarded with a government-protected monopoly—an arrangement that turned out to be very profitable for him. Having opened his camp not long after Grajagan was first surfed by his brother, Bill, and fellow American Bob Laverty in 1972, by 1985 Boyum was grossing approximately $250,000 annually.[112] He was also trafficking cocaine.[113]

Two years later, at approximately the same time that the OM Bali Pro Am was first held in 1980, Garuda Indonesian Airways, the state-owned airline, began offering Australians a twenty-eight-day "budget priced holiday" to Bali that, the airline claimed in recurring two-page advertisements in *Tracks*, was "perfect for surfers." The trip, which the airline dubbed its Easyrider, "gives you the feeling as well as the sights of Bali," where "[y]ou get to know the Balinese people. To absorb their ideas and beliefs. And to understand their gentle ways." Providing airfare, accommodation in various *losmens*, and local transportation, Garuda offered the "value of a package" but "without the strings." "Freedom is the keynote," the government organ pronounced without irony.[114] (Hoping to ensure a steady stream of visitors, the state-owned airline later took to sponsoring Australian performances of *Asian Paradise* [1984], a film about "travel, discovery[,] & sharing the perfect waves" of Java and Sumatra, among other destinations.)[115] Garuda's trip in fact followed a number of those established by independent tour companies in the 1970s. Bali Surfing Tours, for instance, offered eleven-, fourteen-, or thirty-five-day packages that included food, accommodation, and roundtrip airfare on the state-owned Indonesian airline.[116] There were also the previously mentioned trips organized by Qantas, as well as those from other outfits offering nine-, sixteen-, and thirty-day alternatives.[117] Bali Special Encounter upped the ante by including the "services" of a "top local surfer who knows where it's happening every day."[118] While successful in bringing tourists to Indonesia, none of the trips encouraged surfers to move beyond Bali. It was with this concern in mind that the regime sponsored Alan Rich and his group's junket to Lombok, hoping to stimulate dreams of discovery for surfers who had grown tired of the crowds at Kuta and Uluwatu.

Yet there was an unbridgeable tension between such dreams and the authorities' desire for outer-island development. In order for meaningful development to occur, communities outside of Bali had to draw a steady and substantial number of visitors. But this meant crowds, and most surfers wanted to explore Indonesia precisely in order to avoid other surfers. The goal of these tourists was not to create another Bali; it was to find isolated and unnamed breaks where they and a few friends could enjoy the waves together. There was, for many, an unwritten code governing surf exploration: never reveal the location of one's discoveries. Once the secret is out, there is no taking it back. The crowds *will* come. The explosive development of Bali—what *Surfer* called "the great discovery" of the 1970s—offered a case in point.[119] So, too, did Lagundri Bay, the perfect Nias right-hander ridden by the American writer Erik Aeder in the late 1970s. When Aeder chronicled his experience for *Surfer* in 1979, he was careful to not disclose the location of the setup. It was only a matter of time, however, before word filtered out.

Two Californians who traveled to Lagundri just months after Aeder, Bill Finnegan and Bryan Di Salvatore, had heard stories about this "place that promised it all." It was not "a new discovery, but a well kept secret," they noted, a place that was "said to have spawned just the right level of Westernization in the nearby village—a hospitable losmen, with absolutely no hassles."[120] Following a bone-crushing journey by boat and truck, Finnegan and Di Salvatore were startled to discover, upon arrival at Lagundri, that they were not alone; there were already a number of surfers at the break. But at least the crowd was manageable. It was the two Californians and a handful of Australians, "taking turns" on perfect waves in a "glorious bay in the middle of nowhere, twenty miles from the Equator and ten thousand miles from the nearest Taco Bell." It was the kind of place "that stirred fantasies of staying forever," they gushed. The blissful existence continued for days until a new crew of surfers suddenly appeared. This new crew did not "seem to be able to get on the group wavelength at all. Instead of taking turns, there was jockeying, snaking, even a few harsh words." Worst of all, the new arrivals "brought with them The Article. There it was, in living color," Finnegan and Di Salvatore wrote of Aeder's account in *Surfer,* "several full-page spreads, and even a cover, Our Humble Haven." The secret was out. "The villagers were thrilled," the Californians disclosed, "and it was hard not to be perversely fascinated ourselves."[121] But Aeder's piece portended the end—not of exploration, maybe, but certainly of Lagundri Bay. The allure of uncharted Niasan perfection was over.

When the identity of the break was finally revealed to the international surfing community, the response was predictably harsh. "Ex–La Gundhi [*sic*] Traveller," an Australian surfer from Victoria, asked why people would go "fuck it up by telling the whole world." Without public exposure, the bay offered "just good barrels and no crowds." Now it was well on its way to becoming "another Bali." "I suppose if there's money to be made out of it, WHY NOT!" he spewed.[122] David Sumpter, who claimed to have "helped put Bali on the surfing map" in the early 1970s, was put off by the Victorian's bitter complaints. "Today thousands of surfers enjoy [Bali's] magic qualities," Sumpter retorted. "If surf spots become too crowded for you, just keep on moving. There are thousands of surf spots still undiscovered."[123] To be sure, Sumpter's vision was decidedly optimistic. It assumed a finite number of surfers, an abundance of time and money, and a seemingly endless number of breaks. But more people took up the sport, budgets remained tight, and fewer discoveries remained. Places like Lagundri suffered. By 1981, it had made its cinematic debut in *Asian Paradise* (1981) and *Bali High* (1981), films that were followed shortly afterward by Dick Hoole and Jack McCoy's *Storm Riders* (1982). *Asian Paradise,* which went so far as to locate Nias on an on-screen map, perhaps naively asserted that because the break was "hard to reach," only a "special breed of surf adventurer will ever see this wave firsthand."

What may have been true of Lagundri in 1981 did not remain true as the 1980s progressed, however. The early years of the decade were indeed trying for visitors. Clean water was in short supply. Food was scarce. Sanitation was virtually nonexistent. And disease—especially malaria—was widespread. "Ex–La Gundhi [*sic*] Traveller" had pointed to some of these problems in criticizing boosters for spreading visions of a "surfer's paradise" while ignoring "the rip offs, the malaria, the shortage of food, the frequent no swell periods, the many onshores [an unfavorable type of wind] which prevail in this equatorial region." There is "another side of Indonesia" that journalists "don't seem to mention," he asserted.[124] Indeed, two of the first people to ride Lagundri in 1975, the Australian surfers John Geisel and Kevin Lovett, experienced at least one of these issues firsthand. "We wanted to find the perfect wave. We wanted to live the surfer's dream," Lovett would later recall. They found their "perfect wave," but at a price that was tragically high. Both men contracted malaria. Lovett was fortunate and recovered, but nine months later Geisel was dead.[125] Complaints about the disease, as well as dysentery, were heard from numerous travelers in the 1980s. One visitor, mourning the recent death of an Australian after surfing at Lagundri, complained about the chloroquine-resistant mosquitoes that lived at the bay "in plague proportions all year round."[126] Another pointed to the lack of "clean drinking water" and the fact that there were "no toilets." "[G]uys keep shitting behind trees," the surfer remarked in disgust, and "[t]hese days there aren't too many trees left to shit behind."[127]

Some Niasans sensed an opportunity. Ama Dolin, a local entrepreneur, pushed hard to develop surf tourism on the island, and numerous *losmens* and homestays began to sprout up at Lagundri near the break. Restaurants soon appeared, and it was not long before even a deluxe resort opened on the headland overlooking the reef. Within a decade enough infrastructure existed to allow for professional contests featuring contingents from around the world. Despite often-difficult changes to the local community—a nearly complete reliance on seasonal tourism, village youths who refused to work and wanted only to surf, the widespread incidence of petty theft—the case of Lagundri in many ways represented a realization of the Indonesian regime's ambitions for outer-island tourism development.[128] Yet for some people, the transformation was a travesty. By the late 1980s, lamented longtime visitor Peter Reeves, "the magic was gone." Lagundri had become "an eroded, polluted, hygienic nightmare."[129]

. . .

It would be easy to dismiss Reeves's plaint as little more than bitter nostalgia. Yet it taps into a broadly felt sentiment that persists in the international surf community. With its "discovery" by surfers in the 1970s, Indonesia came to symbolize a sense of unbridled freedom. In a state that, paradoxically, was characterized by massive levels of political repression—realities essentially banished from the surfing imagination—these foreign tourists found an enchanted paradise of solitary travel and picture-perfect waves. Even in those rare instances when surfers did in fact acknowledge Indonesian political violence, such as the mass killings of 1965 and 1966, it was acknowledged in a manner that treated the violence as a Communist-induced aberration resolved by the enlightened leadership of the military government. John McLean's *Island of the Gods*, a novel first published in 1990 (it was reissued in 1998) about an Australian in Bali in the late 1970s, serves as a case in point.

Surf fiction enjoys a relatively brief but productive history. From Frederick Kohner's immensely popular *Gidget* in 1957 (and the series of sequels it spawned) to the more recent works of Kem Nunn, Chip Hughes, and Dean Koontz, surfers have been appearing in fictional form for decades. Many of the novels are gripping. Some are even memorable. McLean's *Island of the Gods* is neither. From its stereotypical treatment of subservient Balinese women to its risible portrait of American feminists—"butch looking women . . . with short haircuts, hairy legs[,] and deep, authoritarian voices"— the novel is a literary embarrassment.[130] As a demonstration of how one surfer-writer offered a tortured celebration of the Indonesian regime, however, it is in fact quite valuable. Dealing variously with the two most violent campaigns in postcolonial Indonesian history—the mass killings of the mid-1960s and the Indonesian invasion and occupation of East Timor— *Island of the Gods* in both instances flipped documented reality on its head.

This required a remarkable suspension of one's ability to think beyond simplistic Cold War terms. Beginning with the anti-Communist massacres, McLean offered his most extensive remarks on the bloody destruction of the PKI in an explanation by a respected Balinese elder to Adrian, the novel's Australian protagonist. It is worth quoting at length:

> "It was during the troubles in 1965 when the whole island exploded into a frenzy of killing. The communists tried to stage a coup and overthrow the government. They infiltrated their agents and supporters into the police and army and the schools. Many communists became school teachers so that they could spread their poisonous ideas to the young people in their classes. They tried to undermine our religion and our traditional society. They promised to give free land to the peasants if they joined the party. Many joined but they never got any free land. The only thing that the communists gave was trouble. Then, when they killed the generals in Java and tried to take over the government, the people here decided that they had had enough. They were tired of the communists bringing discord and hatred to our peaceful and well-ordered society.

"It was known which people were communist supporters and they were attacked by bands of villagers who killed them with whatever weapons they could find. *Krises*, swords, clubs. Even rice knives. Then the communists started killing each other. Some of them were deeply ashamed and went to the temple and asked the priest to purify them with holy water. Then they went outside and asked the mob to stab them to death. Which they did.

"Once the killings started it was very hard to stop them. It was a chance for everyone to get rid of all the hatred that had been building up inside them. And that is how the trance killings began. People went into a trance and killed anyone who got in their way. Old enemies killed each other. Moslems in the west of the island were killed just because they were Moslems. Chinese were killed. Even children went into trance and cut people's throats and chopped their arms and legs off.

"One night a group of [communists] who had gone into a trance and were running amok smashed their way into the house where Dayu [Adrian's Balinese girlfriend] was sleeping with her parents. They slashed to death with their sharpened *krises* every one in the house except Dayu. She hid under her bed and in the dark the crazy killers didn't see her. She waited until the daylight and then ran outside to fetch some help. She was brought up here to live with me and she cried for many months. They were terrible and frightening times."

"How many were killed?" asked Adrian.

"Some say it was forty thousand. Some say fifty thousand and some say that it was even as many as a hundred thousand. Who knows? Eventually the army came over from Java and restored order and since then we have not had any political or revolutionary trouble of any kind. Thanks to General Soeharto. He has brought stability to Indonesia and we have all prospered. But it was terrifying to see the demons unleash so much evil power all at once." Adrian listened in horror to the old man's story; it made him realize how fortunate he was to live in such a peaceful land as Australia.[131]

Island of the Gods is certainly unusual in its acknowledgment of the Indonesian mass killings. Yet the acknowledgment is delivered in a way that is both factually perplexing and morally appalling. The PKI membership was not, it turns out, the primary victim of the atrocities; the Communists were, rather, their greatest perpetrators. And when PKI members did die, according to the novel, it was often as a result of Communist fratricide or suicide. The novel is, moreover, silent in at lease one fundamental respect: McLean utterly fails to identify the crucial role of the military in the mass atrocities, transforming the armed forces from instigators (as historians understand them) into peacemakers. Suharto, meanwhile, is the deliverer of not only stability but prosperity. He is, in fact, precisely what Indonesia needs. Democracy, readers learn later, clearly has no place in the country. "They tried democracy and it didn't suit them," insists Adrian to what is perhaps the novel's most distasteful character. "The communists took advantage of it and caused great trouble. Anyway, the Indonesians have just as much personal freedom as anyone else."[132]

It is a dubious assertion. It pales in comparison, however, to McLean's apologia for the genocidal occupation of East Timor. Readers are informed about the situation in Timor through a plotline involving a former Portuguese intelligence officer then living as a restaurateur in Bali who is assassinated by an East German secret agent posing as a West German tourist and doing the bidding of a former officer in the Waffen-SS serving his new "masters in Moscow."[133] The story, like that last sentence, is convoluted and ridiculous—it ends with the gruesome murder of the restaurateur, whose penis is cut off and stuffed down his throat—but the context in which it situates Indonesian actions in East Timor is revelatory, to say the least. Indonesia, according to *Island of the Gods*, was guilty of neither international aggression nor widespread atrocities, which receive no mention. On the contrary, the Suharto government had served freedom admirably by foiling a Communist plot to take over East Timor as part of the Communist conspiracy to achieve "world domination."[134]

The novel suggests that East Timor was significant to the Soviets because, under a government formed by the "Marxist guerrilla movement" masking its "true communist identity" and "guided by experienced KGB operatives," the territory would "lie like a dagger pointing at the heart of Australia. Just like Cuba does to the United States." In the former Portuguese colony, McLean writes, "the Soviets planned to establish a huge airbase . . . with inter-continental ballistic missiles that would threaten both Indonesia and Australia. Then they could neutralize both countries whenever it suited them."[135] The one-time chief of military intelligence in Portuguese Timor who revealed this unquestioned reality to the book's readers was not a morally suspect agent of the former Salazar dictatorship; he was, in McLean's characterization, a kind and gentle man whose "beautiful country was betrayed in 1974" when Portugal's "long established government . . . was overthrown" by "communists . . . carrying out a plan that had been worked out by the KGB in Moscow some twenty years earlier."[136]

But, on Timor, the West was slow to act. A "gullible" but "silly" Australia, believing the Timorese guerrillas' rhetoric of freedom and democracy, failed to take the Soviet threat seriously.[137] Not so the Indonesians. "Their own intelligence supported" what the Portuguese had revealed, "so they sent in a military force to wipe out the guerrillas and so stop Timor from becoming a Soviet base in this part of the world." The Timorese guerrillas were ruthless and brutal—the restaurateur had seen their "mobs murdering innocent Portuguese in the streets," including "priests and nuns"—such that "the Indonesians lost many men" during their campaign to eradicate the Communist threat. But it was worth it. Jakarta recognized what was at stake. Recalling the "very difficult and bloody" effort to repulse the Communist attempt to "take over the whole country" in the mid-1960s, "the present Indonesian government, when they saw what was happening in Timor, decided to nip it in the bud at the earliest opportunity." To the restaurateur, who advised the Indonesians for several months during the operation and is treated in the novel as an exemplar of moral virtue, this was an indisputably beneficial decision for which the world owed Suharto a debt of gratitude. "Thank God they did [decide to nip it in the bud]," the Portuguese pronounces, "and Timor is now part of the Indonesian Republic instead of a little patch of Marxist mischief in this beautiful and safe part of the world."[138]

While *Island of the Gods* was a relatively marginal work of fiction that would be easy to dismiss on both literary and factual grounds, it is the sort of book that appealed to young people—especially surfers and backpackers—traveling in Southeast Asia. One Californian reviewing the book on Amazon, for example, "could not put [it] down" after buying it "while on a military port call in Hong Kong back in the late 90's." It was a "must read for a surfer or non-surfer."[139] The novel's praise of the authoritarian regime makes sense in the context of surfers' desire to imaginatively construct a pacific Indonesia—the "peaceful and well-ordered society" identified by the village elder in one of the passages cited earlier—through which one could travel without the encumbrance of guilt.[140] Such a fantastical view of the country flourished in the 1980s as surfers followed their exploratory instincts to Sumbawa, Lombok, Roti, Sumba, and countless other islands in the archipelago. The promise of endless pleasure rendered it morally convenient to ignore the numerous atrocities then being perpetrated in East Timor, Aceh, and West Papua. Everyday political repression was, to borrow a term from the vernacular of surf culture, something of a bummer. Why concern oneself with it? Too much adventure awaited. Bali, which was "once the secret of Indonesia," in time became "merely the landing dock to paradise."[141]

By the 1990s, the Mentawais, a chain of small islands off the coast of Sumatra, had emerged as the most popular new destination for what was perhaps appropriately being dubbed "surf imperialism."[142] The Mentawais, Matt Warshaw wrote, were "generally considered to be the world's richest wave zone."[143] Most of the surfing in the islands during that decade was done not by tourists trekking on land and encountering local people but by surfers eating, sleeping, and traveling on at times plush charter cruises. Such travel by boat, which coincided with a greater emphasis in the 1990s on high-end surf tourism, had the effect of further removing these visitors from potential exposure to some of Indonesia's less pleasant political and social realities.[144] The charter outfits soon began "sparring among themselves for exclusive reef-use rights" as well as "engaging in endless political dealings with Indonesian officials and politicians."[145] Surfers, in other words, became painfully aware that the possibilities for discovery were not in fact endless. A right to exclusive use of the waves—a form of "surf imperialism," indeed— had become the ideal.

It is hardly surprising, then, that private surf resorts would emerge as one of the most popular forms of surf travel as the twentieth century drew to a close.[146] "The brute reality," explained one celebrated surf traveler, "is that the surf world is now one of increasing demand and diminishing resources. Surf resorts are the inevitable outcome."[147] The first to open was in Indonesia— the resort at Grajagan established by Mike Boyum—but they soon spread to, among other locales, Fiji, Mexico, Costa Rica, Tonga, Panama, the Maldives, El Salvador, the Philippines, and Nicaragua.[148] Not all of them offered exclusive wave-use rights, but their general appeal was nevertheless obvious. They offered comfort, predictability, and fewer crowds. To many surfers, however, the resorts' mere existence was appalling. Only a couple of decades earlier, surfers, envisioning themselves as modern-day explorers, had set out across the Indonesian archipelago in search of unridden waves in what seemed a warm-water paradise. For most foreigners, however, the search had come to an end. The discoveries had been made or were simply no longer worth the hassle. It was now, it seemed, a battle for exclusivity. The enthusiasm of the 1970s had definitely passed.

FOUR

When Surfing Discovered It Was Political

CONFRONTING SOUTH AFRICAN APARTHEID

IT WAS A DECISION THAT STUNNED surfers worldwide. Tom Carroll, having just secured his second world championship while competing at Bells Beach in Australia, disclosed to a *National Times* journalist in April 1985 that he would boycott the South African leg of the next world tour. The reaction was electric. "On the beach at Bells," one reporter noted, "there was practically no other subject of conversation."[1] For Carroll, a solidly built goofyfooter from New South Wales, the choice was not an easy one. With South Africa host to several contests, including the long running Gunston 500, it would make securing a third world title extremely difficult. Still, there were times when one's sense of morality trumped personal ambition. This was one of those times, he believed. The apartheid policies of the South African regime were simply too repugnant. He had no choice but to take a stand. In addition to shunning the South African contests, Carroll would sever his relationship with a major sponsor, the South Africa–based Instinct Clothing, as well as donate $1,000 to "a charity surfing contest . . . in aid of a black famine appeal."[2] It was, collectively, a symbolically powerful statement from a highly visible competitor at the peak of his professional career. "I can no longer turn a blind eye," Carroll explained.[3]

Tom Carroll's decision, which prompted California phenomenon Tom Curren and Durban-raised up-and-comer Martin Potter to likewise join the boycott, may have appeared to mark the beginning of a contentious era in professional surfing history, but it in fact culminated a long period of introspection within the broader surf community about what it meant to seek pleasure—indeed, what it meant to achieve "freedom," as many surfers would have it—in a state characterized by violent racial separation. Were foreign surfers lending aid and comfort to an oppressive regime by visiting South

Africa? What were the implications of surfing at segregated beaches? Were proponents of a boycott being hypocritical in light of widespread racial injustices in the United States and Australia? All of these were questions that divided the surfing community. The case of South Africa forced surfers, often for the first time, to begin conceiving of themselves as global political actors. This is not to suggest that they had avoided political engagement in the past. On the contrary, some had organized on behalf of environmental causes or the preservation of waves and coastal access.[4] But those were issues that had consequences for the enjoyment of their sport. The apartheid case was different. With the institutionalized racism of South Africa, foreign surfers were confronting an issue that, for the most part, did not directly affect them. Given their overwhelming whiteness, they faced no racial barriers in traveling to the country and riding its waves. They could come and go as they pleased. This was true, in fact, even for most foreign surfers of color. Like others before them, the dark-skinned Hawaiian brothers Michael and Derek Ho, for instance, were granted a special provisional "white" status in 1985 to enable their participation in the South African leg of the world tour, though the limitations of their honorary whiteness were soon made apparent: they were still denied entry at certain clubs and restaurants.[5]

So why does any of this matter? Who cares about how surfers responded to apartheid? Most scholarship on international sport in South Africa has centered on rugby, soccer, and cricket, major team sports that garnered substantial media attention. This made them attractive targets for those many anti-apartheid activists who pushed their professional associations—successfully, in the case of soccer and cricket—to endorse the athletic boycott. Professional surfing, conversely, largely operated outside the major media spotlight. The surfing world tour may have been followed by the hundreds of thousands of readers of *Surfer*, *Tracks*, and dozens of other publications, but it was only sporadically covered by the mainstream press. It is precisely this marginality—perhaps not in popular culture terms but certainly with respect to global athletic competition—that renders the case of surfing so significant. As relatively low-profile athletes who competed as individuals in a sport whose professional association refused to heed the boycott call, surfers had to decide independently how to respond. The story of surfing and South Africa thus tells us something about the ways that individual athletes—and especially those too often caricatured as self-absorbed airheads—found themselves unexpectedly wrestling with a deep moral concern.

Those professionals who boycotted South Africa, in the process sparking considerable debate within the wave-riding ranks, raised the consciousness of a notoriously cloistered demographic, forcing surfers worldwide to reckon with a system that, as Durban local Potter later put it, had for too long been made to seem "normal."[6] The reckoning was long overdue. By the 1980s, South Africa was home to one of the most established surf cultures on the planet. The country enjoyed a large and vibrant community of highly skilled wave riders, including 1977 men's world champion Shaun Tomson and four-time women's world champion Wendy Botha; it hosted a number of professional contests, such as the Gunston 500, the second longest-running competition in professional surfing history; it contained what is arguably the world's best pointbreak, the long right-hander at Jeffreys Bay; and it groomed influential leaders such as Peter Burness, who was president of the world tour's organizing body, the Association of Surfing Professionals, when Tom Carroll made his 1985 announcement at Bells Beach.[7] When the professional surfers elected to honor the boycott, they forced the global surf community, including hundreds of thousands of young people in Australia, the United States, and especially South Africa, to confront an issue that they might otherwise have ignored. Much of that youthful demographic had, in the decade following the end of the Vietnam War, retreated inward, embracing an apoliticism that rendered more worldly concerns an unsavory distraction from the pleasure to be found in the ocean. By bringing the politics of apartheid into the surf community, the boycotting professionals forced some of those millions of young people to consider and perhaps contend with the brutality of that racist system. With the professional boycott, one South African attested, "the attention of many surfers (myself included) has been drawn to the pressing political issues in our country."[8]

These were pressing issues that far too many people had found convenient to overlook. To most surfers, the simple act of wave riding is an act that transcends sport, providing, in its elegant exploitation of the natural world, something close to a spiritual experience. This has translated into a sense of "freedom" in the oceanic encounter. To mix political engagement with surfing's inherent "purity" was thus, to many of its enthusiasts, to fatally corrupt the latter. Carroll, Curren, and Potter may have been heeding a global call to arms, their critics conceded, but they were concomitantly undermining wave riding's spiritual foundations. Others disagreed. It was impossible, the boycott's champions maintained, to divorce surfing from the social realities of the littoral world. There was no freedom in surfing if it was done in conditions of unfreedom. Or, as one American percipiently commented in 1966, white South Africans "cannot possibly find freedom in the surf. The only free men in South Africa are in the prisons."[9]

The case of surfing and South Africa can tell us a great deal.

THE DISCOVERY OF SOUTH AFRICA

While the known roots of South African surfing date to the First World War, when visiting American marines, together with local Heather Price, took to the waves at Muizenberg along the Cape Town coast, the country first began to seriously capture the attention of the global surf community in the mid-1960s.[10] It was a film—Bruce Brown's *The Endless Summer* (1966)—that was largely responsible for this attention, though its origins can be traced to the global wanderings of a Southern Californian several years earlier. In 1958, inspired by tales of adventure he had read while working behind the counter of his Huntington Beach liquor store, Dick Metz set out on a world-wide hitchhiking excursion. Beginning with an outstretched thumb in front of his home in Laguna Beach, in the months that followed Metz made his way through Central America, the South Pacific, Australia, and Asia, surfing when he could but otherwise just seeing the sites and meeting the locals. Yet it was the African portion of his journey that proved most consequential to international surfing history. Africa drew Metz because, he recalled years later, he wanted "to see wild game and wild tribes."[11] Disembarking in Mombasa from an Indian labor ship that originated in Bombay, he spent months traveling through Kenya, Uganda, and Tanganyika before catching a ride to Cape Town in 1959.[12] There he serendipitously met John Whitmore, a man often called the "father of South African surfing" and known affectionately to many as "the Oom."[13]

Half a century later, the Southern Californian recalled their chance encounter. Having just spent approximately ten days on the road, Metz was deposited a block from the ocean by a South African driver who had brought him thousands of miles to the continent's southern tip. Metz walked down to Glen Beach and, unaware that surfers even existed in South Africa, noticed a solitary figure in the water. As Metz stood watching, the surfer lost his board—modern leashes would not appear until the 1970s—which washed toward shore. Metz ran to protect the board from the rocks lining the beach. As the man swam in, Metz, board in hand, told him, "This is probably the ugliest surfboard I've ever seen." Offended, the surfer asked, "Well, what the hell do you know about surfboards?" Metz was quick. "By the looks of this surfboard, a whole lot more than you do," he responded. Whitmore, who had detected the visitor's American accent, liked him instantly. The beach-side meeting, which culminated in Metz staying and surfing with Whitmore for the next few months, marked the beginning of a long, close, and mutually beneficial relationship.[14]

Metz, who has been described by journalist Ben Marcus as "one of the founders of the surf-industrial complex," put Whitmore in touch with friends in the United States who, among other things, could supply him with the materials necessary for modern surfboard design, such as polyurethane foam blanks.[15] Whitmore would exploit this pipeline to become what was probably South Africa's most influential surfboard shaper. Whitmore likewise became—again through Metz, who introduced him to John Severson, the publication's founder and editor—the first South African distributor of the California-based *Surfer* magazine.[16] Perhaps most significantly, Metz also facilitated the transatlantic communication of Whitmore and Bruce Brown, setting in motion a longstanding relationship that would result in the filmic sequences of South Africa that appeared in the latter's celebrated classic, *The Endless Summer.*[17]

Following Metz's introduction, Brown visited South Africa in late 1963 with California surfers Mike Hynson and Robert August. Whitmore hosted the group and suggested they look for waves at Cape St. Francis, a long point approximately sixty miles from Port Elizabeth along the country's south-eastern coast.[18] The Americans took his advice. What they discovered was a right-hand pointbreak that looked like something out of a dream. "You can't tell how good a wave is until you actually ride it," Brown told viewers of *The Endless Summer*. "On Mike's first ride—the first five seconds—he knew he'd finally found that perfect wave." Viewers need not have simply trusted his narration; the footage of Cape St. Francis appeared to bear out Brown's gushing claims. As images of blue-water perfection unfolded on-screen, the filmmaker said "the waves looked like they'd been made by some kind of machine." The rides were "so long," he asserted, "I couldn't get most of them on one piece of film." What's more, according to Brown, local fishermen said the waves "always looked like that, day after day," while there were days "when the surf broke big out by the end of the cape, seven miles further [*sic*] out, and rolled all the way in to where we were surfing." Then a question for his captivated viewers: "Can you imagine riding a fifteen-foot wave shaped like this for seven miles?" It was too much. Surfers worldwide began packing their bags for the South African coast.[19] "[I]t's become the dream of every surfer who has seen [*The Endless Summer*]," distinguished filmmaker Bud Browne wrote to a friend and colleague in Durban.[20] Bruce Brown's motion picture represented perhaps "the greatest public relations job imaginable" for South Africa, intoned Bob Evans.[21] "Watch out," *The Endless Summer*'s director warned Durban surfer Harry Bold in 1964. "I expect you to be invaded by Americans on the way to Cape St. Francis."[22]

Cape St. Francis, which would ever after be known as Bruce's Beauties (or just Bruce's), was not in fact as perfect as viewers were led to believe. Brown subsequently revealed that it only worked well for the visiting Americans for an hour or two before the incoming tide shut it down. But "the actual thing doesn't make for a very good soundbite," he maintained, so the film opted for an illusory vision that would play well with its audience.[23] And it worked. "[T]he end result was the most famous scene in the most popular surf film ever made," noted journalists Marcus Sanders and Kimball Taylor.[24] *The Endless Summer* stimulated dreams of exploration and discovery, and in the process it placed South Africa on the global surfing map. Yet the perspective viewers received of the country was a very partial one. The South Africa of *The Endless Summer* is a beautiful, lush, and sparsely populated place of nearly infinite wave potential. One thing South Africa was not, at least according to Brown's film, was a stubborn bastion of white supremacist rule. Apartheid simply did not fit the motion picture's idyllic vision. It is not, to be sure, that *The Endless Summer* defended the country's ignoble politics. Rather, it totally ignored them. Brown's motion picture provided an attractive portrait not only of South Africa's surf but also of its people, geography, and wildlife. Not once, however, did it acknowledge the country's notorious system of racial segregation, including on its beaches.[25] The only black South Africans to be featured in the production were a rickshaw driver and a young boy (several others appeared as a backdrop), both of whom were teased in Brown's comical narration.[26]

Yet the country's system of racial injustice was hardly a secret to the filmmaker. In an April 1965 letter to a white South African friend and colleague, for example, Brown joked about the settler state becoming an "independent African nation run by the Africans," with the white population becoming "refugees" in the United States. "I guess that's not a very funny joke in South Africa," he added.[27] Mike Hynson, one of the film's two traveling American surfers, appeared more celebratory. "I was most impressed with South Africa ... out of the many countries we visited," he disclosed in the film's marketing materials. Situating his impressions—and his identification with the white citizenry—in a familiar American context, Hynson explained, in apparent approval, that "[t]he Union of South Africa is almost as old as the U.S. The first white settlers came to Cape Town about the same time we settled Plymouth Rock. They also had a covered wagon drive through the country which parallels very closely our American History; we fought the Indians and they fought the Zulus."[28] Conquest, in other words, was conquest.

APARTHEID IN THE SURFING CONSCIOUSNESS

Not all surfers overlooked the system of South African segregation, however. The apartheid issue unexpectedly emerged as a point of considerable debate at approximately the same time that *The Endless Summer* opened in theaters nationwide. In 1966, *Surfer*, the sport's flagship American magazine, published a feature on South Africa that highlighted Durban's thriving white surf culture amid the country's omnipresent blackness. It was the sort of piece that typified the genre: photographs of enticing waves in an exotic locale combined with resplendent images of the nonwhite locals. What was unusual about the article in *Surfer*, however, was its explicit engagement with the inevitable politics of surfing on a segregated coast. "There is total and highly enforced racial discrimination in South Africa," the story's Australian author, Ron Perrott, conveyed to readers. "The country is divided into Europeans (white), Indian[,] and native (Negro), and most of the surfers come from the European segment. Just a short distance from the main European beach strip, the Indian and native beaches get some excellent surf, but it's rare to see a non-European surfing, although several Indian life-savers use boards to supplement their normal equipment."[29] Probably more politically incendiary than this passage, however, was one of the photographs that accompanied the text. It showed a young black man standing at water's edge while dressed in slacks, close-toed shoes, and a collared shirt; in the background were several white surfers walking with their boards. The caption, even in its simplicity, proved explosive. "Durban's beaches are segregated[,] so this native youngster can't join these three surfers strolling along Dairy Beach near the West Street Groyne for a little fun in the surf," it read.[30]

FIGURE 12. Did surfing exist outside of politics? Well before the professional surfers' boycott of South Africa in the mid-1980s, this photograph in *Surfer* magazine sparked a fierce debate within the international surfing community about apartheid, South Africa, and racism in the United States. Its 1966 publication, one of the editors wrote, generated "the most reader response" in the magazine's history. Photograph by Ron Perrott. Credit: © *Surfer*.

What followed was a cavalcade of letters that amounted to "the most reader response" in the magazine's history, according to one of its editors. This was particularly "strange," the editor noted, in that "the picture" prompting the mail had, in his opinion, "nothing to do with surfing."[31] The correspondence, which was published over the next fourteen months, represented a lengthy international and multiracial back-and-forth that anticipated, in important respects, the debates that would consume the international surfing community in the years to come. Readers tackled and disagreed about the repugnance or merits of apartheid, the existence of racial injustice in the United States, and, significantly, the question of whether surfing—as a sport, a growing industry, and a lifestyle—should even engage such matters. "No photo previously published by SURFER has ever had a greater impact upon me," confessed a Californian from Orange County in one of the first responses to appear in print. "When are countries like South Africa going to realize that there is no place for segregation in a 'modern' society or 'civilization' as ours? People in the United States are finally realizing the wrongs of segregation and I hope that other countries, including South Africa, follow up quickly. Waves are for everyone to enjoy," the reader maintained, "not just a 'chosen few.' This segregation can do nothing but hurt the world and the sport of surfing."[32] Another Californian shared her compatriot's disgust. "When I saw that picture of the native standing on the beach as three surfers made their way toward the waters from which he was banned, it really got to me," she wrote. "Let's hope we never see this on any of our beaches."[33] A Hawaiian pointed out how different things were in the islands. "This deal about segregated surfing should be dropped," he counseled. "Surfing should be for everybody. In Hawaii, we have no trouble."[34] It took nearly a year and numerous letters, but ultimately the magazine's editorial staff weighed in with its own denunciation of the South African system, asserting that "human dignity and equality" should never be constrained by national borders.[35]

As would quickly become obvious, however, not all Americans felt likewise, either about apartheid or about surfing's alleged politicization. "Since when has SURFER [m]agazine become so divine that they can hand down a verdict that segregation of South Africa's beaches is so bad and evil and should be abolished?" asked a North Carolinian.[36] A surfer from Florida concurred, adding that at the local beaches in Jacksonville "the whites stay with whites and the blacks with blacks. This way everybody's happy. So you see," he concluded, "segregation can't be that bad after all."[37] As would a number of surfers from Durban to Cape Town, the Floridian pointed to this same American segregation to negate the criticism of its South African counterpart. This was not, as apartheid scholar Douglas Booth has pointed out, an unusual tactic. "By drawing attention to discrimination against 'ethnic minorities' in other nations," Booth found, "apologists attempted to create the impression that South Africa was being unfairly singled out and that prejudice is 'normal.'" Such displacement, he argued, has "rightly been called 'comparative trivialization.'"[38] The fact that some of that trivialization originated with Americans lent the phenomenon a fascinating transnational twist. "We are not the ones to criticize South Africa," insisted a New Yorker, for example. "We have many problems concerning the Negro at home."[39] His views were echoed by a Californian who had just returned from his third trip to the apartheid state and who purported to be speaking for himself and "many of the people" in that country. "[D]on't you think it would be a good idea to iron out our own racial problems before we start knocking Africa's[?]" he asked. The Californian was not content to stop there, however. He also offered a spirited defense of the South African status quo. "[T]here is no place in the record books [in South Africa] that says a colored person can't surf; in fact, they have many fine beaches with surfing possibilities which the whites can't use," he wrote. Moreover, his discussions with "the colored people there" indicated that they have no desire to "enter places where only whites are allowed."[40]

Other Americans were appalled by the notion that their country's racial injustices should preclude criticism of the South African system. A young man from Long Beach was especially passionate on this matter. "The United States has faced up to its problems and is attempting to remedy them through the use of effective legislation," he wrote.

> I pity the South African youth. Do they not possess enough intellectual maturity to realize separate but equal facilities are inherently unequal as stated by the United States Supreme Court in 1954! The youth are the impetus of the civil rights struggle in America. We are concerned with our problems, while the South African youth attempts to shun theirs.... The subjugation, minority rule, and the apartheid policy practiced by South Africa belong to the feudal ages.[41]

The Californian was perhaps too optimistic about the extent to which the United States was seeking to remedy the entrenched racism that characterized American life, but he at least recognized that surfing was not above politics. The same was true of a correspondent from Massachusetts. Demolishing a popular self-styled trope that equates surfing with "freedom," he asked whether readers were aware that "the little Negro boy in the Surf Suid Afrika picture could have been arrested, held without trial[,] and perhaps shot if he had surfed that beach? South African surfers are deluding themselves," he insisted. "[T]hey cannot possibly find freedom in the surf. The only free men in South Africa are in the prisons."[42]

Among the most oft-stated views to emerge from American readers was that *Surfer*—and, by implication, surfing—ought not address matters that reeked of politics. Numerous correspondents were incensed that, in acknowledging South Africa's official white supremacy and entertaining the debate that followed, *Surfer* had allowed itself to become a venue for what one writer termed the "political propaganda" of both sides. "How about keeping SURFER free from politics and keep it on the subject," one Floridian wrote. "[I]t should and is supposed to be primarily concerned with surf. If I want to read about integration or segregation or anything else political," he insisted, "I'll subscribe to *National Review* or *Time*."[43] A writer from Los Angeles echoed this view. "I think SURFER has really taken a giant step—downward.... Why can't politics be kept out of surfing. I never thought you would sink to discussing racial discrimination as a topic in your magazine. Why can't SURFER stick to stories about surfing and surfing places that surfers actually surf."[44] There was, in other words, something pure about people riding waves on a board that transcended—or at least should have transcended—worldly concerns. The notion that surfing could exist in an apolitical universe was, to these and other writers, a self-evident truth. Contravening those who were uncomfortable with popular notions of surfers as disengaged "beach bums"—"Do [surfers] surf for twenty-four hours a day and never leave this carefree life like some aquatic animal who has no power to reason and cannot comprehend what's going on in the outer world?" one outraged black reader asked—numerous correspondents insisted that surfing and politics simply should not mix.[45] And though *Surfer* initially agreed in its January 1967 issue that the "segregation issue" should be left to other publications, the magazine reversed itself two months later, rejecting this apolitical formulation.[46] In a tempered yet firm editorial—and one coming just a few years after the editors mistook Senegal for a city in South Africa while making racist jokes about Africans eating visiting surfers—the magazine insisted that should "any force . . . hamper any surfer from enjoying his sport anywhere in the world," the editors were obligated to "call attention to this injustice."[47]

Perhaps not surprisingly, South Africans strenuously objected to *Surfer*'s uncharitable, but accurate, representation of their country. After all, they were far more accustomed to the uncritical paeans of admiring visitors such as Bruce Brown than the full-throated condemnation gracing the pages of the American periodical. Marcus Sanders and Kimball Taylor wrote in 2007 that the South African surf community "mainly did not agree with the rules of apartheid" and "tended to be anti-apartheid."[48] This may (or may not) have been true of the 1970s and 1980s, but I have seen no evidence of the claim for the bustling surf culture of the 1960s. Indeed, the response to Ron Perrott's 1966 piece in *Surfer* unleashed a torrent of vitriol from enraged South Africans. "Why don't you guys think before writing such trash?" asked one.[49] Another suggested, "Why don't all you finks who love to criticize a country about whose ways of life and whose problems you are so ignorant all take a good long vacation. Yeah, leave behind your civil rights unrest and racial violence and come spend a nice, peaceful vacation in nice, peaceful South Africa."[50] In pointing to the racial injustices of the United States, the South African alluded to what he and others clearly considered to be the hypocrisy and foolishness of American denunciations.

If the United States was such an enlightened model, asked a surfer from Cape Town, then "why is it that a picture has been painted of an American G.I. kicking furiously at a Viet Cong who is already down on his knees and completely without defense?"[51] It was difficult to argue with this sentiment, as the United States had, in Vietnam and elsewhere, demonstrated the glaring distance between its professed ideals and the realities of American power. On the question of race, however, the country had in fact moved beyond legal segregation and could thus—on this narrow issue, at least—claim a moral high ground. But this did not stop the challenges. "Why don't we see any photos of Negro surfers in the mag?" asked a South African writer. "I'm not talking of Hawaiians," he clarified, "but real, true Negroes."[52] For he and his compatriots, the answer was obvious: it was a racial thing. "The natives are petrified of the surf," wrote a Durbanite in what would appear, then and later, to be a popular trope.[53] "The fact is that they are terrified of the water and have surrounded it with mysterious myths and legends," asserted another.[54] Of course, the same was said of the Balinese in the 1970s, yet that did not preclude a popular surf culture from emerging there and elsewhere in the Indonesian archipelago.[55]

The belief in a racial explanation was also ahistorical. "From the Age of Discovery through the nineteenth century," concluded historian Kevin Dawson, "the swimming and underwater diving abilities of people of African descent usually surpassed those of Westerners."[56] Some Africans, moreover, had independently developed an affinity for wave riding long before European contact.[57] Still, the challenge was repeatedly made by later white South Africans: "How about featuring a few pictures of Negro surfers in your magazine just to prove that Negroes are all that interested in our sport."[58] In this call, interestingly, the white South Africans were joined by black Americans. "Since there have been Japanese, Hawaiians, Frenchmen, Mexicans, Puerto Ricans[,] and Peruvians written up in your magazine, now why not negroes[?]" asked a New Yorker then living in Tennessee. Yet the American hardly shared the white South Africans' skepticism about blacks' desire and ability to surf. "I am a Negro," he began his letter, "and I surf in Long Island. I am considered by others as an 'above average' surfer on the East Coast. But there are many others, and the few I do know are pretty good."[59]

Throughout the entire fourteen-month exchange, not a single South African took to the pages of *Surfer* to denounce his or her country's brutal system of racial separation. And, in their own media across the Atlantic, it was much the same. *South African Surfer*, a magazine rife with racist imagery that in the mid-1960s was the country's only surf periodical, featured two responses to *Surfer*'s engagement with apartheid.[60]

The first was an interview with Anthony van den Heuvel, a white South African who had just returned from the United States. Asked about the "controversial photo" in the American publication, van den Heuvel offered that, "[b]esides the fact that politics should be kept out of surfing, most people thought it was a lot of bull." In any case, he added, "the whole time I was over there, I only saw two Negro surfers. It[']s just not their game." To this, the magazine's interviewer followed up, "With conditions as crowded as they are, I don't suppose anybody tries to talk them into it either." "That's for sure," van den Heuvel agreed.[61] The second response was an outraged letter. "We really do not need surfing magazines such as the American 'Surfer,' which has lately been printing controversial articles and editorials on South Africa," wrote G. Klug. "Let us," the surfers of South Africa, "stick together and 'cock this magazine a complete deafy,'" he suggested, calling for a formal

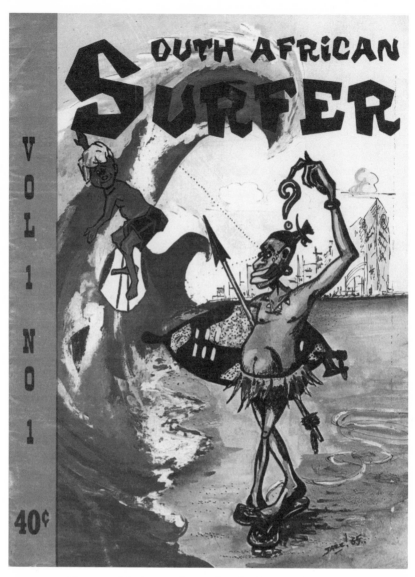

FIGURE 13. The cover of the inaugural issue of *South African Surfer* in 1965 spoke volumes about the racism prevalent in South African society. Credit: © *South African Surfer.*

boycott of the American publication. After all, he noted of the laws surrounding apartheid, "[w]e in [South Africa] have certain regulations to keep."[62]

CONFRONTING APARTHEID

And for decades those regulations were kept. For over twenty years after *The Endless Summer* featured the "perfect waves" of Cape St. Francis as the film's apotheosis of surf travel (with, it should again be noted, nary a word about South Africa's violent system of racial separation), young Americans and Australians ventured to the apartheid state to enjoy its coastal splendor. Some "superstars"—from the Australians Midget Farrelly and Peter Drouyn to the Americans Brad McCaul, Jim Blears, Randy Rarick, and Jeff Hakman—were in fact paid to come by the South African regime.[63] The subsidies appeared to color the judgment of at least some of them. Farrelly, writing glowingly about his travels in the country, spoke frankly about black-perpetrated atrocities while brushing aside apartheid as "not worth talking about."[64] Other touring notables, such as Australian filmmaker and *Surfing World* editor Bob Evans, found South Africa "very good for my soul," having dismissed apartheid in the late 1960s as not such a big deal after all.[65] Those who resisted traveling to the country in light of its "ugly segregation policy," such as longtime surfer Richie Strell of New York, were relatively few in number.[66] Among their ranks, however, were a number of influential figures, including Paul Holmes, the editor of *Surfer* from 1981 to 1989, and, as he reached the end of his tenure at the magazine, reportedly every member of his staff.[67] That such journeys were inherently political became apparent as a global athletic boycott of South Africa gathered steam in the 1970s. As early as the 1950s there had been calls for such a sporting movement, and during the 1960s South Africa found itself barred from the Olympic Games. But it was not until the early 1970s that the athletic boycott became widely endorsed by international sporting federations. It would be several years before amateur surfing honored the call—South Africa was allowed to compete in the amateur world titles through 1978—though major demands for a boycott had emerged as early as 1971, when the Australian magazine *Tracks* went on record in support of such a move.[68] Sport, in other words, became part of the broad-based movement to oppose apartheid in South African life.[69]

To be sure, the boycott was not a static effort that enjoyed only a single goal. As conditions changed on the ground in South Africa, so, too, did the boycott's objectives. In the early 1970s, when South African sport was officially segregated, the goal had been to bring about an end to racialized sport. Athletes should be free to play with and compete against one another regardless of color or background, it was argued. As this objective was slowly realized by the late 1970s—a time when the South African government had made sport, including surfing, a visible element of the country's foreign policy—the boycott's goals shifted.[70] Organizers increasingly took to challenging "the peculiar apolitical ideology of sport and reminded the international sporting community that it could not ignore the broader conditions under which sport is played." Sport, in other words, could not be separated from its social context, they argued. Such a perspective was employed in continuing the boycott as deracialization was realized in the late 1970s. The boycott's goal thus became nothing less than to bring about the end of apartheid. For the international community, then, the sporting boycott became "one strategy, in a raft of many, to shame and isolate the Pretoria regime" in an effort to hasten its transformation or collapse.[71]

It was in the politicized context of this international competition that the issue of apartheid was most obviously addressed by surfers, though it persisted at the grassroots as a recurring theme in articles and letters in surfing magazines and in conversations about the South African state. The relationship of surfing to apartheid, it must be noted, was different from that of rugby, cricket, soccer, or any of the other team sports that have to date received the bulk of scholars' attention. Surfing generally did not witness the same sort of explicit racial division as did those other pursuits. This was, in large part, because there were very few South African surfers of color.[72] Whites in the country were quick to argue that the reason for their absence was that "they don't seem to have either the interest nor aptitude to surf, as basically Blacks in South Africa are scared of the sea."[73] Yet this is much too simplistic—and, with respect to the matter of "aptitude," much too racist— of an explanation.

Anti-apartheid activists developed an appreciation in the 1970s that "sport did not transcend politics" and that, as Douglas Booth put it, "black people would continue to experience discrimination in sport while they suffered mass unemployment and poor living conditions, inadequate health services and transport, housing shortages, inferior education and subsistence wages."[74] So while it may be true that South African blacks demonstrated relatively little interest in surfing in the 1970s, this cannot be divorced from the oppressive realities of apartheid that governed their lives. Unlike the Balinese, who were likewise said to fear the ocean yet began to develop a vibrant surf culture that same decade, nonwhite South Africans faced much greater barriers in adopting the pastime as their own. Surfing is neither inexpensive nor easy. Its learning curve is slow, and it requires equipment that, relative to a more popular sport such as soccer, is both bulky (and thus not easily transportable, especially via public transit) and expensive. It also requires reasonable proximity to the ocean—something that was not always possible when racial housing patterns in South Africa were dictated by the state—as well as abundant leisure time and a flexible schedule. It is thus little wonder that surfing has, in global terms, largely been the purview of the more economically well-off classes. Moreover, in a country such as South Africa, where the beaches were racially segregated and the best breaks were either reserved for or controlled by whites, it could, for surfers of color, have seemed downright terrifying to paddle out past the whites-only signs peppering the sand to be the lone black face in a sea of whiteness.[75]

Many white South Africans may have convinced themselves, as one wrote in the mid-1970s, that "[n]o South African surfer minds sharing his waves and good surf with anyone, regardless of color, them all being equal in the love of their sport," but such an inclusive sentiment was relatively easy to express to an international audience when the number of nonwhites in the water was negligible.[76] Had black or "colored" South Africans taken to surfing in droves, greatly increasing crowd pressures and heightening the competition for waves, it is hardly inconceivable that many whites may have found themselves enforcing the racial privileges they enjoyed under apartheid. After all, even when surfers of color existed only in small numbers, some whites were already doing so. In 1989, for example, the Durban leg of the nonracial South African Surfing Union national championships precipitated what the local press called a "racial 'surf war'" when a group of white teenagers apparently "swor[e] at and racially abused" a "large portion of the 70 coloured and Indian surfers" competing in the event. Approximately sixteen white surfers then refused to leave the contest area, claiming that "blacks were not allowed to surf at the Bay of Plenty," the "'mixed' beach" that served as the contest venue, leading to a fight between a contestant and a white surfer with "a bad racist attitude." It took the intercession of a highly regarded local professional, Tommy Lawson, to defuse the volatile situation.[77]

And the harassment of surfers of color was hardly confined to the "racial 'surf war'" in Durban. Simply entering the water could, for many such individuals, be treacherous. "At places like Muizenberg, Long Beach[,] and later J-Bay [Jeffreys Bay], the cops would arrive and threaten us with arrest if we paddled out," Faeez Abrahams recalled of the 1980s. "At Long Beach, we would pretend to leave, then crawl through the bushes around back and paddle out. But," he noted, "it didn't stop there. Once you were in the water, you had a lot of guys picking fights with us. Most of the time it was hostile, seriously hostile, to a point where we had to defend ourselves physically. It was heavy back then. The other surfers didn't want us on the beach. It was illegal for us to be there. They were defending that law—the board that said, 'Whites Only.'"[78]

While many white South Africans were in fact opposed to apartheid—one, the *Cape Times* editor Tony Heard, even hatched a quixotic plan in the late 1970s to liberate Nelson Mandela from his Robben Island imprisonment on his surfboard—there were enough exceptions to make it dangerous for surfers of color to wander the coast.[79] "You go and surf at places like Long Beach or anywhere, and people would tell you, 'Fuck off back to Ocean View,'" one recalled. "Or you'd surf up in Muizenberg, and people would tell you, 'Fuck off back to Nine Mile.'"[80] Cass Collier, probably the most broadly respected nonwhite surfer in South Africa, once found himself dragged from a beach in Cape Town, according to Matt Warshaw, while Collier's father, Ahmed, recalled being repeatedly detained by the police for venturing onto whites-only beaches.[81] The younger Collier got the message. The "politics at home" made "competing on the local surfing circuit ... not an option for Cass," noted filmmaker Nicolaas Hofmeyr, so he left South Africa to compete on the professional world tour.[82] When he did return to his native country to compete, as he did for the 1990 Cape Surf Pro/Am, he did so strictly as a "disenfranchised citizen."[83]

It would not be until the mid-1980s that several of the world's most accomplished surfers announced their refusal to compete in South Africa, but for years before that the issue percolated, periodically exploding into public consciousness. One of those moments occurred in 1972. The occasion was the Gunston 500 contest in Durban, the city on South Africa's east coast that had emerged as the center of the country's surf culture. Eddie Aikau, a highly regarded Hawaiian—and one who had hosted Ahmed Collier when he went on holiday in the islands in the early 1970s—had won an expense-paid trip to the South African event as a finalist in the 1971 Smirnoff Pro-Am, a prestigious contest on Oʻahu's North Shore that notably was won that year by South African surfer Gavin Rudolph.[84] Aikau was joined by Smirnoff co-finalists Billy Hamilton and Jeff Hakman, both of them haole surfers living in Hawai'i. At the time, the global anti-apartheid movement was beginning to grow, and Hakman was asked by a friend not to make the South African journey. "You can't go, Jeff," pleaded Lee Wy Diu, a surfer and politically active attorney in Honolulu. "You must not go[;] you'll be playing right into their hands."[85] Hakman went. Not only did he consider himself above politics but, like thousands of other Americans, he had seen *The Endless Summer* and had wanted to ride South Africa's famed breaks since the film's release.[86] Hakman was accompanied by Hamilton. The two haoles, enjoying the privileges of their white skin, had a wonderful time at the contest, which Hakman won, as well as on an extensive surf safari in the weeks preceding it.

Not so the dark-skinned Aikau. Arriving in Durban in the South African winter of 1972, the realities of apartheid were made immediately apparent to him. He lost his accommodations when the Malibu Hotel overlooking the Bay of Plenty denied him entry. The contest organizers, moreover, "had to make special arrangements for [Aikau] to compete at the whites-only beach where the contest was held."[87] His racist treatment should hardly have come as a surprise. "While we are aware that the South African Government occasionally and for reasons of its own extends preferential treatment to certain black visitors from a number of different countries," a State Department official had notified Representative Ron Dellums several months before Aikau's visit, "we know of no plan on the part of the South Africans to make this the rule rather than the exception."[88]

What Aikau saw and felt in the country deeply concerned him. "I fear to walk the streets," he told a local black publication. "I get scared to . . . think that someone is going to scream at me because I am walking on the wrong side of the street because it is for Whites only. I fear and am really frightened that someone is going to pick me out. I am looking forward to go[ing] home."[89] That one of the world's top surfers could be treated so appallingly was an embarrassment to the local contest organizers. The "people at the helm of South African surfing" may have been "amongst the most well respected businessmen in Durban," noted Hakman biographer Phil Jarratt, but, he rightly concluded, they suffered a "rather large blind spot" when "it came to understanding their own government's racist policies." Eddie Aikau was "the nearest thing to a pure-blood Hawaiian you could find in the second half of the twentieth century," Jarratt suggested. "Did it not occur to any of them that . . . [he] was not exactly a blue-eyed blond?" Seized by this realization, panic ensued. The local press began asking whether the visiting surfer's treatment might "lead to a boycott of the Gunston by the Hawaiian team."[90]

They need not have worried. Aikau quickly received an invitation to stay in the beachfront apartment of Ernie Tomson, a cofounder of the Gunston contest and the father of future world champion Shaun Tomson, but the message to nonwhites was clear: even world-class surfers were not immune to the racial politics of apartheid.[91] What was worse, perhaps, was the nonchalance with which the episode was dismissed by the Hawaiian's compatriots. Hamilton brushed off Aikau's troubles as little more than an "interesting sidelight" of the South African event—the native Hawaiian "was the target of a few tossed glances from the predominantly white gathering," he wrote—while seeming to accept apartheid as the natural order of things. "Generally, the situation among the dark-skinned people is accepted," Hamilton surmised in the pages of *Surfer*. "[T]hey are content with their working positions and the roles they play in the structure of society along with their European counterparts."[92] Jarratt appropriately referred to Hamilton's article as "something of a public relations coup for the South African government."[93] Aikau was left feeling bitter. "My Hawaiian teammates abandoned me," he told a reporter for the *Honolulu Star-Bulletin*.[94]

The Hawaiian's pain must have only been compounded by the fact that the International Professional Surfers Association (IPSA) announced that same year its decision not to honor a boycott of South Africa, citing a "good faith"—but, frankly, preposterous—belief that the country's beaches were open to all. "We are not going to South Africa to thrust our ideas upon other people," president Ron Sorrell said in a statement. "We do not believe that politics should be entangled with sports. Yet," he continued, "we cannot be unaware that the Union of South Africa has in the past made sports activity with South Africa a political activity—by the imposition of apartheid policies upon South African [s]ports and competitors." But, Sorrell apparently believed, competitive surfing would not fall prey to Pretoria's trap. "We go with goodwill to South Africa and South Africans, white and black. We go to surf." Then, most bizarrely in light of the recent experience of Aikau and the reality of countless "whites only" signs dotting the coast, the IPSA president added that "[w]e go with good faith that surfers, regardless of color, are and will continue to be free to surf on the same beaches, on the same waves, under the same conditions as any other surfer on the beautiful shores of South Africa."[95] It is unclear whether the organization was hopelessly ignorant or purposely deceitful. In the end, however, it did not matter. The international competitions continued.

Most of those foreign visitors who became subject to apartheid's injustices were Hawaiian, among them some of the world's most highly skilled and respected surfers. Hawai'i was one of two "dark nations" identified by a contest organizer for the South African Surfriders Association (SASA) in preparing to host the 1970 world titles, a fact that could have caused the South Africans some trouble. But, happily for the organizers, the government gave the "green light for the holding of a 'mixed' world surfing championship" while it signaled, through the Minister of Sport and Recreation, that "there would be no apartheid problem in 1970."[96] For reasons that remain uncertain, the 1970 titles were not ultimately held in South Africa—they were moved to Australia—but it would soon become apparent that, for visiting Hawaiians, apartheid was to remain a problem for years. The 1972 treatment of Eddie Aikau was one such case. Another came in 1976, when Dane Kealoha was barred from a local restaurant while competing in Durban.[97] Randall Kim also "had a hard time" in the country, according to the former Springbok surfer Martin Potter, while Louie Ferreira got "beaten up" at a disco for "chatting" with a white girl.[98] Then, in 1985, Michael and Derek Ho, two brothers who were highly accomplished professional surfers (Michael finished in the top sixteen for ten straight years, while Derek would win the 1993 world championship), were turned away from various establishments in Durban and Cape Town.[99]

Still, such off-beach indignities were not experienced universally. The Hawaiian standout Reno Abellira, for instance, wrote of how, while in Durban in 1977, "I didn't see the racial friction or feel the bad vibes. I almost expected to go along with the prohibiting signs that read, 'Europeans Only.' People, on the whole, here were curious, kind[,] and courteous. Yet Durban wasn't Soweto," he added. "[I]n this liberal, beach resort city, and amongst the surfing community, it was hard not to feel insulated from the petty injustices of apartheid."[100] Such insulation—made possible by the South African regime's endowment of honorary whiteness on the touring Hawaiians, enabling them to surf on the country's segregated beaches—in fact grated on some South African surfers of color. "The Hawaiians enjoy white privilege while we must suffer," complained one member of the nonracial Wynberg Surf Club.[101] The fact that a number of the visiting professionals did not experience the oppression lived by their South African counterparts—Dane

Kealoha even returned to the country repeatedly after his 1976 experience, winning the Gunston 500 in 1979—allowed the sport's professional organs to sidestep a direct confrontation with the racist policies governing South African life.

The world tour's organizers were also aided by what appeared to be a general indifference to apartheid—or, startlingly, even public sympathy for it—among a number of top professionals. When the student-led Soweto uprising was violently quashed by South African authorities in 1976, with hundreds of casualties, international pressure only escalated for a formal sporting boycott. The Commonwealth of Nations responded in 1977 with the Gleneagles Agreement, a document that built on the Declaration of Commonwealth Principles issued in 1971 in Singapore.[102] The Gleneagles Agreement discouraged athletes from competing in South Africa (or even against South Africans), and it had the effect of once again raising questions about the responsibilities of surfers as competitors in international sport.[103] This was particularly true of Australians. Australia was not only a Commonwealth nation but also, as one South African wrote, the "vortex of international hot surfing."[104] As debates over the South Africa boycott ensued, numerous Australian professionals found themselves deeply troubled by the growing belief that surfing, like sport in general, was not simply an apolitical pursuit, and they took to the media to air their views. It was not their finest hour.

"The power [in South Africa] is in the hands of the people who know how to use it," insisted future Quiksilver executive Bruce Raymond. "That probably sounds morally wrong. I should be saying that everyone is equal and should have a say in their future," he suggested, "but when you look at the country as a whole, rather than the individual, that's just not the case. Some people are more capable than others and they're the ones who should be running the country." Raymond's interactions with South Africans—presumably nearly all of them white—left him with "the impression that majority rule in South Africa will set the country back a hundred years."[105] The status quo should thus remain, he argued. Terry Fitzgerald, who in 1975 divulged that he was "more of a conservative than most people think," was also somewhat sympathetic to the South African government's policies.[106] "I went over there the first time with one set of values and I came home with a new set," he revealed. "I'm not going there to make political judgements but I think what they're doing for the blacks in the Homelands—trying to give them their own sense of identity—is basically a good thing."[107]

The only Australian professional to publicly give any support to the idea of a boycott was Simon Anderson. While confessing that he had not "given the matter too much thought" as a "moral issue," he said that "on principle I suppose we shouldn't be going." Still, Anderson added, the South African contests were "a part of the international pro surfing circuit and it should be up to the governing bodies of surfing to do something about it, rather than the individual."[108] He would thus compete. Among those queried, however, the predominant sentiment appeared to be that regardless of what the Gleneagles Agreement might say, the politics of South Africa should have no bearing on whether foreign surfers competed in the country. "Government intervention in sport really gets me angry," Raymond declared.[109] The recently crowned world champion, Peter Townend, was more blunt: "I don't really give a stuff what our government says." South Africa, he added, was "an unreal place to go. I had more fun there last year than I'd had anywhere for a long time." Townend was adamant that he did not "like the way they treated their black people. . . . It blew me out when I was there." But, he noted ho-hummedly, "you get into the swing of things after a while."[110] Brian Cregan, like Townend, could not have been clearer about his feelings. "Mixing sport with politics is absolute crap," he fumed.[111]

Voices advocating that South Africa be boycotted were, in the late 1970s, rare in the surfing world. Stan Couper, a contest organizer and cofounder of the Australian Surfriders Association, was one such individual.[112] So, too, was Phil Jarratt, the editor of *Tracks* magazine. In a lengthy editorial in August 1977, Jarratt laid out an impassioned yet sober case for why South Africa ought not be included "in the international surfing circuit, both professional and amateur." Surfers, he argued, were being used as "political tools" by the South African government, lending legitimacy to the perpetration of racial injustice. The "powers-that-be," moreover, were shamefully placing Olympic ambition—a desire to see surfing emerge as an Olympic event in the 1980s—before moral principle. The fact that amateur surfing's official body was planning for a 1978 world contest in South Africa was a particular outrage to Jarratt. "Once again," he wrote, "surfing conveniently sticks its official head in the sand and refuses to believe that the thinking people of the world have finally said no to apartheid. No other sporting body would even consider holding such an event in South Africa while apartheid still exists—a fact that has resulted in South Africa's decline in international prestige and caused considerable internal dessent [*sic*]—but surfing clings to the absurd belief that the world isn't watching it." For too long surfers had turned away from the implications of their pastime in South Africa, he argued. "But surfing is too big and the issue is too pressing to get away with that any longer."[113] Jarratt's opposition, at least initially, went nowhere. South Africa continued to serve as a contest venue on the professional and amateur circuits. Indeed, the 1978 world amateur championships went forward at Nahoon Reef in East London, though—in a partial victory for boycott proponents— Australia, due to "government pressure" and "certain political considerations," did not field a team.[114]

Jarratt, like Simon Anderson, believed that anti-apartheid actions should have been spearheaded collectively by organized surfing rather than by individual surfers. There was a logic in this belief: it would have removed the pressure to choose profit over principle from cash-strapped competitors who risked forfeiting prize money, ratings points, and publicity by not competing in officially sanctioned contests. The case of Ces Wilson, a young Australian competing in the country for the second time in 1985, was illustrative. "I don't like what I see here, as far as the blatant racism is concerned, but there's absolutely nothing an individual like myself can do," he said. "Morally I don't think we should be here; financially we have to be. In my position it's necessary to compete in every event. It's up to the ASP [the Association of Surfing Professionals, which organized the world tour]. I'll only come back if I have to—there's no way you'd choose to come back to compete unless it was absolutely necessary."[115] The tour's organizers never favorably acted on the growing anti-apartheid sentiments of many surfers, however, and even when national bodies attempted to do so, the result was underwhelming. The Australian Professional Surfing Association ordered the withdrawal of the Australian team from competition in Durban in 1982, for example. But as noted by the United Nations body tasked with monitoring and combating apartheid, the Australian surfers "continued to participate as individuals."[116]

APARTHEID AND THE ASP WORLD TOUR

With the world tour's perennial failure to act, it was ultimately left to individuals to respond. Tom Carroll, in 1985, was the first professional surfer to do so. His decision was not made lightly. Carroll first competed in South Africa in 1981, and he returned several times before announcing his boycott in 1985. Aware of apartheid before ever stepping foot in the country, he was nevertheless shocked by what he saw, both within the South African surfing community and in South African society more broadly. There were, for example, the country's segregated beaches.[117] There could be no equality among surfers when their sport's venue was not open to all. There were also some South Africans' exterminationist fantasies: the "father of a couple of guys I surf with in South Africa" told him that "we were lucky in Australia— all our Aborigines had been killed."[118] Carroll, as an Australian, was "acutely aware" of the injustices faced by Aborigines in his own country, but the behavior he witnessed in South Africa was unlike anything he had ever seen at home. And then there was the experience of driving with a friend from Durban. Heading to the beach together in the early morning, the South African—a young man Carroll's age who performed his national service by intermittently working as a police officer for four years rather than serving in the military for two—attempted to drive over some of the black housekeepers and other domestic employees making their way to the white homes in which they worked. Carroll was especially troubled that his friend, who one moment was "trying to kill people," was just moments later "really gracious and giving" and "a really nice guy." What could make even seemingly decent people do such things? The experience left the Australian sobered.[119]

By 1984, cognizant of the growing international debates over the relationship between sport and apartheid—proponents were insistent that there could "never be normal sport in an abnormal society"—Carroll was consciously considering the implications of his participation in the South African leg of the world tour.[120] He left the Gunston 500 that year, which he won, feeling "ashamed" that his presence might be contributing in some way to the maintenance of the apartheid regime. Although he "didn't understand all the deeper details" of the issue, he knew that it "just didn't feel right." The time had come, he believed, to move from thought to action. It would be his last trip as a professional competitor.[121] In April 1985, just moments after securing his second world title, Carroll announced that he would boycott the South African contests scheduled for later that year. He initially asked his manager, Peter Mansted, to "write up an agreement so that all the U.S., Australian[,] and Japanese surfers" would similarly agree to boycott the country, though Carroll ultimately backed away from that collective effort.[122] Nevertheless, he was quickly joined by two other top competitors: young California standout Tom Curren and Martin Potter, a British national raised in Durban and highly regarded Springbok surfer. Collectively, these three men would account for six world titles—Carroll won two, Curren won three, and Potter won one—serving as a dominant force in professional surfing from much of the early 1980s to early 1990s. The symbolic significance of their actions was thus great. Indeed, according to Phil Jarratt, the veteran journalist who tirelessly sought to raise surfers' consciousness of the apartheid issue, the surfing precedent was cited by golfer Greg Norman, footballer Glen Ella, and several Australian cricketers in explaining why they chose not to compete in South Africa.[123] Not long afterward, the Australian prime minister, Bob Hawke, pointed to Carroll's "admirable" sacrifice—he was jeopardizing his chances for another world title by forgoing the South African leg of the world tour—when criticizing the decision of tennis star Pat Cash, fresh off a victory at Wimbledon, to play in the apartheid state.[124]

As the first to agree to a boycott and a bright, thoughtful citizen of a country where surfing is not simply dismissed as a disreputable subculture, Carroll's stand received the most attention.[125] He became a focus of debate not only among surfers worldwide but also within the multinational surfwear industry—a primary sponsor of his was Shaun Tomson's South Africa–based Instinct Clothing—and, perhaps most notably, within the Australian political system. Carroll's position generated a great deal of support—"[c]ongratulations . . . for taking an idealistic stance against fascism," wrote Jocko McRoberts of San Francisco—though the support was hardly universal.[126] South Africa's leading surfing publication, *Zigzag* magazine, immediately pooh-poohed his "bombshell" announcement while accusing the young Australian of "turn[ing] nasty."[127] In what looked like a case of petty sniping, Carroll was shortly afterward criticized in the South African press for having "failed dismally in his attempt to attain the lofty heights" achieved by several previous world-title holders, including the South African legend Shaun Tomson; Carroll's "overall contribution to the sport," Nick Williams wrote, has been "negligible."[128] On the tour itself, numerous voices were raised to question why surfing had to be mixed with politics, most notably by Tomson, the former South African world champion and 1984 world tour runner-up, as well as by the future Australian world champions Damien Hardman and Barton Lynch. All opposed the boycott. For Carroll, though, nonparticipation was a "moral obligation."[129] It was about taking "a humanitarian stand."[130]

And it was not without consequences. After announcing his decision to forgo the South African events, Carroll "resigned his contract" with Instinct the next day—there was "no way he could stay with Instinct, a company based in South Africa and employing cheap black labour," he told *Tracks*—prompting the clothing manufacturer to threaten an injunction that would

FIGURE 14. Australian prime minister Bob Hawke saw Tom Carroll as a positive role model for Australian youth and offered the surfer whatever assistance he could. Here, Hawke (left) speaks with Carroll at a 1984 contest in Sydney. Months later, Carroll announced his boycott of South Africa. Credit: Photograph courtesy of Peter Simons.

prevent him from accepting other sponsorships in Australia and the United States for twelve months.[131] (Quiksilver, which had earlier sponsored Carroll but had let him go in the early 1980s, was interested in re-signing the now two-time world champion, and the company subsequently did so.) It was clear the business relationship was over, but the terms of its cessation were uncertain. With the possibility of a lawsuit by the South African firm, the Australian prime minister intervened. Bob Hawke, a veteran trade unionist who was a vocal opponent of apartheid and a self-described sporting fanatic, met with Carroll at Parliament House in Canberra and offered his government's assistance in defending against Tomson's company.

Carroll, Hawke told the surfer, had made a "courageous decision" and was "setting an inspiring example for millions of young Australians." As such, the prime minister promised, "the Government is prepared to provide legal assistance to you by meeting the costs of a legal opinion and advice from senior counsel."[132] Hawke's offer was not without controversy. It was quickly dismissed as "entirely unjustified" by his political opposition, but the issue became moot as Instinct—presumably reeling from a one-two punch of bad publicity and the resources proffered by the Australian government—opted not to seek the injunction.[133] The company quickly signed boycott opponent Barton Lynch.[134]

If Tom Carroll enjoyed the support of the Australian political leadership in shunning South African surfing, Tom Curren, the influential Californian who would win the world title three times between 1985 and 1990, found himself opposing not only the Pretoria government but also the Reagan administration, which counted among its most important African allies the white supremacist regime.[135] Under leadership both Republican and Democratic, it had been so for decades. Indeed, Pretoria had long been considered "a vital Cold War ally" to the United States, a sentiment that only increased in the late 1970s and early 1980s.[136] This followed American expressions of racist contempt for black Africans as the 1970s began. Africans are "childlike," President Richard Nixon explained to Henry Kissinger in 1971. The national security advisor concurred, adding a racist characterization of his own. They are "savages," Kissinger volunteered amidst laughter from Nixon.[137] As anti-Communist sentiment escalated during the Jimmy Carter administration, the president from Georgia, despite his insistence that human rights represented the soul of his foreign policy, proved unwilling "to go beyond symbolic disassociations with apartheid to the level of structural disengagement from South Africa," notes historian Thomas Borstelmann.[138] Carter in fact saw such disengagement as counterproductive, according to Simon Stevens, as the president believed that "American businesses could have a positive impact on race relations in South Africa."[139] This may have frustrated anti-apartheid activists, but Carter faced little political risk for his failure to disengage; one poll in 1979 revealed that only 18 percent of the American public had even heard of apartheid.[140] Carter's successor, Ronald Reagan, showed an even greater inclination to seek accommodation with the Pretoria regime. Whether in its opposition to what Reagan described as the "calculated terror" of the African National Congress or its role in the conflicts in Angola, Namibia, and Mozambique, South Africa essentially enjoyed—albeit uneasily and always with mild opposition intended to fend off tougher congressional action—the steady support of the Reagan White House.[141]

Curren nevertheless bucked official opinion and acceded to the boycott movement, making him one of the more prominent American athletes to individually decide to do so. The Californian had first surfed in South Africa as a member of the U.S. national team during an amateur contest in 1981. Like thousands of other young Americans, he knew of the country because of its waves and its accomplished surfers. The "picture" he developed during that 1981 trip—it was "kind of like California, a lot of good surf, good food"—was "obviously not the whole picture." "Regrettably," Curren said years later, the "political situation was not anything that I really contemplated." By 1985, following several more visits, the realities of the racist system—and his responsibility as an athlete competing in the apartheid state—had begun to dawn on him. "The basis of . . . my decision was . . . knowing that the ANC [African National Congress] were requesting foreign athletes to boycott South Africa," he maintained. "I couldn't ignore that." In light of the ANC's call, as well as an in-law urging the same, Curren found himself contemplating how his role as a professional surfer was not necessarily as apolitical as many of his contemporaries might have imagined. When Tom Carroll announced his boycott at Bells Beach in April of that year, Curren quickly followed the Australian's example. While "I really enjoyed going to South Africa and surfing the waves there," the young Californian noted, "there was a bigger moral issue," and boycotting the country was "the right thing to do." He had no regrets. "I felt good about my decision . . . regardless of how it would affect my ratings."[142]

As a young man raised in South Africa, Martin Potter, who would win the world title in 1989, came to the apartheid issue more personally than did Curren and Carroll. Potter was born in the United Kingdom but moved with his family to Durban—his father had taken a position as an engineer for a South African oil company—when he was two years old. Not knowing any differently, he grew up thinking apartheid was "normal." It was simply "how people lived over there," he recalled. His involvement in surfing showed him otherwise. At the age of fourteen, Potter made the Springbok national team and, in 1980, traveled to California to compete. It was at that point that he realized there was something "different . . . about where I live." Most notably, in California he saw "blacks and whites hanging out together." It began to dawn on him that the situation at home was "not quite right," that there was a serious problem with how whites "showed such disrespect toward . . . blacks." When Potter turned pro the following year, and the frequency of his world travel increased, he began to share with his mother his growing disenchantment with his adopted country. He realized, at the age of sixteen or seventeen, that he "wanted to get the hell out of South Africa and start building my own life somewhere else." While cognizant that racism existed all over the world, including in Australia and the United States, he nevertheless felt a need to distance himself from the apartheid system. After briefly maintaining an official residence in England, he ended up in Australia.[143]

From his new home he was able to ruminate not only on what he had left behind but also on what it meant to be a traveling professional. "Growing up [in South Africa], looking back, I saw a lot of stuff happen that I just brushed off as, 'Oh, well that's just life. That's just how things operate.' And then, the more I grew up and the more I . . . got a bit older and thought about things, I knew that it wasn't right. And [for] me, going and competing in the events in South Africa was almost supporting the way all that stuff was happening." He grew so uncomfortable with the status quo that he said to himself, "I can't keep condoning this. I can't keep condoning the way these people are treated." He decided to "make a stand to not compete in the [South African] events." For the former Springbok, the decision to boycott—a decision that, like Tom Curren's, was announced just after that of Tom Carroll—came at a considerable personal cost. Not only was Potter forfeiting the points he might have earned on the South African leg of the tour, thus jeopardizing his championship aspirations, but he also "lost a lot of friends, a lot of kids I grew up with, a lot of guys I surfed with on the Springbok team." Moreover, he had heard from other South African professionals that his "life was threatened. If I ever went back to South Africa I was going to be murdered," he said he was told. "I had a black mark next to my name."[144]

Potter's actions did not go unrecognized by those active in the anti-apartheid struggle. As a white Durbanite who allowed his sense of morality to trump self-interest, the exiled surfer received a letter from the African National Congress thanking him for his position and notifying him that—unlike "a lot of the others," Potter said the letter stated—he would be welcomed in post-apartheid South Africa. It was "kind of an uncomfortable letter to receive," he confessed, as he wanted "nothing to do with that sort of stuff. I just want[ed] to get on with my life and I want[ed] to try to live it the best I can. And [to] bring my kids up with an open mind." Potter did not, in other words, see himself as a political activist. He made his decision to boycott not for "any press" or "any pat on the back," he said. Nor, he insisted, was he trying to denounce the South African people or hurt competitive surfing. His target was the Pretoria regime. Like Carroll and Curren, Potter boycotted the country for a simple reason: he felt that "it was the right thing to do."[145] The fact that its beaches were segregated, and that surfers of color could not compete under the apartheid system, was appalling.[146] "Just because we're surfers doesn't mean that . . . we're able to forget and not be involved in that kind of stuff," he maintained.[147]

The Association of Surfing Professionals (ASP), the umbrella organization of the surfing world tour, did not penalize or otherwise pressure its boycotting members. At the same time, neither did it move toward—nor, for that matter, did it at first even discuss—a larger professional boycott, as numerous other sporting organizations had done.[148] Indeed, the ASP actually went out of its way to assure South Africa's survival on the tour, sanctioning events in the mid-1980s even when they failed to meet the minimum purse necessary under tour rules.[149] As Phil Jarratt pointed out in *Surfer*, the failure of the South African organizers to provide the necessary prize money afforded the ASP a perfect opportunity to stage an "honorable retreat" from the tour's brush with apartheid sport.[150] (So, too, did the fact that the white government banned one of the surfing world's leading publications, the Australia-based monthly *Tracks*.)[151] But Ian Cairns, the ASP's executive director, was adamant: "We don't have a political position," he stated. Even with the "recently declared state of emergency and well-publicized violence," South Africa would remain on the tour schedule.[152] In professing an apolitical position, the ASP operated under what can only be described as specious logic.[153] To boycott South Africa was political, in its estimation, while to compete in South Africa was somehow apolitical. In fact, *both* positions were political. One was simply more lucrative for professional surfing. The ASP's views represented "self-serving cowardice of the worst kind," one surfer angrily intoned.[154]

While the official position of the ASP was nonacquiescence to the athletic boycott movement—a movement that, by the mid-1980s, encompassed many of the world's most popular sports—some of the ASP's leading members did not hesitate to raise their voices in favor of continued competition. Foremost among these was 1977 world champion Shaun Tomson, a major force in the development of professional surfing. Intelligent, handsome, and articulate, Tomson was South Africa's most accomplished male surfer (his record was surpassed only by that of Wendy Botha) and was considered by many to be an unofficial diplomat for the sport.[155] His good looks and innovative tube riding made him a darling of the international surf press. As a

Jew whose parents fostered respectful, nonracist thinking—it was his father, Ernie, who hosted Eddie Aikau when the Hawaiian was barred from the Malibu Hotel overlooking the Bay of Plenty in 1972—the Durbanite seemed an unlikely opponent of the boycott. He was, after all, opposed to racial separation.[156]

But Tomson maintained that sport and politics should not mix. True, the white South African regime saw things differently. The Springbok national team for which Tomson had surfed as a youth, for instance, had over the years received considerable government support, while government funds enabled the globe-trotting of the country's top talent.[157] Tomson's older cousin Michael, himself an accomplished professional who in 1979 took to the op-ed page of the *New York Times* to lament the global sporting boycott, acknowledged in the 1970s how he and other South African surfers touring California were not simply competing as individuals.[158] They were there, he emphasized, "because the government likes to see *South Africa* going to compete against foreign countries." Prompted about whether surfing was for them a "nationalistic type of thing," there was no doubt in the elder Tomson's mind. "Right! Definitely!"[159] It is thus little wonder that the apartheid government, working through its London embassy—Britain was at the heart of the global anti-apartheid movement—exploited his young cousin's competitive accomplishments as part of its overseas propaganda.[160]

Still, Shaun Tomson maintained, sport was (and should be) divorced from politics. Athletes were goodwill ambassadors who fostered constructive communication.[161] "The South African government had used Apartheid (meaning 'apartness' in Afrikaans) as an instrument of cruelty to separate people, not only whites from blacks (and Indians and Coloureds), but black ethnic groups and social classes from one another," Tomson wrote years later. "Surfers were employing the tactics of the enemy and using the sport of surfing as a political weapon."[162] Tomson also had more personal objections. Boycotting South Africa meant boycotting the Gunston 500. Staying away "would be a slap to a sponsor [the tobacco company Gunston] that had been a longtime supporter of the tour, and also to the memory of my father (he passed away in 1981), who had helped found the event."[163] Finally, Tomson believed, surfing should not be understood in the context of apartheid, as South African surfers had achieved their success strictly on merit. There was no discrimination. Blacks, he said, were simply not interested in surfing.[164]

When Tom Carroll secured his second world title in 1985 and almost immediately announced his boycott of South Africa, "an emotional . . . Tomson," who had finished just behind Carroll in that year's ASP rankings, urged the assembled professionals (as well as contest organizers, industry leaders, and journalists) at a Hall of Fame ceremony in Torquay to "think hard" before they "abandon one of the strongest sections of the pro tour."[165] "Suddenly the surfers have principles. Suddenly we have political aspirations," Tomson spewed in what Matt Warshaw noted was an uncharacteristically sarcastic speech from "the sport's most gracious speaker." Questioning whether the United States should be boycotted because of its sponsorship of the Contras in Nicaragua or whether England should be boycotted over its brutal repression in Northern Ireland, Tomson was outraged by the singular focus on South Africa. "Where will it all end?" he asked. "I'll tell you. It will end with the destruction of pro surfing as we know it!"[166] Most of Tomson's colleagues did not at first need much cajoling. While the three who boycotted were among the sport's highest profile athletes—a fourth, Cheyne Horan, boycotted the events in 1985 but began returning to South Africa in 1986 with "Free Mandela" splashed across his board—they also represented a distinct numerical minority.[167] From South Africa the view was dismissive. The "net result" of the boycott was "negligible," a piece in *Zigzag* insisted.[168]

But by 1986 the movement was in fact showing results. Unprecedented attention was being drawn to apartheid within the surfing community, including among South Africans. One South African surfer, for instance, praised the boycotting professionals for "increasing the political awareness among surfers, thus perhaps in some small way influencing political change." Rather than merely focusing on "wind direction, swell size, [and] bikini-clad bodies," his compatriots were being forced to consider "the pressing political issues in our country." The "efficacy" of the boycott "cannot therefore be disputed," he maintained.[169] The sentiment was echoed by others.[170] Within the professional ranks, in 1986 nearly half of the world's top sixteen surfers stayed away. In addition to Carroll, Curren, and Potter, the dark-skinned Hawaiian brothers Michael and Derek Ho, who had faced discrimination in Durban and Cape Town the previous year, forsook the South African events, as did Mike Lambresi and Chris Frohoff of the United States and Gary Elkerton and Barton Lynch of Australia. Not all of the absent surfers were driven by moral principle—some apparently felt the prize money not worth the hassle or their personal security in doubt—but the viability of the tour's South African leg appeared increasingly questionable.[171]

Safety, more than anything else, imperiled its future. With a number of competitors expressing concerns about the country's violence, *Tracks* wondered "how much hell would break loose if things erupted on a Durban beach during the Gunston and a surfer got hurt." This was not merely fanciful speculation. The city, the magazine noted, had recently been rocked by "a series of bomb blasts," including at "a beachside hotel [and favored after-dark watering hole] where many surfers have stayed over the years." Imagining such violence erupting during the athletes' 1986 visit, the editors derisively suggested that the ASP's "excuse book would run dry with that one."[172] A meeting was thus hastily called. Only "[t]wenty-four hours before the [tour] was to leave for South Africa," *Surfer* magazine reported, "a telephone vote was held to determine whether or not the two events scheduled there would be sanctioned." Despite the fact that the prize money in one of the contests was far below the tour minimum, that a state of emergency had been declared just a couple of weeks before, and that seven of the top sixteen surfers had already said they would stay away, the ASP nevertheless voted to sanction the events and proceed as planned.[173] Perhaps surprisingly, among those voting with the minority was Shaun Tomson, who served as the official representative for the South African and European competitors. But Tomson explained his vote by noting that while he was indeed concerned for the safety of the surfers, he also "felt sure" that the vote would turn out favorably for South Africa.[174] There was thus nothing to lose. "Pro surfing owes the South African events a debt of gratitude," ASP founder and executive director Ian Cairns had declared months earlier amid a collapsing South African economy, "and I'd like to extend the hand of friendship and help them out at a bad time."[175] Still, the absence of many of the top professionals was an undeniable blow to South African sporting interests. Nearly twice as many competitors stayed away in 1986 as did in 1985. "[A]t this rate," Phil Jarratt opined hopefully, "none of the seeded surfers will go in 1987"—if, that is, the tour was even sanctioned.[176]

It was, and some did, but the no-shows continued. In 1987, ten of the thirty highest-ranked professionals announced that they would forgo the South African events, and others, such as Vetea "Poto" David—the Tahitian winner of the 1986 world amateur junior title—also ducked out of the African portion of the tour.[177] One of those who did make the trip was the young Hawaiian (and later world champion) Sunny Garcia. Like some of his fellow competitors, Garcia found himself in what *Tracks* called "a pretty awkward" situation when the first of the two South African contests was temporarily moved to Blouberg, one of the few remaining whites-only beaches in Cape Town. Yet Garcia was unfazed. "If someone tries to stop me surfing on this beach[,] I'll knock his block off," he threatened.[178] Another visiting professional was rumored to have been "forcibly silenced" by South African friends when he began chanting "Free Nelson Mandela" in a Cape Town shopping center.[179] *Surfer* was scathing in its criticism of the ASP. Apart from challenging the organization's stated policy of "separating politics from surfing" as a "questionable distinction," the magazine asked how much "credibility" a "'major' pro surfing event" had "when 33% of the Top 30 doesn't show."[180] If the tour officials were bothered by the media denunciation, they did not let on in planning for the following year. Again two events were scheduled for South Africa. Again a substantial number of the world's top professionals chose not to compete. And again *Surfer* was condemnatory. "World Tour victories are cheap in South Africa," the magazine said of the 1988 contests, whether "from a moral standpoint" or "because the heart of the ASP field stays away altogether."[181] The South African press saw things differently. The events were "a huge success," *Zigzag* opined, as "they were blessed with waves, crowds, great surfing[,] and[,] for the first time in years, the [then-current] world champion," Damien Hardman.[182]

If 1988 showed the boycott to be an ongoing fact of professional surfing life, by 1989 many were wondering whether the writing was in fact on the wall for the tour's South African future. That year a remarkable twenty-five of the top thirty professionals stayed away.[183] Tom Carroll was again at the center of what one journalist called the "bitter political turmoil" that surrounded the boycott, and he was once more personally thanked for his principled position by the Australian prime minister, Bob Hawke.[184] Many of his fellow competitors were no doubt less concerned with the moral stand against apartheid than they were with the lack of prize money and ratings points the trip offered—only one event, the Gunston 500, was scheduled for the South African leg of the tour. Nevertheless, the country's isolation, both politically and geographically, did not bode well for its competitive horizon. "It remains to be seen whether the Gunston will survive another year and celebrate its 21st birthday," Brisbane's *Sunday Mail* suggested ominously.[185] The Durban-based magazine *Zigzag* seemed particularly sobered. Looking back to 1985, it ruefully characterized the boycott's origins as "the beginning of the end" for South African surfing.[186]

By 1989, developments internationally had also begun to weigh on the minds of competitors. South African surfers had long faced difficulties in receiving visas to compete in various contests abroad. In the first such instance, in 1978, recently crowned world champion Shaun Tomson was banned from Brazil in what the Australian surfing press called "the first time that surfing has been caught up in international political barracking of South Africa."[187] Brazil would continue to deny visas to South African competitors into the 1980s, as would at various times Australia, New Zealand, France, and Japan.[188] Some professionals were able to get around the visa restrictions by using foreign travel documents. Pierre Tostee, for instance, traveled to Brazil and Japan by drawing on his Mauritian ancestry, while Shaun Tomson, probably the most famous South African surfer in history, took to using an Irish passport.[189] But the visa restrictions took a toll on South African professionals, leading some to drop out of the international ranks.[190] The country's amateurs likewise found themselves feeling isolated, with their participation in the 1988 and 1990 world championships forbidden by the International Surfing Association.[191] By the late 1980s, however, it was not just South Africans who had to worry. Other surfers began to feel the effects of having previously graced the shores of the apartheid state.[192]

In probably the best-known case of such blowback, in February 1989 the two top-seeded surfers in the ASP East, Americans Rich Rudolph and Charlie Kuhn, were prohibited from competing in the West Indies at the Natural Art/Carib Beer Pro-Am, the first Caribbean professional contest sanctioned by that organization.[193] Prompted by a letter to the editor from a visiting Briton, a local newspaper, the *Barbados Advocate*, had launched an investigation of who, among the more than 125 foreign surfers descending on the predominantly black island, had competed in any South African events.[194] When the paper disclosed just a day before the contest that Rudolph and Kuhn had done so, official investigations were launched by the Barbadian Immigration Department and the Ministry of Sports.[195] "I don't support apartheid or anything like that," Kuhn explained to the *Advocate*. "It is just that when you are a professional you are sometimes forced to do things you wouldn't do normally." Rudolph opted for a different tack, appearing to claim ignorance. "We are not politicians," he told the paper. "When we go to South Africa we are fairly isolated and not allowed to travel around and see what the country is really like[.] [W]e just simply surf."[196] The Barbadian authorities were apparently not impressed. The two Ameri-

FIGURE 15. The *Barbados Advocate* was scathing in its depiction of the American surfers who had traveled to South Africa before competing in the West Indies, running a cartoon that showed a white surfer, cash in hand, riding the wave of apartheid over a drowning black South African.

cans, the government decreed the next day, could not surf in the contest.[197] They quickly decided to leave.

This was an unprecedented development—surfers allowed into a country but then barred from competition—and one that left the organizers extremely displeased. The two top seeds in the ASP East's inaugural Barbadian contest had been disqualified, the Barbados Surfing Association had at least temporarily taken a public drubbing, and a number of sponsors were so upset—not with the surfers but with the *Advocate*—that they had withdrawn their advertisements from a special supplement generated by the newspaper for the three-day event.[198] Bitter contest officials, meanwhile, hindered the *Advocate*'s ability to cover the competition, inviting the condemnation of the Barbados Association of Journalists.[199] In an effort to tamp down the outrage of the local media and authorities, the director of the ASP East, Mike Martin, hastily called a press conference as the contest got under way. His response to what *Surfer* magazine took to calling "The Incident" was, in typical ASP fashion, markedly wishy-washy. When the ruckus had first erupted several days earlier, Martin claimed that his "association does not take its competitions to South Africa and does not encourage sporting links with that country," an initial statement in which he apparently attempted to draw a distinction between the ASP as an umbrella organization and the regional circuit under his charge.[200] But several days later, following a late-night conversation with ASP executive director Graham Cassidy, Martin, while condemning apartheid as "repugnant and indefensible," defended the American surfers by noting that they were technically not in violation of the Gleneagles Agreement; they had competed in South Africa as individual athletes and not as representatives of a signatory nation.[201] Faced with questions about how many of the other surfers in Barbados had traveled to the apartheid state, Martin was skillfully evasive. His performance—a well-mixed combination of prevarication and calm reasoning—demonstrated the "aplomb of a natural diplomat," *Surfer* reckoned.[202]

Controversy would greet the Barbados contest again the following year. Wes Laine, a Virginia Beach local who had been ranked ninth on the world tour in 1983 and 1985 but retired in 1989 to concentrate on the East Coast professional circuit, professed to California-based *Surfing* magazine his absolute refusal to abide by the South Africa boycott. "I'm not going to jeopardize my livelihood or miss out on a good surf trip for anything," he declared. Frankly, Laine gushed, he "loved South Africa, [and] couldn't *not* go there, because the waves are just too good." The boycott, moreover, was a futile effort; it was not going to have "any impact on South Africa's politics, period," the Virginian insisted.[203] None of this pleased Barbadian contest officials, who, upon learning of Laine's comments, promptly told the American that he would be prohibited from entering the country. An angry Laine responded by pledging to disrupt the 1990 contest by, of all things, organizing a boycott of Barbados.[204] It went nowhere.

When combined with the ongoing professional boycott of South Africa, international incidents such as the ones in the West Indies threatened the world tour's continuation in the apartheid state. "The Barbadian government had put the ASP on notice," *Surfer* observed. "Let your surfers know they have a choice. They can compete in South Africa or they can compete here. They can't do both."[205] Just as it appeared that matters had reached a nadir for the embattled South African surfing community, however, a confluence of developments in the months following the tour's 1989 swing through the country proved beneficial to its competitive future. In November of that year, the government of F. W. de Klerk opened the country's whites-only beaches to blacks. Then, in February 1990, the Pretoria regime released Nelson Mandela, ended the ban on the African National Congress, and began the process of formal negotiations to bring about an end to apartheid. "Whether it was a loosening of apartheid laws, or because a few other events have dropped off the '90 schedule, the Gunston was better attended by the international crew than at any time since 1985," *Surfer* noted of the 1990 South African portion of the tour. "Nine surfers of the Top 16 showed up, despite the fact that the Gunston was the only rated event in South Africa this year."[206] Still, even with the improved attendance, seven of the top sixteen continued to stay away, as did several other highly ranked professionals.[207] But sporting views of South Africa were indeed rapidly changing. The fact that the South African government, responding to tremendous international and domestic pressure, had begun the process of dismantling apartheid made it increasingly likely that the professional surfers' boycott, like those of other foreign athletes, would rapidly come to an end. And, as things improved, it did begin to unravel. Tom Curren returned to the country in 1992 after seven years away. Martin Potter came back the following year, where, placing fifth in the Gunston 500—the storied South African contest that witnessed an estimated 250,000 spectators in 1993—he was dubbed a "local hero" by *Surfer* magazine.[208]

Tom Carroll, the Australian professional and two-time world champion who kicked off the professional surfers' boycott, was the last to return. He had nearly been the first, contemplating a 1991 entry in the Gunston as South Africa was beginning the process of serious political change. But ultimately he decided to hold off. "What still bugs me[, . . .] despite all the headway in dismantling apartheid, is the one-man one-vote issue," Carroll told the press just days before the contest. "In the end I couldn't . . . [go] back there this season because that aspect of apartheid has still got to be fully addressed. The blacks have got to have a say." While quite adulatory of the developments under way—"I'm convinced the Pretoria [g]overnment is genuine in what it's doing. I'm sure corporate pressures have a lot to do with it, but even so, President de Klerk has made some very brave moves," he said—Carroll was insistent that South Africa still had some distance to go. "I'll stay away until the vote is given to the blacks," he declared.[209] That vote would not materialize until 1994, the same year Carroll, after a professional career spanning a decade and a half, retired from the world tour. Alas, apartheid ended too late for his third-world-title aspirations. Nevertheless, in 1996 Carroll was given an opportunity to return. When he received a wild-card invitation for that year's inaugural CSI/Billabong Pro at Jeffreys Bay, the world-famous pointbreak forty-five miles southwest of Port Elizabeth, the Australian eagerly accepted. Coming eleven years after he had last set foot in the country, it was a joyful moment in a difficult but distinguished career.[210]

. . .

The boycott initiated by Tom Carroll will strike few surfers, who generally see their sport in apolitical terms, as the high point of the Australian's professional life, but that was not true of the movement to which he contributed. Bob Hawke, for instance, could not praise Carroll enough during a testimonial dinner in 1993. The former prime minister—who would introduce Carroll to Nelson Mandela in 1997 in what the surfer warmly recalled as "a very, very touching moment"—could think of "no example in the history of Australian sport where a champion has been prepared to put principles so manifestly in front of his or her own interests," he told the assembled guests, and there was "no Australian sporting hero or legend" for whom he felt a "greater surge of affection and admiration."[211] While the actions of Carroll, Curren, and Potter forced the political confrontation with South African apartheid into the world of competitive surfing, racial separation in that country had in fact long simmered in the surfing consciousness. Surfers, to be sure, were only marginal players in the world of global sport, and their boycott of South Africa received far less attention than did those of cricketers and soccer players with far larger fan bases. Yet as individual athletes in a sport often associated with "freedom," their participation in the South African saga held considerable symbolic significance.

The boycott penetrated the cloistered and intimate world of competitive surfing, undermining its perceived apoliticism and forcing countless young people to begin reckoning with an injustice that they likely would have otherwise ignored. If the "freedom" of surfing had, since the sixties, meant for many an escape from the world of politics and commerce, the boycott of South Africa—and the years of debate that preceded it—demonstrated that surfers could not so easily disentangle themselves from some of the pressing political issues of the twentieth century. In doing so, they necessarily became, despite their protestations to the contrary, political actors.

FIVE

Industrial Surfing

THE COMMODIFICATION OF EXPERIENCE

RICK KANE IS A SURPRISINGLY popular figure for someone who does not actually exist. Surfers worldwide know his story, and they can quote him and his friends at length. For those readers unfamiliar with contemporary surf cinema—*Point Break* (1991), *Blue Crush* (2002), and the like—Rick Kane is the name of the character played by Matt Adler in *North Shore* (1987), a Hollywood foray into the industrializing world of Reagan-era surf culture. The film is the wildly improbable story of Kane, a teenager from Arizona who, having won a surf contest in a wave pool hundreds of miles from the nearest coast, uses his $500 award, as he proudly announces to a cheering crowd, to go "to Hawai'i to surf the big waves of the North Shore." The time spent on O'ahu is, for the Arizonan, dramatic from the moment of arrival. Within hours he befriends two Australian professionals (Mark Occhilupo and Robbie Page), attends a party with surfing celebrity Lance Burkhart (Laird Hamilton), suffers the theft of his luggage, and finds himself harassed by the Hui—the Hawaiian locals who resent the haole invasion of their islands.

Fortunately for the "barney" from Arizona—a "barney," viewers learn from a beloved character called Turtle, is someone who is "so haole he doesn't even know he's haole"—he serendipitously meets Chandler (Gregory Harrison), a bearded, white board shaper who respects local traditions and embodies the film's conception of "soul." Chandler takes a liking to Kane, a budding artist, and asks him to create a new logo for his business. In return for the design work and some assistance in cleaning up, Chandler provides the young Arizonan with room and board. Chandler, the audience quickly discovers, is everything that the recent arrival is not. He understands the science of waves, he appreciates the ocean's awesome power, and he is sensitive

FIGURE 16. Rick Kane (Matt Adler) and Chandler (Gregory Harrison) embodying soul in *North Shore* (1987). Credit: © Universal Pictures.

to the American colonization of the islands. This initially creates an inherent tension with Kane, a clueless mainlander who is enamored of surfing's neon-infused glitz and aspires to reach the top ranks of the professional circuit. Kane admires the sponsorships and money that have made surfing increasingly mainstream and the celebrity culture spawned by the surf media. Chandler, not surprisingly, sees the sport's professionalization—the quest for fame, wealth, and glory—as destructive of its soul.

But Kane, whose views are clearly presented as misguided, is not beyond redemption. Before long, Chandler, encouraged by his Hawaiian wife, begins teaching the Arizonan what it means to be a true surfer—a "soul surfer." This includes an appreciation for decades of advances in board design, an understanding of underwater topography, and learning to ride *with* a wave rather than to "shred" it. Kane proves a quick and ambitious student. By the film's end, he has emerged as a skilled wave rider; captured the heart of a beautiful Hawaiian woman; earned the respect of the Hui leader, Vince (Gerry Lopez); and nearly won a storied contest at the Banzai Pipeline—a contest Kane lost only because the winner, the same arrogant and obnoxious Burkhart he once idolized, found it necessary to cheat. Chandler, who by that point had gotten swept up in Kane's march toward competitive victory, wanted his young charge to lodge a complaint about the cheating with the

FIGURE 17. Though Rick Kane arrives in Hawai'i a star-struck "barney," creating tension with the Hui, including Vince (Gerry Lopez, third from right) and Derek Ho (fourth from right), he undergoes a transformation into a "soul surfer," earning the respect of those same Hawaiian locals. Credit: © Universal Pictures.

judges. But Kane refuses. "It's only a contest," he reminds Chandler. "It doesn't mean anything, right? Not to us soul surfers."

North Shore may have been a critical and box-office bomb—its American gross, according to IMDb.com, came to approximately $3.8 million—but, with its impressive wave-riding footage and inclusion of numerous surfing personalities (in addition to Occhilupo, Page, Hamilton, and Lopez, Derek Ho and Corky Carroll had speaking roles), it developed a cult following within the surf community.[1] Indeed, the California Surf Museum, to mark the twenty-fifth anniversary of the picture's 1987 release, opened its fifth annual film festival with a tribute screening of what it called a Hollywood "classic" at La Paloma Theatre in Encinitas; in attendance at the 2012 event were the movie's director and writer, and several of its actors, including surfing legends Lopez, Hamilton, and Shaun Tomson.[2] (Tomson made a cameo appearance in the film.) *North Shore*'s plot is undoubtedly hokey and far-fetched, but the film resonated with countless surfers. In large part this was because of its comical story line, impressive cinematography, and, like most surf flicks, overrepresentation of female skin. Yet it also addressed an inevitable tension in the sport at a time when the surf industry was beginning to truly live up to its name: Has surfing been corrupted by its professionalization? Is there a conflict between purity and commercialism? Does the industry threaten the sanctity of the wave-riding experience?

There had long been debates among surfers about what their pastime represented. On one side were "purists," such as *North Shore*'s Chandler and (eventually) Rick Kane, who argued that surfing offered a unique, noncommercial form of communion with the natural world. On the other were competitors who celebrated professionalization as a means to make a living—and an increasingly lucrative one—doing what they most love.[3] If one could be paid by large corporations to travel the world and ride waves, the professionals argued, then why not? What resulted was a seemingly unresolvable tension. What was the place of surfing, which to many afforded an escape from the stresses of modern life, amid a modernity marked by corporate globalization? What did it mean to have a surf industry—scores of corporations and other concerns that too often subscribed to the labor and environmental precepts of the larger industrial world—when the sport itself was a solitary undertaking that, apart from the occasional wave pool, appeared to exist outside mass society? (Surfers tend to overlook the petrochemical mediation on which they rely to experience the outdoors, with modern surfboards, wetsuits, leashes, and boardshorts a veritable stew of industrial chemicals.)[4] Was the development of the surf industry, in other words, antithetical to a pastime rooted in the natural pleasures of the ocean? And if it was inevitable, what values would it embrace?

CORPORATE EMPIRE-BUILDING

Surfing is today big business. By the second decade of the twenty-first century, the surf industry—the surfwear and wetsuit companies, the board shapers and manufacturers, the media producers, the wax and leash makers—was generating economic activity totaling more than $7 billion annually.[5] Surf tourism almost certainly generated billions more.[6] By 1989, the industry had organized its own professional trade group, the Surf Industry Manufacturers Association (SIMA), whose largest member, Quiksilver, Inc., was in 2010 a $2 billion multinational conglomerate with some eight hundred standalone retail outlets in ninety countries.[7] By any measure, the company was no slouch. In 1986, a year before Universal Pictures released *North Shore*, Quiksilver became the first surf-related corporation to go public; its shares are now traded on the New York Stock Exchange. A second industry group, the Board Retailers Association (BRA), formed in 2003 to represent independent board-sport retailers across the United States. By 2012, it boasted some six hundred members. With billions of dollars at stake, SIMA has made it a point since 1997 to meet annually in Cabo San Lucas, Mexico, to address its challenges and chart its future.

Those challenges became steep in the early twenty-first century. It was not that surfing suddenly declined in popularity, threatening the viability of the burgeoning industry. On the contrary, the sport's runaway success, as both a pastime and a cultural juggernaut, attracted the attention of large "non-endemic" corporations seeking a share of the profits.[8] "When we looked at action sports, we saw a unique consumer segment that was underserved in terms of product innovation," Nike president and CEO Mark G. Parker told a shareholder meeting in 2011.[9] Adopting an insistence on corporate "service"—a self-styled beneficent gesture aimed at an "underserved" consumer "segment"—the apparel manufacturer was, by the time of Parker's speech, in the midst of a major bid to capture what it could of the surf market. In 2002, the company bought the surf- and skatewear maker Hurley, and in 2005, it created a sub-brand—Nike 6.0—meant to appeal to surfers, snowboarders, and skaters. In 2009, Nike took a major step, purchasing and sponsoring the world's largest surf competition, the U.S. Open of Surfing (which then became the Nike U.S. Open of Surfing), a weeklong extravaganza held every summer in Huntington Beach, California, that typically attracts hundreds of thousands of spectators and considerable media attention.[10] By 2011, action sports represented a $390 million business for Nike. The company hoped to see that number double within five years.[11]

Other "non-endemic" corporations recognized and sought to emulate Nike's success. Most significantly, in July 2009 Target signed sixteen-year-old professional surfer Carissa Moore, who in 2011 would win the ASP Women's World Tour, in an implicit recognition of the growing popularity of women's surfing. "I love Target and I am honored to make my relationship with them official," the Honolulu-born Moore gushed in a press release. "Target opened two stores in Hawaii this year and it's been great to have one so close to home."[12] Months later the big-box retailer added to its athletic roster the fifteen-year-old up-and-comer Kolohe Andino, son of former professional surfer Dino Andino. "It's a brand I support and I'm proud to be surfing with the bullseye on my board," the young Californian said.[13] To be sure, the marriage of surfing and corporate America—or at least that segment of it outside the organic surf community—was not exactly new. Laird Hamilton, the strikingly handsome big-wave rider from Hawai'i, was by 2006 a spokesperson for American Express and the Davidoff Cool Water fragrance line.[14] Well before that, Shaun Tomson, the 1977 world champion, had exploited his wave-riding notoriety and good looks to model for Calvin Klein.[15] And even earlier, surfers had promoted cars, shoes, and beer.[16] But this was different.

Or was it? Origin stories are often shrouded in myth, and the origins of modern surfing are no exception. To hear some of the sport's more established figures tell it, the white Americans who traveled to Hawai'i in the 1950s were postwar revolutionaries taking on the capitalist system. "That was the counterculture of its day," contest organizer Randy Rarick maintained. "You know, you were bucking the system, and you went to Hawai'i, and you rode waves. They were the pioneers, not only of riding big waves, but of the culture of surfing. They're the ones that set the pace, this kind of free and easy lifestyle." Big-wave legend Greg Noll was even more adamant. "[A]ll of a sudden a bunch of guys come along and they go, 'Screw the money. You know, I'm having all the fun I could possibly have.' [. . .] [And] the more fun we were having, the more it would piss off society." Resistance can of course be fun—just ask the Yippies, the Yes Men, or Billionaires for Bush—but this was different. This was fun *as* resistance. "For the first time ever," Noll continued, "they had a group of guys that didn't give a rat's ass, dropping out of the basketball team or the football team, and just giving the whole thing the finger and going, 'Oh, I don't give a shit about that. I want to go surfing.'" Bill Hamilton, one of the young men who accompanied Eddie Aikau to South Africa in 1972, at least had the good sense to temper his claims. We were "almost rebellious," he said of those early postwar years.[17]

That "almost" is important. While surfers may have envisioned themselves as young radicals "bucking the system," their objectives were entirely selfish. Life was about unrestrained hedonism, not social transformation. The desire to surf may have been laced with an implicit critique of 1950s conformity culture, but the critique remained implicit. These early surfers lacked the political vision, however muddled, of the Beats or even the hippies, two countercultural movements to whom they have at times been compared. When filmmaker Stacy Peralta opined that "[f]or this new generation of surfers, surfing wasn't just something you did, but something you became; not just a sport, but a statement," it was fair to wonder just what that statement might have been.[18] It certainly was not political—or at least not self-consciously so. Postwar society did not consider surfers rebellious; it considered them lazy. Surfers were called "beach bums," not radicals. Yes, surfing was fun. But fun, in a capitalist society, is hardly subversive. Individual acquisition—whether of money, consumer goods, or pleasure—is what drives the American system.[19] There would come a time, especially in the 1990s, when surfing was ascribed an edginess, a sense of rebellion—though without actually being either of those things. Edginess does sell, however, and surfing thus became a brand—or, better yet, a branding vehicle, and one that businesses did not hesitate to exploit.[20]

But that would come later. For much of the early 1960s, as surfing was taking the United States (and the world) by storm, *Surfer* magazine, probably the leading voice of the fledgling American industry, endeavored to rebut the "beach bum" image and improve the sport's fragile reputation. There was a "surfing crisis," the magazine worriedly pronounced, and it was being caused by those "few misplaced 'ho-daddies' and a lot of misinformed 'gremlins'"— that is, hooligans and school-aged troublemakers—who swear loudly, undress in public, trample lawns, make wisecracks, destroy property, and otherwise engage in antisocial behavior. "The surfer has become the UGLY SURFER," founding editor John Severson fumed, "and while a surfboard sticking out of your car once labeled you as something unique—a real sportsman—or possibly just 'one of those crazy guys that rides waves,' it now seems to carry the label of 'bum'!" This was disconcerting. Beaches were being closed to surfers, and surf films were being banned from school and civic center auditoriums. "The real surfers are disgusted and have reached the end of their patience," Severson told his readers. If the sport did not clean itself up, "it's *the end of surfing!*"[21]

The magazine's concern was undoubtedly overblown. But it did go to the heart of how the sport would define itself as it stumbled into the mainstream. To emphasize the gravity of the crisis he envisioned, Severson commissioned a guest editorial by what he called an "acknowledged authority in the field of juvenile delinquency." The Honorable Robert Gardner was a surfer, the father of a surfer, and a judge in the juvenile court system in Orange County, California. As a board-riding enthusiast, Gardner was outraged by "that strange breed which has attached itself to surfing and is giving this great sport a bad name." Whatever the merits of his concern—there have been "juvenile delinquency" scares throughout U.S. history—his understanding of, and prescription for, addressing the "crisis" was chillingly eugenicist. Those few delinquents responsible for tarnishing surfing's image are "nature's inadequates"—"physically, mentally, morally, and personality-wise"—and it was the responsibility of "legitimate surfers" to drive these long-haired "freaks" from the sport.[22] If they did not, beaches might close, new surf spots would not be made accessible, and the "general bad image of surfers in the eyes of the non-surfing public" would continue. Fortunately, a solution was at hand. The United States Surfing Association (USSA) was founded in 1961 precisely in order to encourage "the 'clean-up' campaign" and fight the "misguided legislation" it spawned. With the strong likelihood that surfing would be "outlawed in most cities if not the whole [s]tate [of California]" if "nature's inadequates" continued their nasty ways, support for the USSA was essential, *Surfer* said. Creation of the organization was thus a necessary step away from "a branding of 'ugly surfer' " and "the disapproving looks of the general public."[23]

While the USSA eventually morphed into an organizational arm of competitive American surfing, which seems fitting given the extent to which organized surfing appeared to legitimize the pastime, young wave riders attempted to demonstrate their social worth.[24] When Genevive Hunter of Costa Mesa suffered a flat tire along an isolated stretch of the Pacific Coast Highway, for example, "she was approached by two teen-aged boys clad in soggy beach attire," a local newspaper reported in 1963. Such a scenario may have conjured the opening sequence of a Hollywood slasher movie, but this was a story with a happy ending. The two teenagers were joined by two other young men, all of whom worked together to promptly fix Hunter's tire. When she offered to pay them, the quartet refused. "No thanks, ma'am," the stranded motorist was told. "Just remember, we're surfers."[25] This and other actions—surfers rescuing boaters, surfers saving swimmers, surfers organizing charity drives—were small efforts to counter the negative manner in which society sometimes held the sport. *Surfer* weighed in, too, not only railing against juvenile delinquency and highlighting positive deeds but also attempting to put a respectable face on those who rode waves. In 1965, for instance, the magazine ran a feature on three such individuals: a doctor, a lawyer, and the eldest son of the Juaneño rights activist Clarence Lobo.[26] These, the magazine suggested, were the true faces of surfing.

As the cleanup campaign got underway, the seeds of the modern surf industry began to sprout. Wetsuit makers emerged, board shapers proliferated, and surf-tourism operators started to appear. This was not, for the most part, the large corporate capitalism that one associates with the twenty-first-century surf industry. This was, rather, something much closer to the eighteenth-century version envisioned by Adam Smith: small markets of local owners and producers. There were exceptions, such as the shapers who drew on the aircraft and aerospace technologies that fueled the Southern California economy to mass-produce thousands of boards for the burgeoning American market.[27] But even these operations were not the billion-dollar corporations of today. They remained rooted in coastal communities, drawing on local outlets to sell their products. Surf shops thus arose as social anchors in beachside neighborhoods from San Diego to Sydney. These were places where customers could buy a board, a magazine, a wetsuit, or a bar of wax. As businesses owned by surfers, they were seen as organic outgrowths of an exploding surf culture that increasingly viewed itself in national or international terms. This was in part because of the rise of a locally situated yet globally panoramic surf press, one that aided these local enterprises while developing a variety of cultural vehicles over the decades (magazines, videos, websites) through which surfers could shape, and at times contest, their sport's fluid borders. As media that came to rely on advertising revenue, their content was defined by their symbiosis with the growing industry. They featured the surfers who were sponsored by surf-related businesses that advertised in surf publications. This media-industry nexus would become only tighter as the magazines—and the corporations whose advertising dollars made them possible—grew from a relative handful of periodicals in the 1960s to dozens or even hundreds by the twenty-first century.

If the 1960s were marked by the diffusion of spatially grounded surf entrepreneurs, the 1970s heralded something quite different: the fledgling industry's concentration, professionalization, and globalization. Quiksilver, which by 2010 was the world's largest organic surfwear conglomerate, offers a case in point. The company began, as did many in the industry, with its founders looking to subsidize their surfing habit. Alan Green, Carol McDonald, and Tim Davis were based in Torquay, a small city on the southern Victorian coast through which tourists pass on their way to Australia's famous Great Ocean Road. Just past the edge of town, these tourists see signs for Bells Beach. Most today keep going, but Bells—despite being considered by many an inferior break to neighboring Winkipop—put Torquay on the global surfing map. Green, McDonald, and Davis developed a yoke-waist boardshort with snaps and Velcro that, tapping into local surf shops as apparel retailers, quickly became a hit in Torquay and elsewhere in Victoria. That was in 1969. In 1976, Americans Jeff Hakman and Bob McKnight—the latter a recent graduate of the University of Southern California with a degree in business administration—licensed the brand from Green and his colleagues, and Quiksilver USA was born. America, surf entrepreneurs understood, was where the real money was to be made. The population was exponentially larger, it had embraced what Lizabeth Cohen called a "consumer's republic," and—as the popularity of *The Endless Summer* in Wichita suggests—the surfing bug had bitten even those Americans living hundreds of miles from the nearest coast.[28] Within several years, Quiksilver USA's annual sales had reached millions of dollars, and by the mid-1980s subsidiaries had formed in France, Japan, Brazil, and South Africa, among other places. Before long, Quiksilver branched out beyond surfing, developing lines for skiing, snowboarding, windsurfing, and skateboarding. The company entered the wetsuit market in 1990.[29]

Quiksilver was not alone in being a sizable surf corporation, but it was the largest and arguably the most influential. By 2010, it was a publicly traded multibillion-dollar conglomerate. McKnight, its CEO, was in 2002 named by *Surfer* the single most powerful figure in the sport.[30] Quiksilver understood, perhaps better than others, that surfing was "hip" and that hip, as Thomas Frank would have it, was "official capitalist style."[31] There was, in other words, money to be made—a lot of it—from selling the perceived hipness, or—given the idea's importance to youth culture—what Bill Hamilton might have called the "almost rebelliousness," of surfing. Quiksilver got that, and Bob McKnight exuded it. I'm a "non-garmento, non-Wall Street type," he told the guests assembled for the SIMA Surf Summit in Cabo San Lucas in 2000.[32] But McKnight was being disingenuous. The Quiksilver CEO may have preferred a tropical reefbreak to a New York social club, but he was paid like a Wall Street executive—the dramatic increase in his salary from the already substantial $2.9 million in 2010 to over $10.2 million in 2011 in fact spawned two shareholder investigations—and Quiksilver made its money the same way most other apparel corporations do: it employed First World professional talent and Third World manufacturers.[33]

The company had, by the time of McKnight's 2000 comments, already begun its ascent as a global marketing powerhouse, creating a brand that seamlessly fused the surf experience with surf consumerism. It wedded itself to Hawaiian tradition by founding, in 1984, the Quiksilver in Memory of Eddie Aikau big-wave contest on Oʻahu. It encouraged the surfing-as-insanity sentiment by, in 1999, inaugurating the cold-water Quiksilver Maverick's Men Who Ride Mountains contest near San Francisco. In 2011, it successfully tapped the New York media market by sponsoring the world's most lucrative contest—it had a $1 million purse—just miles from Manhattan, on the western tip of Long Island.[34] The company became synonymous with competitive success by signing the sport's most high-profile athletes, from Tom Carroll in 1986, which made the Australian goofyfooter the first million-dollar surfer, to the eleven-time world champion Kelly Slater, whose unprecedented record led the *New York Times* to ponder whether he might be the greatest athlete of all time.[35] It fostered the rise of female surfing through Roxy, the Quiksilver subsidiary that uses almost invariably thin, bikini-clad riders to market to women (and hormone-frenzied young men) worldwide. And it incessantly exploited the free-spending ways of the youth demographic with its endless global stream of contests, surf camps, and films.

The company sought, in other words, to naturalize the Quiksilver brand as an indispensable marker of the board-riding lifestyle. Quiksilver Entertainment was created in 2002 for precisely this reason. Headed by longtime surfer Danny Kwock and Matt Jacobson, a former executive with News Corporation and the talent firm Creative Artists Agency, the new Quiksilver division produced movies, television shows, and books that celebrated what it meant—at least according to Quiksilver—to be a surfer, skater, snowboarder, or other board-riding enthusiast. This included backing MTV's hit series *Surf Girls*, creating the daily action-sports show *54321* on Fox Sports Net, working with Boost Mobile and Motorola to create the Roxy phone, teaming with Harper Collins to produce the Luna Bay series of books for teenage girls, aiding in the launch of the video-on-demand board-riding channel Union, and, perhaps most notably, developing a number of popular films that presented surfing as not only hip but edgy.[36] Its most significant accomplishment in this regard was *Riding Giants* (2004), the earlier-quoted Stacy Peralta production that featured Greg Noll, Randy Rarick, and Bill Hamilton propounding on surfing's allegedly subversive history. *Riding Giants* opened the 2004 Sundance Film Festival and grossed over $2.2 million at the box office, a not inconsiderable sum for a documentary picture.[37] In most of the Quiksilver Entertainment films, noted the trade publication *Advertising Age* admiringly, there are "end credits and subtle logos, but this is not about product placement or even brand integration." Rather, it is about selling the board-riding lifestyle. "If girls in Kansas adopt the lifestyle of girls in California, we're bound to benefit," Jacobson told the magazine. So would other surfwear companies, of course, but "that's what benevolent market leadership is all about," he continued, "and we believe there's enough upside in the category for all of us."[38]

If Quiksilver had masterfully wed its brand to the board-riding tradition, that only partially explains its corporate success. "Benevolent market leader[]" or not, the raison d'être of the modern corporation is to turn a profit, and to do this Quiksilver embraced the same practices of corporate globalization that countless other clothing and equipment manufacturers had adopted. Most obviously, it turned from the First World to the Third in search of cheap labor for the assembly of its products. This has created something of a paradox in the surfing imagination, for it has meant the establishment of grossly unbalanced relationships with those same brown-skinned peoples that surfers have romanticized during their numerous global jaunts. It has meant, that is, exploiting the poverty and desperation of those who personify the exotic Other. One result has been occasional bad press. In light of Quiksilver's self-styled association with "freedom, fun, and individual expression"—an association posited, in this case, by its subsidiary Roxy— such unwanted scrutiny has threatened to undermine the corporation's painstakingly developed brand identity.[39] In 2003, for instance, the *New York Times* reported on the imposition of a company union—a notable lack of "freedom" and "individual expression"—in a factory producing gear for both Quiksilver and Billabong. "Local authorities sacrifice workers for investors," Liu Youlin, a twenty-nine-year-old organizer who had worked at the factory as a clothing cutter for seven years, told the newspaper. "They do not respect or enforce the laws."[40] And in 2007, China Labor Watch revealed that Quiksilver had contracted with apparel factories "incapable" of compliance with Chinese labor laws.[41] Such laws were notoriously weak, but even that minimal bar was not met. "Watch the costs and the profits will take care of themselves," the industrial titan Andrew Carnegie once counseled.[42] Quiksilver evidently got the message.

The company's manufacture of its goods also raised troubling environmental questions. "We're all guilty," CEO McKnight confessed in 2006. "Making apparel is not exactly the most environmentally friendly industry."[43] This was a concern. There is perhaps no graver sin among surfers than environmental insensitivity. One apparel manufacturer, the high-end clothier Patagonia, thus consistently sought to prove McKnight wrong. The Southern California-based firm, which became known for outdoor clothing but later expanded into surfboards, wetsuits, and boardshorts, oozed the sort of environmentalism that had long appealed to the surf community. Conservation of the wilds—"protect[ing] habitat, wilderness[,] and biodiversity"— was emphasized in its publicity materials.[44] Environmental injustice—the placing of toxic industries in communities of color, for instance—was not. Neither, for that matter, was its onetime interest in creating an artificial reef just minutes from the company's Ventura headquarters by dumping large plastic sandbags offshore.[45] Patagonia regularly touted its activism and its contributions to nonprofit organizations worldwide, and its ecofriendly sourcing and manufacturing practices justifiably earned it accolades. In 2002, it cofounded the business group One Percent for the Planet.[46]

In the 1990s, Patagonia had made a concerted push into the surfing market, introducing a line of surfboards in 1997. By 2010, the company had signed the brothers Chris, Keith, and Dan Malloy, a trio of well-exposed wave riders who until then had been sponsored by Hurley. "Patagonia is a company we have a great deal of respect for because of their support of the environment and other philanthropic efforts," Chris explained.[47] Patagonia did not hesitate to market the passion of its "ambassadors" for all things green. "Home base for Chris is a working ranch in California, where he lives close to the land with his wife and kids ... [in] a blend of tradition, conservation[,] and creativity," declared the company's online profile of the eldest Malloy.[48] Another surfing "ambassador," Dan Ross, "speaks out for environmental causes" while offering consumers this advice: "live simply, eat organic, give back[,] and have fun."[49] Cynics might have noted that there was a missing directive—"buy Patagonia"—but such explicit marketing would have been superfluous. By fusing the brand and a green ethos, Patagonia seemed to successfully bridge capitalism and environmentalism. By buying Patagonia, consumers could believe, one was being green.

Patagonia marketed itself not only as an ecofriendly outfit but as one whose brand transcended corporate culture. The company's relaxed workplace policies, including generous flextime arrangements and leaves for its corporate employees, garnered it national publicity as a human resources model.[50] Indeed, its founder titled his 2005 memoir-cum-business manifesto *Let My People Go Surfing*.[51] At the same time, the Third World workforce that actually made most of Patagonia's clothing did not fare nearly as well as its white-collar staff. Patagonia did manufacture some products in the United States, but most of its operations were located in Asia—especially China, Sri Lanka, Thailand, and Vietnam. In 2012, it began producing outerwear in Bangladesh, which had the world's lowest wages, a network of virtually union-free export processing zones, and an abysmal workplace safety record; indeed, in April 2013 Bangladesh became a focus of international media attention when a factory collapse resulted in 1,127 people losing their lives in the deadliest such incident in history.[52] Closer to its California headquarters, a Salvadoran factory that produced apparel for Patagonia through the last quarter of 2007 came under fierce criticism from the Institute for Global Labour and Human Rights (formerly the National Labor Committee) for paying wages so paltry that they precluded its largely female workers from climbing "out of misery and at least into poverty." The young women making the expensive clothes were, according to the institute, unable to "afford milk and other basic necessities for their children."[53]

Patagonia became a "participating company" in the Fair Labor Association (FLA) in 2001 and a fully accredited member in 2008. As impressive as this sounds, the FLA has repeatedly come under criticism from United Students Against Sweatshops, the Worker Rights Consortium, and other labor activists and organizations for its coziness with its corporate funders and board members and its often inadequate regulatory regime.[54] Still, if Patagonia had at least joined the FLA, Quiksilver could not be bothered to take even that perfunctory step. While the story of sweatshops in the global economy may by now be an old story, surfing's role in what critics have dubbed the "race to the bottom" has received remarkably little attention. This oversight—one of surfing's dirty little secrets—is particularly glaring in light of surf culture's romanticization of Third World peoples and its reflexive equation of surfing with "freedom." But decent wages are one thing and green or hip branding another.

By the second decade of the twenty-first century, Quiksilver and Patagonia occupied competing ends of the industry spectrum. One was a publicly traded board-sports behemoth with no real record of social responsibility of which to speak; the other was a privately owned firm that appeared to take seriously the notion of responsible corporate citizenship—even if, as the company readily admitted, it often fell short of that ideal.[55] But the more progressive-minded Patagonia remained a bit player in the surf industry. It was dwarfed by its organic competitors, and these organics were themselves dwarfed—though perhaps not yet in the surf community—by Nike, Target, and other "non-endemics." Whatever surfing may have once represented—pleasure and cultural survival in early twentieth-century Hawai'i, spiritual attainment in the sixties-era West, "tasty waves [and] a cool buzz" in the Spicoli-inflected 1980s—there was no disputing that, by 2010, the sport was a marketing powerhouse, cultural heavyweight, and money-generating machine. "It is possible," wrote the *New York Times*, "that no sport practiced by fewer people has ever had the influence of surfing on American style."[56]

What had once been a tension between purity and commercialism increasingly seemed but a quaint memory, having been subsumed by a fierce contest over which corporations would be most successful in defining, and then commodifying, the surfing experience. The race was on.

Despite its exploitation of the low-wage global trade regime and its consistent marketing prowess, Quiksilver—together with Billabong, Rip Curl, O'Neill, and others—faced, by the dawn of the twenty-first century, a considerable threat. "Tommy Hilfiger, Nike, Guess, Old Navy, and [the] Gap" were "the enemy," Bob McKnight warned his industry colleagues in 2000, "sucking off us [surfers], trying to take away our customers, creeping in and copying our vibe with checkbook marketing."[57] This was a carefully cultivated "vibe," as McKnight very well knew, and it was imperiled by the deep pockets—the "checkbook marketing"—of corporations such as Nike. McKnight may have seen the organic surf industry in something of a David-and-Goliath battle, but that seems an ill-fitting analogy when talking about a corporation the size of Quiksilver. It was really more like Goliath versus God. Yet McKnight was right about the threat. As early as 2002, Nike had announced its intention to enter the surf market through its $120 million purchase of Hurley International. In doing so, it powerfully sought to tap into that surfing "vibe."

Rob Machado, a perennial contender on the ASP World Tour—he had finished fifth in 1994, second in 1995, fourth in 1997, and third in 2000—became Exhibit A for Nike's campaign. The stylish Californian was a staple of Hurley's marketing efforts, and in 2009 he starred in *The Drifter*, a promotional vehicle for Hurley (and Sire/Warner Bros. Records, which produced the soundtrack) that masqueraded as a documentary about Machado's Indonesian journey of self-discovery. Less subtly than most other works in the genre, the film identified and marketed surfing, through Hurley-sponsored Machado, with countercultural rebellion. Machado had quit the World Tour in 2001 and, with his long, wavy hair and wild goatee, assumed the life of a corporate-sponsored "soul surfer."[58] (In addition to Hurley, Machado rode for Reef and Nixon and had his own line of Channel Islands Surfboards; indeed, he proved such a recognizable figure in the surfing world that he was one of only two surfers—the other was Kelly Slater—to appear as "himself"

FIGURE 18. With his trademark locks, full goatee, and distant gaze, Rob Machado sought to display both soul and rebelliousness in *The Drifter*, his 2009 film for Hurley and Sire/Warner Bros. Records. Credit: © Rob Machado.

in the Oscar-nominated animated picture *Surf's Up* [2007].) A "living icon" with a "down-to-earth, approachable aura," Machado is "[k]nown for his Zen-like flow both on land and in the water," according to his official website.[59] *The Drifter* exudes this soulfulness.

The film unfolds over the course of several months in the Indonesian archipelago, where Machado grows displeased with the hypercommercialization and crowds of Bali before setting out "alone"—he in fact traveled with a film crew and at least occasionally a helicopter, which filmed him surfing from above—to various outer islands. The audience is presented with a portrait of surf rebellion, and viewers quickly become familiar with its aesthetic. Soul surfers read books by the Dalai Lama, ride motorcycles, assume Eastern poses, keep journals, lay backwards in bed, ditch their cell phones, play the acoustic guitar, pose in fields with children, and connect—though generally on only the most superficial level, as most surfers do not speak the relevant languages—with the brown-skinned locals of the Third World destinations they visit. By the end of the film, Machado has discovered a deep lesson: "I thought that being completely isolated would bring me peace of mind. But now I realize that it's the people around us who bring our experiences to life." Like other countercultural types who have looked to Asia for enlightenment, this was something he learned from the Indonesians. "They live the simplest of lives out here," Machado says of those he encountered, "but they make so much of them."[60]

The Drifter's romanticization of poverty seems a striking choice in a film presented by Nike-owned Hurley. At no point does it hint at Nike's notorious use of Indonesia as a low-wage assembly platform or the company's vigorous contribution to the "race to the bottom"—the global competition encouraged by multinational corporations to drive down wages, weaken working conditions, and dilute environmental protections. Informed cynics watching *The Drifter* might have noted that the mostly female Indonesian industrial workforce led "the simplest of lives" because their dead-end jobs left them with little choice. But such critiques of the global trade regime did not make it into Machado's story. Instead, as is true of countless films and magazine articles, the dark-hued locals served as a colorful and romantic backdrop that helped illustrate Machado's soulful embodiment of a manufactured surfing vibe.

Yet Nike's efforts extended well beyond Rob Machado. The company launched Nike 6.0 as an "action sports" sub-brand in 2005, and it sought to disrupt the surf-industry status quo. It became involved, for instance, in a fierce campaign to sign South African phenomenon Jordy Smith. Smith, who was then nineteen years old, was considered the most talented up-and-comer since Kelly Slater when, in 2007, he claimed that his contract with his longtime sponsor, Billabong, had expired. Billabong, for which the young South African had ridden for ten years, disagreed and pursued legal action; it ultimately released him in exchange for an undisclosed sum.[61] When Smith arrived in Huntington Beach for the U.S. Open of Surfing in July 2007, he was, the *Orange County Register* wrote, "the most prized free agent in recent surfing history."[62] Nike entered into a bidding war that for the first time had the company competing by name—rather than as Hurley—against the major surfwear brands. And Nike threw everything it could into signing him. Smith was offered approximately $5 million per year. He was wooed by Nike athletes Michael Jordan and Tiger Woods. He was given a set of Wood's golf clubs and a shoe that Brazilian footballer Ronaldo used to score a goal in a World Cup final. He was shuttled to Nike's headquarters on a private jet to meet Nike cofounder Phil Knight. He was promised, in a play on Nike's earlier "Air Jordan" campaign, a worldwide "Air Jordy" marketing effort that would showcase the South African's aerial talents.[63] But it was not enough. In the end, Smith turned the "non-endemic" Nike down. He signed with O'Neill—the wetsuit and apparel company founded in Santa Cruz, and one of the largest and most well-established players in the industry. In doing so, the South African still received a seven-figure salary, though reportedly about three million dollars less than what Nike was willing to pay him per year. But O'Neill was, importantly for Smith, an organic surfing brand.[64]

Yet not all was lost for Nike. It signed twenty-two-year-old Australian professional Julian Wilson to a five-year deal that made him, according to one report, "surfing's youngest million-dollar-a-year man."[65] And Wilson proved a good bet: in 2011 he was named rookie of the year on the ASP Men's World Tour. Indeed, by late 2011, Nike was sponsoring three of the tour's ten highest-ranked male surfers; ominously for the organic companies, all three had previously been under contract with Quiksilver.[66] Nike also made a considerable investment in women's surfing, nabbing former world junior champion Laura Enever, 2011 world title holder Carissa Moore, Hawaiian standout Coco Ho, and young Californian Lakey Peterson, among others. It wasted no time in promoting the women through *Leave a Message*, a Nike-made film that featured its most talented female surfers riding waves, dancing, and, well, just looking attractive in bikinis. That last element of the film was not unintended. The Nike team, the company claimed, offered an enviable "collection of talent and beauty."[67] These women could surf, and they looked good while doing so.

In a move that surprised some observers, in late 2012 Nike announced a major change of course: it would fold nearly its entire surf-related operation into its more established Hurley brand. The 6.0 experiment was coming to an end.[68] Nike did not reveal its reasons for doing so, but it was understood by many that Hurley, even while owned by the giant apparel corporation, enjoyed something that Nike did not: authenticity. Hurley had roots in the surf community; its founder was board shaper and longtime Billabong USA executive Bob Hurley. Nike, conversely, was an interloper. A number of surfers were only too happy to see the swoosh go. "Good riddance," wrote "Jimmy the Saint" in an online comment board for *Surfer* magazine. "I would never buy a wetsuit or anything surf related with the Nike logo on it. Guess its [*sic*] silly, but I still don't mind Hurley." "Screw nike and there [*sic*] little swoosh!" added someone called Rob. "I would never purchase a nike surf product. . . . [S]tick with what ya know."[69]

During the several years that Nike attempted to overtake its surfwear competitors, and even as it apparently failed to connect with the surfing grassroots, the company recognized something that had long been appreciated by the organic establishment: yes, professional surfers were athletes, but more than anything they were promotional vehicles through which the industry might tap the massive nonsurfer market. "How many people actually surf?" asked California wetsuit maker Ryan Buell. "Not many. How many people pretend to surf? A lot."[70] Nike's sport marketing—whether for basketball, golf, or track and field—was deeply rooted in notions of authenticity, and this authenticity came from its sponsored athletes and their appeal to the larger sporting communities from which they hailed. It was not a wholly one-sided arrangement. Nike's athletes were generally well compensated, and, just as significantly, the sponsorships lent the athletes legitimacy. Sponsorships in fact became totems of success, a symbolic currency on which surfers traded—and one that undoubtedly opened doors. They provided the equipment that surfers needed, from boards and wetsuits to wax and sandals. They covered entry fees in contests, allowing young riders to climb through the competitive ranks. And they enabled travel to exotic places, travel that would be documented by photographers whose work would then expose the surfers to the larger consuming public. There was, in other words, something of a mutually self-serving authenticity/legitimacy loop in the sponsor/surfer relationship.

Surfers, whether sponsored or not, served an important function as what the industry called "image leaders." For instance, the Australian company Billabong, which with Quiksilver and Rip Curl has for years been considered one of surfing's "Big Three," estimated that "board sport fanatics" and "board sport participants" accounted for only 19 percent of its customer base. But, wrote JP Morgan analyst Shaun Cousins, that 19 percent "drive[s] the sales of the remaining 81 percent of customers and hence any loss of interest from the image leaders would have a detrimental impact on sales."[71]

Maintaining authenticity—an organic connection to surfers themselves—was thus important. Or at least that was the impression under which the industry functioned. It is the reason that Nike so aggressively sought to sign Jordy Smith, Carissa Moore, and other top-ranked competitors. And it is the reason that the Big Three, O'Neill, and other industry members tried so hard to keep them. Where Nike failed was in believing that sponsorships alone would endow the company with authenticity; the larger surfing community never fully embraced the footwear behemoth. And where its organic competitors erred was in believing that authenticity needed to be rooted in reality. As the strange saga of an American retail chain reveals, it most certainly did not.

. . .

No surfer would be caught dead wearing a T-shirt from Hollister, but millions of landlocked Americans have proudly done so. Hollister is, for the uninitiated, the "surf company" subsidiary of American retailer Abercrombie & Fitch, the massive clothing chain that in 2010 was unceremoniously elected to the International Labor Rights Forum's "Sweatshop Hall of Shame."[72] Mike Jeffries, Abercrombie's eccentric and controversial CEO, established Hollister as a surfwear complement to his decidedly land-bound flagship brand.[73] By 2012, Hollister was an apparel juggernaut, capturing an enormous share of the surfwear market by selling what its website dubbed "So Cal inspired clothing for Dudes and Bettys."[74] At the core of its identity, and the foundation for its authenticity, was its storied brand history. Hollister, according to a document provided to new employees, was founded in 1922 by one John M. Hollister.[75] That year proved important, as it was the basis for the "22" that became an integral marker of the Hollister brand—a marker for which the company even sought trademark protection from its retail competitor American Eagle in 2003.[76]

The Hollister brand history is brief but vivid. According to the company, John Hollister was a 1915 graduate of Yale University "with an unquenchable thirst for adventure, travel, and beauty." Rejecting the New York establishment for which he had been groomed, Hollister journeyed to the Dutch East Indies—what later became Indonesia—in 1917, where he bought a rubber plantation and fell in love with Meta Van Gilder, the "beautiful daughter" of the plantation's previous owner. Hollister sold the land not long afterward and used a share of the proceeds to purchase a fifty-foot schooner.

He and Meta then "spent the next two years sailing the South Pacific." Hollister, the official history continues, "treasured the entire South Pacific and the works of the artisans that lived there." In 1919, the young couple arrived in Los Angeles, where they married, settled, and had a son, John M. Hollister Jr. Still stricken by the travel bug but with a family to now consider, the elder Hollister spent two years close by, "discovering California and himself" before turning his "lust for the sea" into a commercial venture. In 1922, he founded Hollister Co. in Laguna Beach as a "small trading company that sold imported goods from the South Pacific." John Jr., "an avid and now legendary surfer," took over the business for his father in 1953 and expanded it to include "surf apparel and equipment." It is thus little wonder, as this evocative past reveals, that "Hollister Co. is a story of passion, youth[,] and love of the sea," one that "carries the harmony of romance, beauty, [and] adventure" into a "lifestyle brand for those with an insatiable lust for adventure—both on land and off."

The brand history is indeed stirring, drawing on the pleasures of exploration and discovery in pursuit of self-realization. There are even hints of the fabled early years of California surf culture. Hollister, it seems, was nearly present at the creation. But—and this is surprisingly underappreciated—not a single word of it is true. John M. Hollister was a figment of CEO Jeffries's imagination, a contrivance intended to lend the company a faux authenticity. The original Hollister store did not open in Laguna Beach in 1922; it was unveiled at the Easton Town Center in Columbus, Ohio, in 2000. Within a decade, the company had expanded to roughly five hundred stores built to resemble beachside shacks, most of them in chain-laden shopping malls far from the nearest coast. These were, in essence, simulacra. They contained strictly decorative surfboards and were scented with Hollister's "signature So Cal fragrance." They had lounges furnished with chairs, surfing magazines, and potted palm trees. They occasionally featured shirtless "lifeguards" flown in by the company for their grand openings. And in 2007, they sprouted flat-screen televisions that featured live feeds of the pier-side surf in Huntington Beach.[77] "As far as a mall store goes, and who their customer is, which is the aspirational consumer, they couldn't do a better job building stores that appeal to that consumer," Mitch Kummetz, a senior retail analyst at Robert Baird, told journalist Josh Hunter. "[A] lot of it is contrived and pretentious to someone who is of the industry and participates in the sports, but to somebody who is in the mainstream and is aspirational, their stores are going to look more like the real deal than a PacSun or a Zumiez, or a core shop for that matter. […] [I]f you're just some mainstream kid living in Ohio, or wherever, this seems as authentic as anything."[78]

For Hollister, the market for "So Cal inspired clothing" was not national but global; the company moved beyond the United States and Canada to Europe, Asia, and Australia. With its projection of a "timeless and effortlessly cool" lifestyle, Hollister "brings Southern California to the world," the mall hosting its Sydney store proudly exclaimed.[79] Hollister's reception in Britain—at least at the level of the press—was less fawning. The rapid expansion of the chain in the United Kingdom spurred a BBC investigation of the company's brand history and the "1922" found on its labels. Both were "fictitious," the BBC discovered, as was the alleged date of founding (1932) of another Abercrombie subsidiary, Gilly Hicks. The company opted not to respond. "Due to our policies regarding press, we choose not to provide any comment on your questions," a Hollister representative told the BBC. "[S]ome people might consider Hollister to be treading a fine line," the academic director of the Oxford Institute of Retail Management suggested, but "[i]t's a moot point." To the brand's core demographic, the deceit did not matter. Teenage shoppers interviewed by the BBC were "oblivious to the historical license taken by the stores" but "unconcerned when they were told about it."[80] The case of Hollister, in other words, strikingly revealed the extent to which a widely embraced *appearance* of authenticity could in fact outweigh authenticity itself.

Brand attachment—and sales figures—bore this out. In October 2007, the investment firm Piper Jaffray announced the results of its fourteenth biannual proprietary research survey. For the sixth consecutive time, Hollister was American teens' favorite clothing brand.[81] What Piper Jaffray called "West Coast Brands" or "Action Sports Brands"—groupings that included Quiksilver, Volcom, and Zumiez—would collectively claim the top spot in 2008, but Hollister, as a stand-alone brand, remained a close second.[82] Indeed, Hollister's 2010 sales of $1.55 billion surpassed those of the Australian company Billabong.[83] And Hollister captured this share of the market without sponsoring a single surfer or contest. Nike, in its effort to break into the market in the early twenty-first century, at least poured millions of dollars into the sport. But not so, Hollister. Its association with surf culture was a matter of artful fabrication.

The Hollister phenomenon—and it is, indeed, a phenomenon—offers a fascinating challenge to the meaning of authenticity in corporate capitalist society. Quiksilver and its organic competitors sought to essentially colonize surf culture in the late twentieth century by demarcating the board-riding experience. Outside of Hollywood, professional surfing, which was wholly dependent on the sponsorships of these corporate brands, became the dominant public representation of the sport. By the early 2000s, however, the industry faced unprecedented challenges. Some of these were to be expected. As the profitability of surf culture was made manifest with the growth of a multibillion-dollar industry exuding rebelliousness, edginess, and cool—the likely attraction to that army of corporate executives who, as a host of media outlets from *Forbes* to the *Wall Street Journal* reported, had essentially made surfing the new golf[84]—deep-pocketed "non-endemics" such as Nike and Target wooed professional surfers with lucrative contracts in an effort to purchase cultural authenticity. Nike's retreat suggests they may not have succeeded. But Hollister did something different. It did not attempt to purchase its authenticity through the subsidization of athletes or contests; the company simply manufactured it, creating an entirely fictional past that rendered Hollister an outgrowth of early twentieth-century California surf culture. This was, of course, a corporate artifice. But it worked. If success under capitalism is ultimately measured by profitability, Hollister's billions evince the rise of a master. Cultural capital, the company understood, need not be earned; it can be single-handedly contrived. Surfing, in other words, was just another brand. Welcome to industrial surf culture.

EPILOGUE

A New Millennium

IF, AS HENRY LUCE WOULD HAVE IT, the twentieth century belonged to the United States, it did not seem unreasonable to wonder whether the twenty-first might be Chinese.[1] The Cold War enemy that had so distressed American policymakers had, under Communist Party leadership, emerged by 2010 as a capitalist juggernaut with a hand in seemingly every facet of the global consumer culture. Just as the vast Chinese market had captivated the economic powerhouses of centuries past that favored an "open door" for international trade, so did the low wages and the expansion of the Chinese middle class more recently usher in a stampede of foreign profit seekers determined to strike a fortune. Surfing was hardly immune from this draw. "To a surf industry that seems to be absolutely wallowing in stagnancy at the moment, tapping into China's mushrooming middle class ocean of income would be a massive boon to boardshort sellers, flip-flop makers, and mass-produced surfboard factories," the sport's flagship American magazine noted in 2013.[2] The industry appeared to be doing precisely that. In addition to birthing a board-riding culture—first skating, then, it was hoped, surfing—surfwear manufacturers exploited cheap Chinese labor, foreign surfers started Chinese tourism operations, and Chinese exoticism—at least as perceived by those in the West—colored corporate marketing campaigns.[3]

Red Bull, for instance, sponsored an expedition and contest on the Qiantang River that featured a number of visiting surfers tackling the long, legendary waves of the Silver Dragon, a large tidal bore that advances up the river through the populous city of Hangzhou. Footage of the contest, including strategically located brand placements, appeared not only across China but on CNN, the BBC, *Surfline*, and all over YouTube.[4] Nike-owned

Hurley likewise exploited the West's fascination with the East, sending its sponsored rider Curren Caples to Hangzhou to showcase his skating and surfing acumen, slickly produced videos of which were then placed online.[5] And Quiksilver, like other industry titans who hoped that Chinese youth would adopt board riding as their own, arranged for a sponsored skater of its DC Shoes subsidiary, Danny Way, to jump over the Great Wall and into marketing gold. Videos of the feat, which included a faux introductory news segment by the "Chinese Minister of Extreme Sports," garnered millions of Internet views. It was thus not long before the ASP, with the financial backing of Quiksilver and other corporations, began running surfing contests on the island of Hainan—more, it appears, as a way of getting its organizational feet in the Chinese door than in recognition of world-class Chinese waves.[6]

The industry and the ASP were not in fact breaking new territorial ground. Surfing had been attempted in the then British colony of Hong Kong in the early 1960s, and Australian surfer Peter Drouyn briefly relocated to Hainan in 1985 in a Beijing-sponsored effort to introduce surf culture to Chinese shores.[7] Perhaps most famously, a small group of American surfers—Jon Damm, Matt George, Willy Morris, and Rell Sunn—had, together with photographer Warren Bolster, traveled to China in October 1986 on what they envisioned as a grassroots effort to foster cross-cultural understanding and bridge a Cold War divide between the capitalist West and the communist East. Their updated version of "ping-pong diplomacy"—the 1971 visit to China by the U.S. table tennis team that helped to thaw Cold War tensions and set the stage for Richard Nixon's historic trip to Beijing a short while later—may have succeeded in generating political goodwill, but it did not immediately spawn the potential Chinese surf culture with which Drouyn had flirted.[8] That would perhaps come later.[9] Nevertheless, it became clear from these early American and Australian encounters that waves most certainly did exist.

By the early twenty-first century, Hainan, with its uncrowded breaks and relatively affordable flights, had emerged as a popular destination for Japanese surfers. Much of this popularity was attributable to Hiroshi Yonekawa, who moved to the island shortly after the new millennium and founded the Mon Ran Surf Club as a combination surf tourism operator, surf school, and board and equipment manufacturer.[10] By the time the ASP entered China in 2011 with the Swatch Girls Pro, followed just months later by the Hainan Classic—a 4-Star Men's World Tour event—Chinese authorities had begun to appreciate the potential economic spillover that surfing might deliver. In

2008, Surfing China was founded as the government-sanctioned body to promote the sport "and the related lifestyle industry." One of the organization's first actions was to join Chinese officials, Wabsono International, and Gerard Sports Marketing (GSM) in opening up Hangzhou's Silver Dragon tidal bore to professional surfing. This was followed by live coverage of wave-riding demonstrations on CCTV, visits by government delegations to the United States and Brazil, summits and festivals featuring Quiksilver and Billabong, and the establishment of a Silver Dragon Skateboarding Series in Beijing, Shenzhen, Chengdu, Hangzhou, and Shanghai.[11] On Hainan, where the government hoped to hatch a "Chinese Waikiki," the World Surf Cities Network flirted with the idea of adopting the island, while Chinese authorities facilitated the development of the local infrastructure—roads, airports, and resorts—and made it possible for foreign visitors to receive on-arrival, fifteen-day tourist visas.[12] This frenzy of activity, in combination with China's substantial economic growth amid a global economic crisis, prompted *Surfer* to unexpectedly wonder in 2012 whether China might just represent surfing's next frontier.[13]

Yet while the surfwear industry and ASP officials both viewed China as a great prize with the potential for untold profits, not all surfers shared their enthusiasm. In 2011, Cori Schumacher, a three-time women's world longboard champion, announced that she would boycott that year's ASP world tour. "I have deep political and personal reservations with being a part of any sort of benefit to a country that actively engages in human rights violations, specifically those in violation of women," she told the organizers.[14] The ASP response was prosaic. "[We] would like to see Cori compete . . . as the defending ASP Women's World Longboard Champion, but we respect her personal decision in choosing to withdraw from the contest," the organization said in a statement to *Surfer*, more tellingly adding that "[t]he action sports scene is growing in China and a women's World Longboard Tour event is a great opportunity [to] integrate surfing into the world of Chinese action sports."[15] How was it that a sport that reputedly embraced rebellion could so eagerly jump into bed with a regime responsible for widespread political repression? Such a relationship seems less surprising when one considers the extent to which surfing had, by the late twentieth century, openly embraced its industrialization. With its diverse cast of characters—the ASP, the surfwear industry, tourism providers, and local and national Chinese officials—the case of China starkly illustrates the nexus between organized surfing, soft power, global neoliberalism, and modern state policy. Cori

FIGURE 19. Cori Schumacher announced in 2011 that she would boycott the ASP World Tour because of its decision to hold a contest in China. Schumacher would have been defending her third world title, which she was celebrating here at the 2010 Roxy ASP Women's World Longboard Championships in Biarritz, France. Credit: Photograph courtesy of Maria Cerda. © Maria Cerda.

Schumacher understood as much.[16] When she announced her decision to forgo the professional circuit, she did so in relative isolation. While activists worldwide had grave concerns about Chinese human rights abuses, there was not—unlike the case of South Africa in the 1980s—a major athletic boycott of China. But for Schumacher, that did not matter. Principle, she felt, should trump professional ambition.

Schumacher's decision drew the notice of the *New York Times*, and it started a conversation within the global surf community about not only China and human rights but the role of women in surfing. While women had been respected surfers in pre-twentieth-century Hawai'i, the globalization of surf culture had produced a largely male-dominated sport. There *were* female surfers, including professional competitors, but, for much of the twentieth century, women were more often viewed by men as babes on the beach than as equals in the water. The fact that, by the early twenty-first century, there even *was* a women's world longboard champion was a testament to the sport's evolution.[17] Yet women's professional surfing still played second fiddle to that of men. Women were on average paid far less than their male counterparts, and they received nowhere near the respect that men did. There was also an unspoken assumption that they must look beautiful in a bikini—or at least that thin figures and tiny swimsuits could increase their paychecks. When Quiksilver's female subsidiary, Roxy, released a trailer for the 2013 Roxy Pro in Biarritz, France, for instance, there was not a single image of someone riding a wave. Instead, the video featured a thin, topless, faceless young woman in bed, in the shower, and in a bikini in what could not have seemed any more blatant of an attempt to titillate male viewers. "[S]oft-core porn posing as surf content" has become "a staple of our era," wrote *Surfer* managing editor Janna Irons, but this one, which was ostensibly promoting a women's World Tour event that might decide the 2013 world champion, left her "bewildered."[18] Schumacher had spoken out against the sexism rampant in her sport. She had also, as a lesbian, worked to combat what she called a "massively homophobic" surf culture. She wrote occasionally for *The Inertia* and the *Guardian* of London on these and other issues, and she demonstrated the depth of her seriousness by participating in various protest movements. She had, moreover, refused the corporate sponsorships that are the lifeblood of her profession.[19]

Schumacher, in other words, embodied many of the tensions inherent in twenty-first-century surf culture. She loved to surf—she devoted much of her life to it—but she also recognized that surfing merited a more critical appraisal than it had traditionally received. The smug hosannas were too much. This not only meant criticizing the gender inequities and industrialization of her cherished pastime; it also meant using her elevated profile to attack what she saw as broader social and political injustices. In this, Schumacher was not alone. Leading surfers had spoken out against apartheid in South Africa in the 1980s, and they had organized Surfers Against Nuclear Destruction (SAND) at roughly the same time. By the early twenty-first century, surfers were engaged in a wide range of activist causes, most of them centered on environmental concerns. Although the bulk of this work unfolded outside the mass media spotlight, not all of it did—indeed, among those politically engaged surfers was probably the highest-profile waterman of them all.

Kelly Slater is no marginal figure. With more than ten world championships to his name, he is considered by many to be the greatest surfer in history. He is also a noted ambassador for the sport. His good looks landed him

FIGURE 20. At the 2007 Rip Curl Pro Search in Arica, Chile, then eight-time world champion Kelly Slater exploited his appearance in a country that suffered a U.S.-backed coup in 1973 to criticize contemporary U.S. foreign policy, using the artwork on his board to express his opposition to the American war in Iraq. Credit: Photograph courtesy of the Association of Surfing Professionals. © ASP/Covered Images.

a recurring role on the television serial *Baywatch*, while his eloquence and professionalism have led to appearances on everything from National Public Radio and *Chelsea Lately* to the computer-animated film *Surf's Up* (2007) and MTV's *Total Request Live*.[20] As an American surfer with a foot in American celebrity culture, it may have thus seemed surprising to some that, in June 2007, the then eight-time world champion went public with his deeply held criticism of American foreign policy. He did so in a onetime outpost of the American empire. Chile, which occupies much of South America's western seaboard, contains some of the most consistent left-hand pointbreaks in the world, but the country is perhaps best recognized by international historians today for the U.S.-backed coup that overthrew the elected socialist government of Salvador Allende, ushering in the seventeen-year military dictatorship of Augusto Pinochet. That coup got under way along the Chilean coast on September 11, 1973. More than three decades later, Slater used his appearance at the Rip Curl Pro Search along the same Chilean coast to criticize the American "war on terror" so closely associated with another September 11.

Entering and exiting the water in the city of Arica while mobbed by the local and global press, the artwork on Slater's board was, to those versed in Iraq War iconography, unmistakable. It transformed images of the conflict, from a militant holding an RPG to a widely circulated photograph of the torture by American forces at Abu Ghraib, into an iPod-style advertisement for a product called the "iRaq." There is, to be sure, something joltingly incongruent about the images' appearance under the logos of Slater's corporate sponsors, but the politics of the world champion's action were nevertheless patent. "Why is Paris Hilton going to a halfway house for three weeks bigger news than 500 Iraqis . . . being killed in their own country everyday as well as lots of American troops?" he asked in a piece for *Surfline*. "This is not to mention the injured, which is about ten times higher than the fatalities. It's life-changing for so many people. A crime of humanity." Slater noted that the artwork, by his friend and traveling partner Bruce Gilbert, "was originally made with numbers of troops and Iraqis killed to date but it's far outdated and the numbers are way up there now—around 3,500 U.S. troops and between 700,000 and a million Iraqis killed since the beginning of the war!" This was not the sort of commentary that typically accompanied a sporting event, nor was it what one might have expected from a surfer who used to date Pamela Anderson and Gisele Bündchen. But for Slater, who reputedly had four such "iRaq" boards made, it was a moment of "[p]op culture meets political awareness."[21] And Chile seemed like the perfect place to do it. After all, Slater explained, it was the government of that "democratic country that thirty-five or so years ago the United States covertly helped to overthrow."[22]

It is in fact not that surprising that Kelly Slater would level such criticism. Athletes are not often touted for their intellectual prowess, but Slater possesses a thoughtfulness and intelligence that belies the stereotypes typically associated with his sport. Phil Jarratt described him—not unreasonably, I think—as a "deep and diverse thinker."[23] Slater has criticized not only the recent U.S. war in Iraq but also the years of sanctions and bombing that preceded it.[24] He is self-critical of his environmental footprint.[25] He has spoken in favor of divorcing competitive surfing from its corporate underwriters.[26] He quotes Noam Chomsky.[27] And, in 2007, he cofounded Surfing 4 Peace, which works to "bridge cultural and political barriers between surfers in the Middle East."[28]

Surfing 4 Peace was established following the appearance of a July 2007 article in the *Los Angeles Times* on the difficulties endured by the small and largely unknown community of Palestinian surfers. "If surfing is a quest for freedom," the writer for the *Times* noted, "nowhere is such a pursuit more relevant than in Gaza, an overcrowded, poverty-stricken strip of land on the Mediterranean controlled by Hamas and cut off from the rest of the world by Israel." It is not difficult to appreciate surfing's appeal to a Palestinian people living under occupation and siege. "We go to the beach to forget about the suffering," twenty-year-old surfer Mohammed Juda told the newspaper. The waves offer a temporary escape. "Gaza is like a prison," added cafe owner Bashire Watfa. "There's nowhere to breathe except the beach."[29] One of those who read the article was Dorian "Doc" Paskowitz, a Jewish physician and legendary Texas-born surfer—his popular renown was only enhanced when he and his family were the subject of the critically acclaimed 2008 film *Surfwise*—who introduced the sport to Israel in the 1950s. Paskowitz brought a board with him to Tel Aviv those many years ago, hoping, he later said, "to get Arabs and Jews surfing together."[30] It did not happen. But in 2007, when he read the piece in the *Times*, Paskowitz reached out to Slater, Israeli action-sports executive Arthur Rashkovan, and his son David in an effort to do something.

What resulted was Surfing 4 Peace. Its premise was simple. "People who surf together can live together," Paskowitz believed.[31] The organization immediately set out to facilitate the delivery of fourteen surfboards to the Palestinian surfers in Gaza; they were delivered, with crucial assistance from the peace group OneVoice, on August 21, 2007. Weeks later, in early October, Slater arrived in Israel to participate in several Surfing 4 Peace events. He provided lessons to Israeli Arab and Jewish children in Herzliya. He then traveled to Tel Aviv to participate in a hundreds-strong paddle-out and surfers' circle at Dolphinarium Beach. And he performed in a Surfing 4 Peace benefit concert—Slater is a musician as well as an athlete—attended by more than three thousand people, where he was joined by several members of the Paskowitz family, Hawaiian surfer Makua Rothman, and the Israeli band Malka Baya.[32] America's leading surf magazine commended Slater for exploiting his celebrity in the cause of peace. "In an era in which larger than life sports champions walk the marketing tight rope and rarely take a social stand," *Surfer* noted, "Slater's actions are refreshing and have the stamp of true world champion—in the greatest sense of the phrase."[33]

Slater was not a radical critic. To the almost certain disappointment of some, he did not publicly denounce the Israeli occupation or the siege of Gaza. Neither did he condemn the billions of dollars in U.S. aid or the U.S.

diplomatic support that enabled the Israeli policies. But his participation in Surfing 4 Peace was nevertheless significant. It was significant, of course, because of the obvious publicity his involvement brought to the endeavor. That is to be expected when the world's highest-profile surfer wades into one of the world's most intractable conflicts. Yet it was also significant because of its symbolic value. Unbeknownst to most of his fans, Slater—like consumer advocate Ralph Nader, radio personality Casey Kasem, Apple cofounder Steve Jobs, and others who often go unrecognized as such—is an Arab American. (Slater's father, Steve, was of Syrian descent.) Surfing 4 Peace thus exemplified the vision of ethnic and religious coexistence that the organization identified as its objective—an objective that was shared both by Gaza Surf Relief, a group founded by Poland-born American Seweryn "Sev" Sztalkoper that worked tirelessly to deliver boards and other equipment to Gaza-based Palestinians at roughly the same time, and by Explore Corps, the U.S.-based nonprofit organization that helped launch the Gaza Surf Club and, with Surfing 4 Peace, the Gaza Surfer Girl Project.[34]

None of these efforts will, in and of themselves, fundamentally remake the politics of the Middle East. But that is not the point. Taken together, they demonstrate the emergence of what Irish scholar Stephen Boyd calls a "postnationalist wave" in surfing, one in which surfers have attempted to form a global fraternity that transcends extant national, political, or religious divides.[35] However inconsequential such actions may seem, they represent a grassroots effort to bring people together across a political chasm—to employ, that is, modern surf culture in pursuit of an explicitly political end. This is not to suggest that skepticism should be abandoned. Such efforts are open to the same sorts of critiques that have been leveled at, for example, Daniel Barenboim and Edward Said's West-Eastern Divan Orchestra. Critics might ask whether surfing, like Western classical music, can truly transcend the deep political divisions that have separated historically aggrieved peoples. Or they might wonder whether the organizations do more to appease their supporters than those they are ostensibly seeking to help. And, critics may perplexingly inquire, should surfing really be considered a useful instrument for peace-building? There is, after all, nothing inherently benevolent about the act of wave riding. Surfing is clearly capable of bringing out the worst in people; from Lunada Bay in California to Maroubra in New South Wales, certain beaches have been plagued with a violent localism that has brought the sport into disrepute. But surfing is also capable of the opposite. If riding waves is ultimately about the pursuit of pleasure, there is something about sharing that experience with others that has created a surprisingly intimate community unbound by national borders.

This worldwide surfing community had, by the turn of the twenty-first century, come a long way. What had been an exotic pastime exploited for its colonial utility by Alexander Hume Ford in post-annexation Hawai'i had, by the end of the Cold War era, evolved into a complex industrial brew of exploration, discovery, and neoliberalism. Surfers had set out across the planet in search of waves, and in doing so they had created a vibrant and profoundly global cultural phenomenon. There was inevitably a politics to this process. While those who advocated the boycott of South Africa in the 1980s recognized that their sporting activities were not without political consequences, that seemed but a fillip to the flowering of grassroots critical introspection that characterized the early twenty-first century. Departing from the unidimensional tales of discovery that for years marked the genre, surf filmmakers began to explore the ways that surfing intersected with drug trafficking in Indonesia (*Sea of Darkness* [2008]), the Vietnam War (*Between the Lines: The True Story of Surfers and the Vietnam War* [2008]), race in the United States (*White Wash* [2011]), and the Israeli siege of Gaza (*God Went Surfing with the Devil* [2010]). Not everything changed, of course. Filmic and print travelogues continued to be a commercial staple, with explorations to Russia, Norway, Iceland, and Lake Superior among the more startling examples. But even amid these accounts there were periodic efforts to subvert the conventions of the genre. *Sliding Liberia* (2008), for instance, sought to situate surfing in the broader context of war and peace in West Africa while encouraging surfers to take seriously the notion of "responsible travel."

This was a remarkable departure from the odes to an Indonesian paradise that marked the bulk of the Suharto era.[36] Those tensions that for years lay dormant in global surf culture began to find expression in the films, the athletes, and the organizations that forced a more comprehensive view of surfing's history and traditions. There was, to be sure, a frequent temptation to portray the sport in exceptionalist terms: surfing was not only unique but uniquely salvific. If surfers had for years harbored a self-satisfied belief in their inimitable collective transcendence, there was a conceited tendency to see surf travel as inherently distinct from, and somehow purer than, most other manifestations of contemporary mass tourism. Their footprints, many surfers appeared to believe, were innately smaller and less harmful. It is not difficult to imagine why they may have clung to such illusions. After all, surfing is, at root, about something natural and deceptively simple: catching a wave, standing on a board, and harnessing the energy of a moving mass of water. Countless people do it every day. But one cannot speak of this phenomenon as if it occurs in a vacuum. Surfing exists in a political universe. Yes, it is about pleasure. And yes, it is about escape. But escape is fleeting and pleasure political. Surfing may be a pastime enjoyed by millions of people worldwide, but it is simultaneously a multibillion-dollar industry that relies on global networks of manufacturing, marketing, and travel. Surfers, in other words, are inevitably tied to the political economy of a continually globalizing planet. With this comes the messiness—but also the hope—of a complex and complicated world.

NOTES

INTRODUCTION

1. Rafael Lima, "Combat Surf: The Last Expedition to El Salvador?" *Surfer* 24, no. 10 (October 1983): 76, 80.

2. Ibid., 72, 76.

3. Ibid., 76.

4. Ibid., 76, 80.

5. Ibid., 80.

6. Ibid., 72, 78, 80. Militaristic language is hardly unique to stories such as Lima's; from "bashing the lip," "shooting the curl," and "exploding off the top" to "bombs" and "big-wave guns," it is ubiquitous in surf culture.

7. Guy McCullough, "El Salvador," *Surfer* 25, no. 1 (January 1984): 11.

8. Rick Humphrey, "Combat Surf II," *Surfer* 25, no. 5 (May 1984): 13.

9. Isaiah Helekunihi Walker, *Waves of Resistance: Surfing and History in Twentieth-Century Hawai'i* (Honolulu: University of Hawai'i Press, 2011).

CHAPTER ONE

1. Nathaniel B. Emerson, "Causes of Decline of Ancient Hawaiian Sports," *The Friend* 50, no. 8 (August 1892): 57.

2. Ibid., 57–58.

3. Ibid., 60.

4. Although more complex than can be adequately addressed here, the Makahiki festival was a series of ceremonies and practices marking the new year, while the kapu system was essentially a Hawaiian code of conduct that governed everyday behavior.

5. Emerson, "Causes of Decline," 59.

6. Ibid. Emerson was not the only person in 1892 to comment on the decline of surfing; see also "Surf Bathing," *Paradise of the Pacific* 5, no. 1 (January 1892): 1.

Eight years later, S. E. Bishop, the editor of *The Friend*, claimed that surfing was "now nearly forgotten." S. E. Bishop, "Old Memories of Kailua," *The Friend* 58, no. 12 (December 1900): 102. Assuming a more optimistic perspective, *Paradise of the Pacific* published a brief article in 1896 asserting that the "exciting pastime of surf-riding is enjoyed"—note the use of the present tense—"by both sexes." "From Picturesque Hawaii," *Paradise of the Pacific* 9, no. 10 (October 1896): 146.

7. Emerson, "Causes of Decline," 59.

8. For more on "sensuous surf," see John R. K. Clark, *Hawaiian Surfing: Traditions from the Past* (Honolulu: University of Hawai'i Press, 2011), 45–49.

9. Isaiah Helekunihi Walker, *Waves of Resistance: Surfing and History in Twentieth-Century Hawai'i* (Honolulu: University of Hawai'i Press, 2011), 26–31. It is less clear to what extent the sport "was done in the 1890s at various breaks throughout the Hawaiian Islands," as Walker wrote. He cited, for instance, a photograph reputedly shot in Hilo of two men either exiting or entering the water with boards in hand. Ibid., 30. The source in which the photograph appears, however, said that Hilo "cannot be [the] correct" location, citing the color of the sand, and suggested that Waikiki was "the more plausible site." DeSoto Brown, *Surfing: Historic Images from Bishop Museum Archives* (Honolulu: Bishop Museum Press, 2006), 22. A more recent source firmly claimed that the image was from Hilo. Timothy Tovar DeLaVega, *Suring in Hawai'i, 1778–1930* (Charleston: Arcadia Publishing, 2011), 33. Offering additional support to the existence of surfing on islands other than O'ahu in the 1890s, DeLaVega's book contains previously unpublished photographs of several surfers on Ni'ihau in 1890. Ibid., 27–28. And Ben Finney and James D. Houston wrote, though without citation to evidence, that "[a]s the twentieth century began ... [o]nly a few surfers were actively riding the waves off Maui, Kaua'i[,] and tiny Ni'ihau (the small, privately owned island near Kaua'i reserved exclusively for Hawaiians). Surfing on the once popular Kona coast of the Big Island had virtually disappeared." Ben Finney and James D. Houston, *Surfing: A History of the Ancient Hawaiian Sport* (Rohnert Park, CA: Pomegranate Artbooks, 1996), 59. Likewise, Duke Kahanamoku wrote in his autobiography that, by 1900, "surfing had totally disappeared throughout the Islands except for a few isolated spots on Kauai, Maui[,] and Oahu, and even there only a handful of men took boards into the sea." Duke Kahanamoku with Joe Brennan, *Duke Kahanamoku's World of Surfing* (New York: Grosset & Dunlap Publishers, 1968), 30. I am indebted to Walker's important and novel scholarship for its contribution to my own thinking on surfing and empire in nineteenth- and twentieth-century Hawai'i, as well as to the extensive research undertaken by Finney for its identification of a number of important sources.

10. *Haole* is the Hawaiian term for "whites." On the contextual politics of what it means to be haole, see Judy Rohrer, *Haoles in Hawai'i* (Honolulu: University of Hawai'i Press, 2010).

11. David E. Stannard, *Before the Horror: The Population of Hawai'i on the Eve of Western Contact* (Honolulu: Social Science Research Institute, University of Hawai'i, 1989); Walker, *Waves of Resistance*, 26. Stannard writes that the "first cred-

ible missionary census" found that "the native population of Hawai'i was about 130,000 in the year 1832, and probably at least a few thousand more in 1828—50 years after Western contact." Stannard, *Before the Horror*, 45.

12. Stannard, *Before the Horror*, 45; Andrew F. Bushnell, "'The Horror' Reconsidered: An Evaluation of the Historical Evidence for Population Decline in Hawai'i, 1778–1803," *Pacific Studies* 16, no. 3 (September 1993): 155.

13. Bushnell, "'The Horror' Reconsidered," 115–61.

14. On the presumed benevolence of Indian reformers and the material realities of the imperial project, see Scott Laderman, "'It Is Cheaper and Better to Teach a Young Indian Than to Fight an Old One': Thaddeus Pound and the Logic of Assimilation," *American Indian Culture and Research Journal* 26, no. 3 (2002): 85–111.

15. Hiram Bingham, *A Residence of Twenty-One Years in the Sandwich Islands; or, the Civil, Religious, and Political History of Those Islands: Comprising a Particular View of the Missionary Operations Connected with the Introduction and Progress of Christianity and Civilization among the Hawaiian People*, 2nd ed. (Hartford: Hezekiah Huntington; New York: Sherman Converse, 1848 [1847]), 81.

16. Ibid., 17–18.

17. For an early account by a Hawaiian author that discusses wagering in surfing, see David Malo, *Hawaiian Antiquities (Moolelo Hawaii)*, trans. Nathaniel B. Emerson, 2nd ed., Bernice P. Bishop Museum Special Publication 2 (Honolulu: Bishop Museum Press, 1951 [1898]), 223–24. Malo, "a Hawaiian scholar whose early background was old Hawaiian" and "whose later life was influenced by missionary teaching and beliefs," wrote the original text in Hawaiian. Ibid., xix. He died in 1853.

18. W. D. Alexander, *A Brief History of the Hawaiian People* (New York: American Book Company, 1891), 90. Timothy Tovar DeLaVega also credited "the popularity of a new thrill," horses, with the declining popularity or visibility of surfing. DeLaVega, *Surfing in Hawai'i*, 18–19.

19. Lilikala Kame'eleihiwa, *Native Land and Foreign Desires / Ko Hawai'i 'Aina a me Na Koi Pu'umake a ka Po'e Haole: Pehea La E Pono Ai? / How Shall We Live in Harmony?* (Honolulu: Bishop Museum Press, 1992), 170.

20. Lucia Ruggles Holman, *Journal of Lucia Ruggles Holman*, Bernice P. Bishop Museum Special Publication 17 (Honolulu: Bishop Museum Press, 1931), 17–18.

21. Patricia Grimshaw, *Paths of Duty: American Missionary Wives in Nineteenth-Century Hawaii* (Honolulu: University of Hawai'i Press, 1989), 33.

22. Holman, *Journal of Lucia Ruggles Holman*, 32–33.

23. Sheldon Dibble, *A History of the Sandwich Islands* (Honolulu: Thos. G. Thrum, 1909), 97, 99, 101–2.

24. *Ke Kumu Hawaii*, October 24, 1838, quoted in Clark, *Hawaiian Surfing*, 18.

25. *Ke Kumu Hawaii*, January 31, 1838, quoted in ibid., 17.

26. *Ke Kumu Hawaii*, February 4, 1835, quoted in ibid.

27. *Ke Kumu Hawaii*, October 24, 1838, quoted in ibid., 18.

28. *Ka Nonanona*, February 15, 1842, quoted in ibid.

29. Matt Warshaw, *The History of Surfing* (San Francisco: Chronicle Books, 2010), 35.

30. William Samuel W. Ruschenberger, *Narrative of a Voyage Round the World, during the Years 1835, 36, and 37; Including a Narrative of an Embassy to the Sultan of Muscat and the King of Siam* (Folkestone, UK: Dawsons of Pall Mall, 1970), 2:373, 375.

31. Noenoe K. Silva, *Aloha Betrayed: Native Hawaiian Resistance to American Colonialism* (Durham, NC: Duke University Press, 2004); Walker, *Waves of Resistance*.

32. Emerson, "Causes of Decline," 59.

33. Charles Nordhoff, "Hawaii-Nei," *Harper's New Monthly Magazine* 47, no. 279 (August 1873): 402. Timothy DeLaVega wrote that Hilo offered "Hawai'i's longest rideable surfing wave" before completion of the breakwater in 1926. DeLaVega, *Suring in Hawai'i*, 33.

34. Henry T. Cheever, *Life in the Sandwich Islands; or, The Heart of the Pacific, as It Was and Is* (New York: A. S. Barnes & Co.; Cincinnati: H. W. Derby & Co., 1851), 66–67.

35. Bingham, *A Residence of Twenty-One Years*, 136–37.

36. On Hawaiian resistance to the American imperial project, see, most obviously, Silva, *Aloha Betrayed*.

37. Kame'eleihiwa, *Native Land and Foreign Desires*.

38. U.S. Department of State, *Foreign Relations of the United States, 1894: Affairs in Hawaii*, 53rd Congress, 2nd sess., House Executive Document 48 (Washington, DC: Government Printing Office, 1895), 397. (The document also appears in U.S. Department of State, *Foreign Relations of the United States, 1894: Affairs in Hawaii*, 53rd Congress, 2nd sess., House Executive Document 47 [Washington, DC: Government Printing Office, 1895], 866.)

39. As Noenoe K. Silva has shown, over 38,000 signatures were collected from Hawaiians who opposed annexation at a time when the Hawaiian population totaled approximately 40,000 people. Silva acknowledged that some people likely signed more than one of the petitions then in circulation, but, even so, the total number of signatures remains "impressive," she wrote. Silva, *Aloha Betrayed*, 151.

40. J. Kehaulani Kauanui, *Hawaiian Blood: Colonialism and the Politics of Sovereignty and Indigeneity* (Durham, NC: Duke University Press, 2008), 28; and Kauanui, "Precarious Positions: Native Hawaiians and U.S. Federal Recognition," *Contemporary Pacific* 17, no. 1 (Spring 2005): 3–4.

41. *Hawaii: The Year Round Playground* (Honolulu: Hawaii Tourist Bureau, August 1922), 1, Tourism Brochures (Uncataloged) [hereafter TB], Box 1, Hawaiian Collection [hereafter HC], Hamilton Library [hereafter HL], University of Hawai'i at Manoa [hereafter UH]. For a problematization of the idea ubiquitous in tourist literature of Hawai'i as a "paradise," see Elizabeth Buck, *Paradise Remade: The Politics of Culture and History in Hawai'i* (Philadelphia: Temple University Press, 1993).

42. *Daily Bulletin*, quoted in Ralph S. Kuykendall, *The Hawaiian Kingdom*, vol. 3, *The Kalakaua Dynasty, 1874–1893* (Honolulu: University of Hawai'i Press, 1967), 110.

43. On the transformation of surfing from a moral threat to the colonial order in nineteenth-century Hawai'i to an important component of colonial development in the early twentieth, see Robin Canniford, "Culture Clash: Economic Reconstructions of Hawaiian Surfing," in *On the Edge: Leisure, Consumption, and the Representation of Adventure Sports*, ed. Joan Ormrod and Belinda Wheaton (Eastbourne, UK: Leisure Studies Association, 2009), 3–16.

44. Robert C. Allen, *Creating Hawai'i Tourism: A Memoir* (Honolulu: Bess Press, 2004), 162. The others were *Hawaii Five-O*, Don Ho, and the Polynesian Cultural Center. Allen had served as president of, among other entities, Gray Line Hawaii, Shoreline Cruises, and the Hotel Operating Company; general manager of the Inter-Island Travel Company; executive vice president and managing director of the Hawaii Visitors Bureau; and chairman of the Pacific Area Travel Association Marketing Committee. For Allen's obituary, see Venus Lee, "Former POW Pioneered Hawaii Tourism," *Honolulu Star-Bulletin*, June 3, 2005, http://archives.starbulletin.com/2005/06/03/news/story13.html, accessed July 28, 2011.

45. Joel T. Smith, "Reinventing the Sport, Part II: Alexander Hume Ford," *Surfer's Journal* 12, no. 2 (Spring 2003): 30–31. One of Ford's friends claimed that he actually arrived in Hawai'i in 1905; see Walker, *Waves of Resistance*, 184 (note 9). Jim Nendel wrote that Ford moved to the islands in 1906. Jim Nendel, "Surfing in Early Twentieth-Century Hawai'i: The Appropriation of a Transcendent Experience to Competitive American Sport," *International Journal of the History of Sport* 26, no. 16 (December 2009): 2435. Most accounts are in agreement, however, that Ford arrived in 1907.

46. Alexander Hume Ford, "The Genesis of the Pan-Pacific Union," *Mid-Pacific Magazine* 31, no. 1 (January 1926): 13.

47. Alexander Hume Ford, "Riding the Surf in Hawaii," *Collier's* 43, no. 21 (August 14, 1909): 17.

48. Oscar F. Davis, "Surf-Riding: A Vivid Description of the National Pastime of Hawaii," *Wave* [San Francisco] (December 17, 1898): 8, Newspapers Collection, Box: NEWS 76, Hawai'i State Archives, Honolulu. Davis experienced his wave riding in an outrigger canoe, not on a surfboard. "[W]hite men" rarely "become expert" on the latter, he wrote. Ibid., 8.

49. Alexander Hume Ford, "A Boy's Paradise in the Pacific," *St. Nicholas* 35 (August 1908): 878.

50. Ibid.

51. Joseph "Skipper" Funderburg, "Alexander Hume Ford: Early Life, 1868–1886," Surfing Heritage Scrap Book, 3, http://scrapbook.surfingheritage.org/Main .php?MagID=2&MagNo=6, accessed August 25, 2011; Smith, "Reinventing the Sport, Part II," 31; Ben Marcus, *Surfing USA! An Illustrated History of the Coolest Sport of All Time* (Stillwater, MN: Voyageur Press, 2005), 36. For additional works addressing Ford's early twentieth-century contributions, though often in a more

nuanced manner, see, among others, Finney and Houston, *Surfing*, 60–61; Malcolm Gault-Williams, "Alexander Hume Ford (1868–1945)," *LegendarySurfers.com*, http://files.legendarysurfers.com/blog/ahford.doc.pdf, accessed August 25, 2011; Drew Kampion, *Stoked: A History of Surf Culture*, rev. ed. (Salt Lake City: Gibbs Smith, 2003), 37; Leonard Lueras, *Surfing: The Ultimate Pleasure* (New York: Workman Publishing, 1984), 68–74; Nendel, "Surfing in Early Twentieth-Century Hawaiʻi," 2435–37, 2439–40, 2442; Grady Timmons, *Waikiki Beachboy* (Honolulu: Editions Limited, 1989), 25–26; and Warshaw, *The History of Surfing*, 44–47. For an important corrective to the "revival" narrative, see Patrick Moser, "Revival," *Kurungabaa: A Journal of Literature, History, and Ideas from the Sea* 3, no. 1 (July 2010): 54–57.

52. "Although Ford and [Jack] London did seek to promote surfing and tourism to other haole visitors," Walker writes, "they have been erroneously credited with restoring surfing in general at the time. In reality, the two were merely boosters—promoters who saw the economic potential of marketing the sport and Waikiki to other tourists. Rather than being innovators, Ford and London in fact learned to surf from an already established cohort of Hawaiian surfers in 1907. By that time surfing's resurgence was well underway, led by Hawaiians who formed the Hui Nalu club in 1905." Walker, *Waves of Resistance*, 31–32.

53. William Cottrell provided a list of the "old timers" who "encouraged" the "true revival of the sport" from 1903 to 1908; see Tom Blake, *Hawaiian Surfriders 1935* (Redondo Beach, CA: Mountain & Sea Publishing, 1983), 60. This is a reprint of Blake's *Hawaiian Surfboard*, which was originally published in 1935.

54. Walker, *Waves of Resistance*, 57.

55. Jack London, "Riding the South Sea Surf," *Woman's Home Companion* (October 1907): 9. Ford, London wrote, was "my guardian angel" in the waves. Ibid., 9. When London reproduced this article as a chapter ("A Royal Sport") in his *Cruise of the Snark*, "a black Mercury" became "a brown Mercury." Jack London, *The Cruise of the Snark* (New York: Macmillan Company, 1928), 76.

56. For one of the rare exceptions, see Kristin Lawler, *The American Surfer: Radical Culture and Capitalism* (New York: Routledge, 2011), 31–32, 182 (note 43). On Ford's propagating the view that he revived or at least ensured the perpetuation of surfing, see Alexander Hume Ford to Frank Atherton, December 26, 1930, Folder 17 (Related Activities: Outrigger Canoe Club), Box 7, Pan Pacific Union Records [hereafter PPU Records], Archives and Manuscripts, HL, UH; Alexander Hume Ford to the Directors of the Outrigger Canoe Club and the Trustees of the Royal Hawaiian Hotel, September 18, 1931, Folder 17 (Related Activities: Outrigger Canoe Club), Box 7, PPU Records, Archives and Manuscripts, HL, UH; and Biography of Alexander Hume Ford, Folder 2 (Background Materials: Origins—Late 1930s), Box 1, PPU Records, Archives and Manuscripts, HL, UH.

57. Gary Y. Okihiro, *Island World: A History of Hawaiʻi and the United States* (Berkeley: University of California Press, 2008), 60.

58. Christine Skwiot, *The Purposes of Paradise: U.S. Tourism and Empire in Cuba and Hawaiʻi* (Philadelphia: University of Pennsylvania Press, 2010), 49–86.

59. Daniel Logan, *The Hawaiian Islands: A Handbook of Information* (Honolulu: Department of Foreign Affairs, 1899), 3.

60. Jean West Maury, "Interesting Westerners," *Sunset* 38 (March 1917): 40.

61. Alexander Hume Ford, "Russia's Field for Anglo-Saxon Enterprise in Asia," *Engineering Magazine* 19 (June 1900): 354, 368.

62. Alexander Hume Ford, "The Triumph of the American Idea," *New England Magazine* 25, no. 1 (September 1901): 7, 13, 16.

63. Alexander Hume Ford, "Our American Colony at Jerusalem," *Appleton's Magazine* 8, no. 6 (December 1906): 644–45. For more on Ford's views of socialism—he saw some positive aspects to the "probably . . . most socialistic form of government on earth to-day" in New Zealand but still, at that time, seemed to prefer American capitalism—see Alexander Hume Ford, "Creating a New Dominion," *World To-Day* 14 (February 1908): 205–8. (The quoted material appears on page 208.) By 1915, Ford was referring to Jack London and his wife, Charmian, as "fellow Socialists." Alexander Hume Ford to Jack London and Charmian London ("Mr. and Mrs. Jack London"), August 25, 1915, Jack London Papers, JL 6197–6208, Huntington Library, San Marino, California.

64. Alexander Hume Ford, "Three Eastern Easters," *The Traveller* 3, no. 4 (April 1904): 248, Folder 1 (Background Materials: A. H. Ford), Box 1, PPU Records, Archives and Manuscripts, HL, UH.

65. Alexander Hume Ford, "The Congressional Tour of the Hawaiian Islands," *World To-Day* 13 (August 1907): 800, 804. Several of the congressmen and their aides tried their hand at surfing. Arthur C. Verge, "George Freeth: King of the Surfers and California's Forgotten Hero," *California History* 80, no. 2–3 (Summer–Fall 2001): 153 (note 12).

66. Ford elsewhere drew on the language of savagery and civilization in contrasting the "heathen natives" of the New Hebrides with the English, French, and other white settlers ridding them of their barbarous practices. Alexander Hume Ford, "The New New Hebrides," *Red Funnel* 6, no. 6 (July 1, 1908): 575–82. (The quoted material appears on page 580.)

67. Ford, "The Congressional Tour of the Hawaiian Islands," 800; Ford, "Our Japanese Territory," *Collier's* 43 (July 24, 1909): 13.

68. Ford, "The Congressional Tour of the Hawaiian Islands," 800.

69. Ibid. For more on Kuhio, see Walker, *Waves of Resistance*, 67–70.

70. Ford, "Our Japanese Territory," 12.

71. See, for example, Lawrence Culver, *The Frontier of Leisure: Southern California and the Shaping of Modern America* (Oxford: Oxford University Press, 2010).

72. Ford, "The Congressional Tour of the Hawaiian Islands," 806–7.

73. *Official Proceedings of the First Annual Session of the Pan-Pacific Congress Held at Honolulu, Hawaii, February 20–28, 1911* (Honolulu: Paradise of the Pacific Print, 1911), 20–21, Folder: 9-4-60 Haw. Promotion-Comm. Pan Pac. Congress, Box 662, Central Classified Files, 1907–1951, Office of the Territories, Record Group [hereafter RG] 126, National Archives II, College Park, Maryland [hereafter NA II].

74. *Hawaii: Now or Any Season* (Honolulu: Hawaii Tourist Bureau, January 1924), 2, Folder: Hawaii—Travel Brochures, Box 4, TB, HC, HL, UH. A similar view was earlier articulated by Lorrin A. Thurston; see Skwiot, *The Purposes of Paradise*, 36.

75. "Outrigger Club Is Flourishing," *Evening Bulletin* [Honolulu], August 18, 1909; Walker, *Waves of Resistance*, 61.

76. Alexander Hume Ford, "Out-Door Allurements: The Outrigger Canoe Club," in *Hawaiian Almanac and Annual for 1911* (Honolulu: Thos. G. Thrum, 1910), 144, 146. A portion of Ford's article was reprinted decades later as Alexander Hume Ford, "The Hawaiian Outrigger Canoe Club at Waikiki," *Paradise of the Pacific* 48, no. 10 (October 1936): 21. An official history of the Outrigger Canoe Club indicates that A. S. Herbert and Guy H. Tuttle served as "acting" presidents between Ford and Dole's terms. Harold H. Yost, *The Outrigger Canoe Club of Honolulu, Hawaii* (Honolulu: Outrigger Canoe Club, 1971), 39, 44.

77. "[A]ll Club records before the 1930s were lost," noted a centennial history of the institution in explaining the difficulty in reconstructing its early years. Barbara Del Piano, *Outrigger Canoe Club: The First One Hundred Years, 1908–2008* (Honolulu: Outrigger Canoe Club, 2007), ix. See also Yost, *The Outrigger Canoe Club of Honolulu*, 29–33.

78. This language is from an April 7, 1908, solicitation sent by Ford and other haoles in Honolulu to various organizations in the city. The letter is reproduced in Yost, *The Outrigger Canoe Club of Honolulu*, 38.

79. Ford, "Out-Door Allurements," 143.

80. Ford to the Directors of the Outrigger Canoe Club and the Trustees of the Royal Hawaiian Hotel, September 18, 1931. "Surfboard riding did *not* die out, and when it does, your hotels suffer," Ford wrote Frank Atherton of Castle & Cooke, owners of the Royal Hawaiian, in 1930. Alexander Hume Ford to Frank Atherton, December 26, 1930, Folder 17 (Related Activities: Outrigger Canoe Club), Box 7, PPU Records, Archives and Manuscripts, HL, UH.

81. "Hawaiian Water Sports Delight Great Crowd," *Hawaiian Gazette* [Honolulu], July 21, 1908; Del Piano, *Outrigger Canoe Club*, 9–14.

82. Ibid.

83. Ibid. It is "doubtful," suggested the club's internal history, whether plans for the Outrigger's formation "would have progressed so expeditiously had not the looming arrival of the fleet been a strong impetus." Ibid., 11. On the visit of the Great White Fleet, see also Yost, *The Outrigger Canoe Club of Honolulu*, 41.

84. Alexander Hume Ford to Joseph J. Cotter, February 27, 1920, Folder: 9-4-60 Haw. Promotion-Comm. Pan Pac. Congress, Box 662, Central Classified Files, 1907–1951, Office of the Territories, RG 126, NA II. Surfing and outrigger canoeing, Ford wrote in 1931, are "the most athlete making and health preserving sports in the world" and "the greatest health giving, giant building sports in the whole world." Ford to the Directors of the Outrigger Canoe Club and the Trustees of the Royal Hawaiian Hotel, September 18, 1931.

85. Alexander Hume Ford to Roy J. Banks, November 10, 1930, Folder 17 (Related Activities: Outrigger Canoe Club), Box 7, PPU Records, Archives and Manuscripts, HL, UH; Alexander Hume Ford to R. Q. Smith, October 30, 1930, Folder 17 (Related Activities: Outrigger Canoe Club), Box 7, PPU Records, Archives and Manuscripts, HL, UH.

86. Ford, "Out-Door Allurements," 146. While names are not necessarily an accurate measure of racial or ethnic identity, only one name on the original membership list for the club explicitly suggests Hawaiian descent: the "junior" member H. L. Kinelea. "Original List of Charter Members [of] Outrigger Canoe Club, 1908," Folder 17 (Related Activities: Outrigger Canoe Club), Box 7, PPU Records, Archives and Manuscripts, HL, UH. Ford later wrote that "[i]n organizing the Outrigger Canoe Club in March, 1908, my idea was to bring together the Anglo-Saxon and the Hawaiian surfboard riders and aquatic athletes. The time was not then ripe for including other nationalities," he conceded, "but when the Outrigger Canoe Club was two months old I made the first of many attempts to interest the men of all races living in Hawaii in organizing a permanent Pan-Pacific Olympiad of native athletic games, including those of all Pacific countries, both ancient and modern. We are still working it out." Ford then sidestepped responsibility for the segregation of the club by writing that the "white and part Hawaiian boys did not wish the full Hawaiian boys as members, and jointly they wished to taboo the Portuguese and the Oriental." Ford, "The Genesis of the Pan-Pacific Union," 11, 14. Paul Hooper wrote in 1980 that, "so far as can be determined," the Outrigger had "refused to accept people of Asian ancestry as members" from "the time of its inception to the present." Paul F. Hooper, *Elusive Destiny: The Internationalist Movement in Modern Hawaii* (Honolulu: University Press of Hawaii, 1980), 74.

87. Ford, "A Boy's Paradise in the Pacific," 877.

88. William A. "Knute" Cottrell, quoted in Walker, *Waves of Resistance,* 62.

89. Alexander Hume Ford, "Riding the Surf in Hawaii," *Collier's* 43, no. 21 (August 14, 1909): 17. The earlier belief that only Hawaiians were capable of surfing was articulated perhaps most famously in 1866 by Mark Twain, who insisted in *Roughing It* that "[n]one but natives ever master the art of surf-bathing thoroughly." Mark Twain, *Roughing It* (New York: Harper and Brothers Publishers, 1913 [1871]), 2:288. For more on non-Hawaiian surfers in the nineteenth and early twentieth centuries, see Clark, *Hawaiian Surfing,* 60–66.

90. Ford, "Riding the Surf in Hawaii," 17.

91. Alexander Hume Ford, "Surf Riding for the Motion Picture Man," *Mid-Pacific Magazine* 4, no. 3 (September 1912): 278.

92. The reasons that Hawaiians did not always compete in contests, Warshaw added, are unclear. Warshaw, *The History of Surfing,* 45.

93. Walker, *Waves of Resistance,* 66. See also Sam Reid, "When the Hawaiians Ruled the Waves," *Surfer* 9, no. 3 (July 1968): 63–64.

94. Ford, "Riding the Surf in Hawaii," 17; Ford, "A Boy's Paradise in the Pacific," 876–82; Ford, "Famous Seaside Resorts Around the Globe," *Travel* 14, no. 11

(August 1909): 515–18; and Ford, "Aquatic Sports," *Paradise of the Pacific* 21, no. 12 (December 1908): 19–20.

95. "Experts to Catch Pele in Auction [*sic*]," *Hawaiian Star* [Honolulu], March 1, 1910; Ford, "Surf Riding for the Motion Picture Man."

96. Duke Paoa [Kahanamoku], "Riding the Surfboard," *Mid-Pacific Magazine* 1, no. 1 (January 1911): 3–10. (For a continuation of the article, see Duke Paoa [Kahanamoku], "Riding the Surfboard [continued]," *Mid-Pacific Magazine* 1, no. 2 [February 1911]: 151–58.) Patrick Moser (and others) have concluded that Ford was in fact the author of the article attributed to Kahanamoku, a young man soon to be recognized as the world's fastest swimmer and, according to Ford's introduction to the inaugural piece, "the recognized native Hawaiian champion surf rider." Paoa, "Riding the Surfboard," 3; Patrick Moser, ed., *Pacific Passages: An Anthology of Surf Writing* (Honolulu: University of Hawai'i Press, 2008), 336; and Moser, "Revival," 55. This is almost certainly true. In joking about his exhaustion in running *Mid-Pacific Magazine*, Ford confessed to Charmian London that he wrote "half the articles myself under assumed names, and beg, borrow or steal the others." Alexander Hume Ford to Charmian ("Mrs. Jack") London, January 10, 1913, Coll MS 10, Box 12, Folder 2, Jack London Papers, Special Collections and Archives, Merrill-Cazier Library, Utah State University, Logan, Utah. The same letter can be found in the Jack London Papers, JL 6197–6208, Huntington Library, San Marino, California.

97. A. L. Brick, "The Americanization of Hawaii," *Mid-Pacific Magazine* 1, no. 1 (January 1911): 77–78. Contemplating the infrastructure needed to advance this vision, Brick noted that "[i]f Honolulu and Pearl Harbor are fortified [with breakwaters], five thousand American workmen with their families will doubtless be brought to the islands, and the question of the white man's supremacy settled." Ibid., 80.

98. Valerie Noble, *Hawaiian Prophet: Alexander Hume Ford* (Smithtown, NY: Exposition Press, 1980), 57.

99. Alexander Hume Ford, "Hawaii: The Young Man's Land," *Van Norden Magazine* 5 (August 1909): 523. Ford reprinted the article two years later in his *Mid-Pacific Magazine*, citing the author as "Van Norden" and changing the title to the blunter and more explicitly racial "Hawaii for the White Man"; see Van Norden, "Hawaii for the White Man," *Mid-Pacific Magazine* 1, no. 6 (June 1911): 629–34.

100. Alexander Hume Ford, "Hawaii Calls for the Small Farmer," *Van Norden Magazine* 5 (November 1909): 173, 181.

101. Ford, "Hawaii," 529.

102. Noble, *Hawaiian Prophet*, 57.

103. Yost, *The Outrigger Canoe Club of Honolulu*, 41.

104. "Experts to Catch Pele in Auction [*sic*]."

105. *To the Hawaiian Islands, the Paradise of the Pacific* (Canadian-Pacific Railway and Canadian-Australian S.S. Line, October 1898), 1, 7. The photograph is an oft-reproduced image of Hawaiian surfer Charles Kauha. See, for one example of its reproduction, the cover of DeLaVega, *Surfing in Hawai'i*.

106. *History of the Hawaiian Islands and Hints to Travelers Visiting the Hawaiian Islands* (Honolulu: Hawaiian Gazette Co., 1899). The surfing images appear in two unnumbered montages of photographs with "Davey Photo Co., Ltd., Honolulu" and "Scenes at Hawaiian Hotel Annex, Waikiki Beach" written underneath.

107. Ferdinand J. H. Schnack, *The Aloha Guide: The Standard Handbook of Honolulu and the Hawaiian Islands for Travelers and Residents with a Historical Resume, Illustrations, and Maps* (Honolulu: Honolulu Star-Bulletin, 1915), 1. On "surf-riding," in which "[n]o visitor should leave the Islands without having participated in this popular and exhilarating pastime," see page 56.

108. *Aloha from Honolulu* (Honolulu: Hawaiian Jewelry and Novelty Co., 1915), 25. Another photograph showed Waikiki Beach, where "[a]t all hours of the day bathers and surf riders can be seen in the surf." Ibid., 31.

109. For postcards, see, for example, Brown, *Surfing*, 22–23, 28, 30–33, 48–49, 64–65, 82–83; DeLaVega, *Surfing in Hawai'i*, 32–35, 42, 50; and Lueras, *Surfing*, 67. For surfing in early promotional materials, see, for numerous examples, the pamphlets and other documents found in TB, Boxes 1 and 4, HC, HL, UH.

110. Hooper, *Elusive Destiny*, 69, 199 (note 14). For more on the Hands-Around-the-Pacific Club, the Pan Pacific Union, and the internationalist activities of Alexander Hume Ford, see ibid., 65–104.

111. Thomas Kemper Hitch, *Islands in Transition: The Past, Present, and Future of Hawai'i's Economy* (Honolulu: First Hawaiian Bank, 1992), 301.

112. A. P. Taylor to Franklin K. Lane, August 11, 1917, Folder: 9-4-60 Haw. Promotion-Comm. Pan Pac. Congress, Box 662, Central Classified Files, 1907–1951, Office of the Territories, RG 126, NA II. See also "'Pacific American Union' Plan Launched; A. P. Taylor Fathers an Ambitious Plan," *Pacific Commercial Advertiser*, January 7, 1917, Folder: 9-4-60 Haw. Promotion-Comm. Pan Pac. Congress, Box 662, Central Classified Files, 1907–1951, Office of the Territories, RG 126, NA II. The purpose of the Pacific American Union, Taylor wrote to Secretary of the Interior Franklin K. Lane, was to advance "the exploitation of the American territories and possessions in and bordering upon the Pacific." After all, he reminded Washington, "[t]hese [t]erritories and dependencies of the United States [Hawai'i, Alaska, the Philippines, Guam, and Samoa] dot the great Pacific Ocean region," which was "now looked upon by students of commerce as the great future trading region of the world." A. P. Taylor to Franklin K. Lane, July 17, 1917, Folder: 9-4-60 Haw. Promotion-Comm. Pan Pac. Congress, Box 662, Central Classified Files, 1907–1951, Office of the Territories, RG 126, NA II; and A. P. Taylor to Franklin K. Lane, August 11, 1917. For more on Taylor's plans for a Pacific American Union, see A. P. Taylor, "The Proposed Pacific American Union," *The Friend* 75, no. 2 (February 1917): 36.

113. Noble, *Hawaiian Prophet*, 227.

114. Freeth was not, in fact, the first person to surf in California, though he appeared to leave a more significant legacy than those who preceded him. Most notably, in 1885 three young Hawaiian princes attending boarding school in San Mateo put on a demonstration of "surf-board swimming" in Santa Cruz at the mouth of

the San Lorenzo River. "Beach Breezes," *Daily Surf* [Santa Cruz], July 20, 1885. And there is some evidence of Hawaiian surfer John Ahia being paid by La Jolla hoteliers to provide surfing exhibitions in 1893; see "Earliest Surfing on the Mainland Revised?" *Surfer's Journal* 22, no. 2 (April/May 2013): 126. One of the three princes in 1885 was Jonah Kuhio Kalaniana'ole, who would later become Hawai'i's delegate to Congress. On the significance of the Santa Cruz demonstration, see Geoffrey Dunn and Kim Stoner, "Riders of the Sea Spray," *Good Times* [Santa Cruz], March 31, 2010, www.goodtimessantacruz.com/good-times-cover-stories/936-riders-of-the-sea-spray.html, accessed August 27, 2011. There also was surfing in the first years of the twentieth century in the state of Washington; see Gavin Kogan, "Aloha Washington: An Unlikely Discovery of Pre-Freeth Mainland Surfing," *Surfer's Journal* 15, no. 5 (Fall 2006): 92–97. For more on Freeth, see Joel T. Smith, "Reinventing the Sport, Part III: George Freeth," *Surfer's Journal* 12, no. 3 (Summer 2003): 90–95; Verge, "George Freeth," 82–105, 153–55; and Ian Whitcomb, "The Beach Boy," *American Heritage* 51, no. 4 (July–August 2000), www.americanheritage.com/content/beach-boy, accessed August 31, 2011.

115. "George Freeth Off to Coast," *Pacific Commercial Advertiser* [Honolulu], July 3, 1907.

116. London, "Riding the South Sea Surf," 10.

117. Huntington quoted in James Thorpe, *Henry Edwards Huntington: A Biography* (Berkeley: University of California Press, 1994), 205.

118. Verge, "George Freeth," 88.

119. "Surf Riders Have Drawn Attention," *Daily Outlook* [Santa Monica], July 22, 1907. It is unclear why the report referred to "Hawaiians" in the plural, as Freeth was, according to all accounts I have seen, the only surfer in California—Hawaiian or otherwise—at that time.

120. Kahanamoku statues have been erected on Kuhio Beach in Waikiki, as the centerpiece of the Surfers' Hall of Fame in Huntington Beach, on the headland at Freshwater Beach in Sydney, and at the Field Museum in Chicago. On the Chicago statue, see "Chicago Has Statue of Duke Kahanamoku," *Honolulu Star-Bulletin*, August 4, 1953, Folder 18.9 (Hawaiian Surfing: Vol. I), Box 18, Charles Kenn Collection, MS Group 361, Bishop Museum, Honolulu, Hawai'i [hereafter BM].

121. John Williams, "Duke Kahanamoku Recalls the 'Old Days' at Waikiki Beach," *Honolulu Star-Bulletin*, January 23, 1937, Folder: 9-4-63 Press Clippings, Box 663, Classified Files, 1907–1951, Office of the Territories, RG 126, NA II. Kahanamoku was in fact later cast as "a Red Man with feathers" by Hollywood; for a photograph of him as "Indian Chief" in *The Pony Express* (1925), see DeLaVega, *Surfing in Hawai'i*, 92. On Kahanamoku's swimming records, see Joseph L. Brennan, *Duke: The Life Story of Duke Kahanamoku* (Honolulu: Ku Pa'a Publishing, 1995 [1994]), 4–13. Brennan also touches on the racist treatment Kahanamoku repeatedly experienced while traveling on the American mainland; see Brennan, *Duke*, 39–41. On the racial aspects of Kahanamoku's visit to Australia and New Zealand, see Gary Osmond, "'Honolulu Maori': Racial Dimensions of Duke Kahanamoku's

Tour of Australia and New Zealand, 1914–1915," *New Zealand Journal of History* 44, no. 1 (2010): 22–34.

122. The 1916 Olympics scheduled for Berlin was canceled because of the First World War. Kahanamoku's bronze medal at the 1932 Olympics was for water polo, not swimming. Sandra Kimberley Hall, *Duke: A Great Hawaiian* (Honolulu: Bess Press, 2004), 67.

123. Timmons, *Waikiki Beachboy*, 73. See also Brennan, *Duke*, 93–94. Testifying to the existence of an Australian surf community, an account from Sydney of Kahanamoku's "cavorting the waves" noted that "a nation of surfers" was growing "in this section of the continent," though "[e]xperts at the pastime" declared that Kahanamoku had "no equal." "The display is said to be perfection, and is like nothing our best surfers do," the *Sun* reported. W. F. Corbett, "Surfer and Swimmer / Kahanamoku's Doings / The High Divers," *Sun* [Sydney], December 22, 1914, Scrapbook (Visit of Duke Kahanamoku and George Cunha to Australia and New Zealand, 1914–1955, Hui Nalu) [hereafter Scrapbook], Box 9 (1994.204.373), Duke Kahanamoku Collection [hereafter DKC], MS Group 354, BM. Another account from Corbett credited Fred C. Williams with being "the pioneer. He picked up the art from a South Sea Islander, and spread knowledge of it among the surfers on the most favored beaches of the time—Freshwater, Curl Curl, and Maroubra." W. F. Corbett, "A Great Surf Shooter / Kahanamoku Talks / Methods and Conditions," *Sun* [Sydney], January 8, 1915, Scrapbook, Box 9 (1994.204.373), DKC, MS Group 354, BM. The "South Sea Islander" was presumably a young man identified as "Tommy Tanna," whose actual name is unknown. As the *Manly Biographical Dictionary* noted, "'Tommy Tanna' was a common nickname for any Kanaka male, derived from the fact that a significant proportion of indentured labourers in Australia came from the island of Tanna in the South Hebrides, now part of Vanuatu"; see "Tommy Tanna," *Manly Biographical Dictionary*, www.manly.nsw.gov.au/library/local-studies-collection/people-of-manly/, accessed January 20, 2012.

124. W. F. Corbett, "Wonderful Surf Riding / Kahanamoku on the Board / A Thrilling Spectacle," *Sun* [Sydney], December 24, 1914; "Surf-Board Riding / Kahanamoku's Display," *Sydney Morning Herald*, December 25, 1914; and "The Human Motor Boat / Duke Kahanamoku's Way of Shooting the Breakers / Wonderful Water Feats / Hawaiian in His Element," *Sunday Times*, December 27, 1914, all of which can be found in Scrapbook, Box 9 (1994.204.373), DKC, MS Group 354, BM.

125. "Carnival at Dee Why / Kahanamoku Attracts Thousands," *Sunday Times*, February 7, 1915, Scrapbook, Box 9 (1994.204.373), DKC, MS Group 354, BM.

126. Advertisement of the Queensland Amateur Swimming Association, Scrapbook, Box 9 (1994.204.373), DKC, MS Group 354, BM.

127. "Swimming / Duke Kahanamoku / World's Greatest Swimmer / A Man of Few Words," *Canterbury Times*, March 3, 1915, Scrapbook, Box 9 (1994.204.373), DKC, MS Group 354, BM.

128. "Swimming / Kahanamoku's Carnival / Record Attendance at Te Aro Baths / Civic Reception to Champion," *New Zealand Times*, March 8, 1915, Scrapbook, Box 9 (1994.204.373), DKC, MS Group 354, BM.

129. "Swimming / Maori Welcome to Kahanamoku," *Dominion* [Wellington], March 13, 1915, Scrapbook, Box 9 (1994.204.373), DKC, MS Group 354, BM. Kahanamoku's surfing exhibitions in New Zealand are also mentioned in Brennan, *Duke*, 95.

130. Corbett, "A Great Surf Shooter." Corbett's interview of Kahanamoku was later reprinted in the New Zealand press; see W. F. Corbett, "A Great Surf Shooter / Kahanamoku Talks," *Weekly Press* [Christchurch], March 17, 1915, Scrapbook, Box 9 (1994.204.373), DKC, MS Group 354, BM.

131. On his 1916 wave-riding demonstrations in Atlantic City, New Jersey, and Nassau, New York, see Timmons, *Waikiki Beachboy*, 73. Matt Warshaw discusses a 1912 exhibition in Atlantic City while returning from the Olympic Games; see Warshaw, *The History of Surfing*, 55, as well as Reid, "When the Hawaiians Ruled the Waves," 59; and "The Duke," *Surfer* 6, no. 1 (March 1965): 18. On California, see Blake, *Hawaiian Surfriders 1935*, 61; Hall, *Duke*, 41; Finney and Houston, *Surfing*, 81; Nancy N. Schiffer, *Surfing, Surfing, Surfing* (Atglen, PA: Schiffer Publishing, 1998), 54; Matt Warshaw, *The Encyclopedia of Surfing* (Orlando: Harcourt, 2003), 309; and Warshaw, *The History of Surfing*, 55. On Kahanamoku's evangelizing for surfing to young Americans, see Duke Kahanamoku, "Full Speed Ahead," *Youth's Companion* 102, no. 7 (July 1928): 330.

132. On race and Kahanamoku's body, see Michael Nevin Willard, "Duke Kahanamoku's Body: Biography of Hawai'i," in *Sports Matters: Race, Recreation, and Culture*, ed. John Bloom and Michael Nevin Willard (New York: New York University Press, 2002), 13–38.

133. Jane C. Desmond, *Staging Tourism: Bodies on Display from Waikiki to Sea World* (Chicago: University of Chicago Press, 1999), 122; on the magazine covers, see, for a number of examples, *Holiday* (February 1931); *La Paree* (September 1934); *New Yorker* (January 1933); *St. Nicholas* (September 1930); *Sunset* (August 1916); *Travel* (September 1937); *Travel* (June 1939); and *Vogue* (December 15, 1938). These and other covers have been reproduced in Timothy DeLaVega's invaluable *200 Years of Surfing Literature: An Annotated Bibliography* (Hanapepe, Kaui, Hawai'i: Timothy T. DeLaVega, 2004), 32–62.

134. "Mrs. Mary L. Rice, Home in Oakham After Four Years, Talks of Hawaii," *Worcester Telegram* [Massachusetts], October 24, 1920, Folder: 9-4-63 Press Clippings, Box 663, Classified Files, 1907–1951, Office of the Territories, RG 126, NA II.

135. "In the Land of Sweets Where Romance Reigns," *Waterville Sentinel* [Maine], October 12, 1920, Folder: 9-4-63 Press Clippings, Box 663, Classified Files, 1907–1951, Office of the Territories, RG 126, NA II. On "Surf Riders, Hawaii," a painting by the English watercolorist Charles W. Bartlett that was featured in Detroit's Carper Galleries in 1920, see "India, Hawaii, Japan in Colorful Exhibition,"

Detroit News [Michigan], October 31, 1920, Folder: 9-4-63 Press Clippings, Box 663, Classified Files, 1907–1951, Office of the Territories, RG 126, NA II.

136. For 1936 and 1937, see George T. Armitage to Joseph B. Poindexter, June 13, 1938, Folder: 9-4-2 Reports-Annual-Hawaii Tourist Bureau, Box 564, Classified Files, 1907–1951, Office of the Territories, RG 126, NA II. For 1938, see Annual Report of Hawaii Tourist Bureau for the Fiscal Year 1938–1939 to the Governor of Hawaii, Folder: 9-4-2 Reports-Annual-Hawaii Tourist Bureau, Box 564, Classified Files, 1907–1951, Office of the Territories, RG 126, NA II. For 1939, see Annual Report of Hawaii Tourist Bureau for the Fiscal Year 1939–1940 to the Governor of Hawaii, Folder: 9-4-2 Reports-Annual-Hawaii Tourist Bureau, Box 564, Classified Files, 1907–1951, Office of the Territories, RG 126, NA II.

137. Ruth Hampton to George T. Armitage, December 20, 1939, Folder: 9-4-118 Tourist-Hawaii Tourist Bureau, Box 730, Central Classified Files, 1907–1951, Office of the Territories, RG 126, NA II. "In a war torn world," she added several weeks later, "Hawaii offers inducements to travelers." Ruth Hampton to George T. Armitage, February 2, 1940, Folder: 9-4-118 Tourist-Hawaii Tourist Bureau, Box 730, Central Classified Files, 1907–1951, Office of the Territories, RG 126, NA II.

138. Desmond, *Staging Tourism*, 129.

139. Press Release [?] from George T. Armitage, December 1, 1941, Folder: 9-4-118 Tourist-Hawaii Tourist Bureau, Box 730, Central Classified Files, 1907–1951, Office of the Territories, RG 126, NA II.

140. For details on lessons and rentals, see, for example, *Tourfax* 128 (Summer 1941), Folder: 9-4-118 Tourist-Hawaii Tourist Bureau, Box 730, Central Classified Files, 1907–1951, Office of the Territories, RG 126, NA II.

141. "The Royal Hawaiian Hotel in War and in Peace," [*Newsweek*'s Special Picture Review], n.d., Folder: 9-4-118-Tourist-Hawaii Visitors Bureau, Box 730, Central Classified Files, 1907–1951, Office of the Territories, RG 126, NA II. On the lease to the U.S. Navy, see "Resort History," www.royal-hawaiian.com/resort/history, accessed November 16, 2011.

142. "Waikiki Beckons Water Sport Fans," *Honolulu Advertiser*, February 22, 1948, TB, Box 1, HC, HL, UH. For more on tourism and war, see Richard Butler and Wantanee Suntikul, eds., *Tourism and War* (London: Routledge, 2013).

143. Don James, *Prewar Surfing Photographs* (Santa Barbara: T. Adler Books, 2004), 5. See also Don James, *Surfing San Onofre to Point Dume, 1936–1942* (San Francisco: Chronicle Books, 1996), 10.

144. See, for example, C. R. Stecyk, "Introduction: 1936 to 1942. Left of Eden," in James, *Surfing San Onofre to Point Dume*, 16.

145. Stecyk, "Introduction," 16; Warshaw, *The Encyclopedia of Surfing*, 679; and Peter Westwick and Peter Neushul, *The World in the Curl: An Unconventional History of Surfing* (New York: Crown Publishers, 2013), 81–102.

146. Warshaw, *The Encyclopedia of Surfing*, 693; Westwick and Neushul, *The World in the Curl*, 91–97; and advertisement for "Surf Shop," *The Surfer* 1, no. 1 (1960): 29.

147. For footage of the OSS personnel using the boards—though they appear to be doing so for reasons having more to do with pleasure than preparation—see "West Coast Schools Maritime Activities," Film 226.D.6089, RG 226, NA II.

148. "Newest for 'Frogmen': Underwater Surfboard," *Paramount News*, March 9, 1953, Film 200.PN.12.59, RG 200, NA II.

CHAPTER TWO

1. Brendan McAloon, introduction to *To the Four Corners of the World: The Lost Journals of the Original Surf Explorer*, by Peter Troy (Jan Juc, Victoria, Australia: Flying Pineapple Media, 2010), 15, 18–19, 22. Troy wrote in a July 1964 letter that it was "Hawaiians" who introduced the new board design to Australia. Troy, *To the Four Corners of the World*, 195.

2. Brandan McAloon, "World Tour: The Lost Journals of Peter Troy," *Surfer's Journal* 20, no. 4 (Summer 2011): 34.

3. "Peter Troy: Around the World on a Surfboard," *Surfer* 9, no. 3 (July 1968): 120.

4. "Peter Troy," *Times* (London), October 4, 2008.

5. Eugene Burdick, *The Ninth Wave* (Boston: Houghton Mifflin, 1956); Eugene Burdick and William J. Lederer, *The Ugly American* (New York: Norton, 1958); Eugene Burdick and Harvey Wheeler, *Fail-Safe* (New York: McGraw-Hill, 1962); and Tom Wolfe, *The Pump House Gang* (New York: Farrar, Straus & Giroux, 1968).

6. For more on the U.S. military in Hawai'i, see Brian Ireland, *The US Military in Hawai'i: Colonialism, Memory, and Resistance* (Houndmills, Basingstoke, UK: Palgrave Macmillan, 2011).

7. Matt Warshaw, *The Encyclopedia of Surfing* (Orlando: Harcourt, 2003), 86, 530, 679.

8. Troy, *To the Four Corners of the World*, 139.

9. Ibid., 34–35, 60–61.

10. Ibid., 42–43, 45.

11. Ibid., 50.

12. Ibid., 56, 59–60. Ellis would later speak out against surfing's relationship with South African apartheid; see chapter 4.

13. Rennie Ellis, "Odyssey of a Surfer," *Surfing World* 4, no. 1 (March–April 1964): 46, reprinted in Troy, *To the Four Corners of the World*, 64.

14. Troy, *To the Four Corners of the World*, 59.

15. Ibid., 92.

16. Ibid., 115.

17. Ibid., 117–18.

18. Ibid., 123–24, 126.

19. Ibid., 136–37.

20. Warshaw, *The Encyclopedia of Surfing*, 455.

21. Troy, *To the Four Corners of the World*, 144–45.

22. Ibid., 255.

23. Ibid., 256.

24. Ibid., 183.

25. Ibid., 208.

26. Kevin Lovett, quoted in Troy, *To the Four Corners of the World*, 342.

27. R. Paul Allen & Associates, "Documentary Surfing Film, 'The Endless Summer,' Scheduled for New York City Opening in June," News Release, n.d., Clippings File: *The Endless Summer*, Margaret Herrick Library [hereafter MHL], Academy of Motion Picture Arts and Sciences, Beverly Hills, California [hereafter AMPAS].

28. Allen Rich, "Surf Film Rides a Wave of Money," *Hollywood Citizen News*, July 6, 1969, Clippings File: Bruce Brown, MHL, AMPAS.

29. Ibid.

30. Ibid.

31. Andy Marx, "After 26 Endless Years, Surf's Up Again," *Los Angeles Times*, May 24, 1992.

32. Kevin E. Cullinane, "With a Wave from the Past, Surf's Still Up for 'Endless Summer's' Creator," *Washington Post*, September 2, 1991.

33. Velma West Sykes, "'The Endless Summer' (Cinema V) Wins Jan. Blue Ribbon Award," *Boxoffice Showmandiser* (February 13, 1967): 3, Clippings File: *The Endless Summer*, MHL, AMPAS.

34. "Surf's Up," *Time*, July 8, 1966, Clippings File: *The Endless Summer*, MHL, AMPAS; and Peter Bart, "Fellini of the Foam," *New York Times*, June 12, 1966, Clippings File: Bruce Brown, MHL, AMPAS.

35. Cullinane, "With a Wave from the Past."

36. My use of the term "subculture" to describe surfers is attributable to Steve Hawk, the former editor of *Surfer* magazine. *The Endless Summer* ended "the myth that we were all goateed Gilligans," he claimed. "It legitimized the sport of surfing and let people in middle America know about this subculture in Southern California." Cullinane, "With a Wave from the Past."

37. "WB's 'Down Staircase' Going to Fest in Moscow After Tortured Protocol on Subject Matter by State Dept.," *Variety*, May 17, 1967, Clippings File: Moscow Film Festival (1967), MHL, AMPAS; "Valenti to Head U.S. Moscow Fest Delegation," *Film Daily*, May 16, 1967, Clippings File: Moscow Film Festival (1967), MHL, AMPAS; Vincent Canby, "'Up the Down Staircase' Entered by U.S. in Moscow Film Festival," *New York Times*, May 16, 1967; and Vincent Canby, "Surfing Film Earns Its First Million," *New York Times*, June 13, 1967.

38. On tourism and the Cold War, see, for several examples, Christopher Endy, *Cold War Holidays: American Tourism in France* (Chapel Hill: University of North Carolina Press, 2004); Christina Klein, *Cold War Orientalism: Asia in the Middlebrow Imagination, 1945–1961* (Berkeley: University of California Press, 2003), 100–42; Scott Laderman, *Tours of Vietnam: War, Travel Guides, and Memory* (Durham, NC: Duke University Press, 2009), 15–45; and Dennis Merrill, *Negotiating Paradise:*

U.S. Tourism and Empire in Twentieth-Century Latin America (Chapel Hill: University of North Carolina Press, 2009).

39. U.S. Embassy in Moscow to the Secretary of State, May 31, 1967, Folder: MP 8, 1/1/67, Box 377, Central Foreign Policy Files, 1967–1969, Culture and Information [hereafter CFPF], Record Group [hereafter RG] 59, National Archives II, College Park, Maryland [hereafter NA II].

40. Department of State to U.S. Embassy in Moscow, June 3, 1967 ("For Marc Spiegel from Jack Valenti"), Folder: MP 9, 6/1/67, Box 378, CFPF, RG 59, NA II. The film was made by Robert Cohn, son and nephew of Columbia cofounders Jack and Harry Cohn, respectively. (The Cohns founded Columbia with Joe Brandt.)

41. U.S. Embassy in Moscow to Secretary of State, July 21, 1967, Folder: MP 8, 6/1/67, Box 377, CFPF, RG 59, NA II.

42. Report of the United States Delegation to the Fifth International Film Festival (Submitted by Jack Valenti to the Secretary of State), August 17, 1967, 7, Folder: MP 8, 8/1/67, Box 377, CFPF, RG 59, NA II. While barred from festival presentation, *The Young Americans* was shown by the American ambassador to the Soviet Union at Spaso House ("at the request of Mr. Robert Cohn of Columbia Pictures") for an audience "composed of Embassy officers, a few Soviet guests, the American press, and some members of the American delegation." U.S. Embassy in Moscow to Department of State, July 28, 1967, Airgram A-120, Folder: MP 8, 6/1/67, Box 377, CFPF, RG 59, NA II.

43. U.S. Embassy in Moscow to Secretary of State, July 21, 1967. In addition to the hundreds of thousands of viewers at the festival, the Soviets requested that a number of the American films be shown across the Soviet Union after the festival concluded. Foy D. Kohler to Jack Valenti, July 20, 1967, Folder: MP 8, 6/1/67, Box 377, CFPF, RG 59, NA II; see also U.S. Embassy in Moscow to Secretary of State, July 17, 1967, Folder: MP 8, 6/1/67, Box 377, CFPF, RG 59, NA II.

44. Jack Valenti to William Rogers, February 3, 1969, Folder: MP 8, 5/1/68, Box 377, CFPF, RG 59, NA II.

45. "US Pavilion: Fact Sheet," n.d., Folder: US PAVILION JAPAN WORLD EXPOSITION OSAKA 1970/PRESS KIT, Box 3, Entry #A1 1054-A: Files of the Press Office, 1967–1970 [hereafter A1 1054-A], Office of the Director/Osaka World Exhibition Office [hereafter OD/OWEO], RG 306, NA II; "Expo '70: Foreign and Domestic Participation," n.d., Folder: US PAVILION JAPAN WORLD EXPOSITION OSAKA 1970/PRESS KIT, Box 3, A1 1054-A, OD/OWEO, RG 306, NA II; Joy Hendry, *The Orient Strikes Back: A Global View of Cultural Display* (Oxford: Berg, 2000), 64–65; John R. Gold and Margaret M. Gold, *Cities of Culture: Staging International Festivals and the Urban Agenda, 1851–2000* (Burlington, VT: Ashgate Publishing Company, 2005), 133. An AP dispatch upon the fair's opening claimed that 77 nations were participating in Expo '70. John Roderick, Associated Press dispatch, n.d. [March 14, 1970?], Folder: EXH 8-1 Reaction Reports, Box 1, Entry #A1 1054-C: Files of the Japan and Washington Liaison Administrative Office, 1967–1972 [hereafter A1 1054-C], OD/OWEO, RG 306, NA II.

46. See, for several examples, Robert W. Rydell, *All the World's a Fair: Visions of Empire at American International Expositions, 1876–1916* (Chicago: University of Chicago Press, 1984); Rydell, *World of Fairs: The Century-of-Progress Expositions* (Chicago: University of Chicago Press, 1993); and Jack Masey and Conway Lloyd Morgan, *Cold War Confrontations: U.S. Exhibitions and Their Role in the Cultural Cold War* (Baden, Switzerland: Lars Müller, 2008).

47. Howard L. Chernoff to Frank Shakespeare, October 30, 1969, Folder: Design: Correspondence Gen., Box 7, Entry #A1 1054-B: Files of the Design Office, 1967–1972 [hereafter A1 1054-B], OD/OWEO, RG 306, NA II.

48. "World Expositions: US Participation," n.d., Folder: US PAVILION JAPAN WORLD EXPOSITION OSAKA 1970/PRESS KIT, Box 3, A1 1054-A, OD/OWEO, RG 306, NA II; "US Pavilion: Fact Sheet," n.d.

49. Michael Scott Moore, *Sweetness and Blood: How Surfing Spread from Hawaii and California to the Rest of the World, with Some Unexpected Results* (New York: Rodale, 2010), 296–300; Warshaw, *The Encyclopedia of Surfing*, 301.

50. "Surf Spots," *Surfer Quarterly* 3, no. 1 (Spring 1962): 14; P. A. Drips, "Surf Spots," *Surfer Bi-Monthly* 3, no. 4 (November–December 1962): 31; "Pipeline: Bruce Moves Fast," *Surfer Bi-Monthly* 5, no. 1 (February–March 1964): 40–41; Del Cannon, "Japan," *Surfer* 5, no. 3 (July 1964): 53–60. See also "Surf Spots," *Surfer Bi-Monthly* 4, no. 4 (August–September 1963): 56.

51. "Japan," *Petersen's Surfing Yearbook No. 3* (Los Angeles: Petersen Publishing Company, 1966), 52; Steve Perrin, "Japan: Land of Rising Surf," *Surfer* 9, no. 3 (July 1968): 132–39, 141, 143.

52. Warshaw, *The Encyclopedia of Surfing*, 301. Most of the surf shops were "surf-flavored boutiques," Warshaw noted. On the Japanese embrace of baseball, see especially Sayuri Guthrie-Shimizu, *Transpacific Field of Dreams: How Baseball Linked the United States and Japan in Peace and War* (Chapel Hill: University of North Carolina Press, 2012).

53. Moore, *Sweetness and Blood*, 303.

54. Jack Masey to Mary Kirkland, September 22, 1969, Folder: E6, SPORTS: Introductory Photo Panel, Box 3, A1 1054-B, OD/OWEO, RG 306, NA II; "Press Campaign/Sports Exhibits," n.d., Folder: P 1 General Policy, Plans, Box 1, A1 1054-A, OD/OWEO, RG 306, NA II. Surfing was not alone in its uniqueness, gadgetry, and polish. The Americans saw "[s]ky diving, . . . the gyrocopter, the dune buggy, the chromed motorcycle and the snomobile [*sic*]" as sharing these attributes.

55. "Sports Exhibit [Pat's Copy]," n.d., Folder: E 61, AMERICAN SPORTS/ GENERAL, Box 3, A1 1054-B, OD/OWEO, RG 306, NA II.

56. Patricia R. Ezell to Mr. Skora, December 4, 1969, Folder: E6, SPORTS: Films/Chaparos Productions Ltd., Box 3, A1 1054-B, OD/OWEO, RG 306, NA II; Nick [Chaparos?] to Pat Ezell, November 17, 1969, Folder: E6, SPORTS: Films/ Chaparos Productions Ltd., Box 3, A1 1054-B, OD/OWEO, RG 306, NA II.

57. "Sports Exhibit [Pat's Copy]," n.d.; "*Sports Illustrated* Photos for U.S. Pavilion," n.d., Folder: E6, SPORTS: Introductory Photo Panel, Box 3, A1 1054-B, OD/ OWEO, RG 306, NA II.

58. Jack Masey to Robert H. White, April 18, 1969, Folder: E6, Bob White Surfboards, Box 4, A1 1054-B, OD/OWEO, RG 306, NA II; Notes on "Hawaiian Boards," n.d., Folder: C, SPORTS—Surfboards/Dewey Weber, Inc., Box 4, A1 1054-B, OD/OWEO, RG 306, NA II; "Office Research: Surfboards," n.d., Folder: C, SPORTS—Surfboards/Dewey Weber, Inc., Box 4, A1 1054-B, OD/OWEO, RG 306, NA II.

59. Henry Loomis to USPAV EXPO, June 11, 1970, Folder: P2, GENERAL REPORTS (Reaction report—USPAV), Box 1, A1 1054-A, OD/OWEO, RG 306, NA II. On praise for the sports exhibit in particular, see, for a number of examples, Howard L. Chernoff to Frank Shakespeare, March 12, 1970, Folder: P2, GENERAL REPORTS—Press Preview (3/10/70)/Media Reaction, Box 1, A1 1054-A, OD/OWEO, RG 306, NA II; Howard L. Chernoff to USIA [2 of 3], June 12, 1970, Folder: P2, GENERAL REPORTS (Reaction report—USPAV), Box 1, A1 1054-A, OD/OWEO, RG 306, NA II; "Exhibits [Excerpts from Press]," n.d., Folder: PR13, Public Opinion (Criticisms, commendations), Box 7, A1 1054-A, OD/OWEO, RG 306, NA II; the attachments to Howard L. Chernoff to Henry H. Gosho, n.d., Folder: PR13, Public Opinion (Criticisms, commendations), Box 7, A1 1054-A, OD/OWEO, RG 306, NA II; Durward G. Hall [O. K. Armstrong], "America's Exhibit at the World's Fair," *Congressional Record*, April 23, 1970, E3492, Folder: Press Clippings Regarding U.S. Pavilion—Misc., Box 8, A1 1054-A, OD/OWEO, RG 306, NA II; and Mike Schaefer to Frank Shakespeare, July 28, 1970, Folder: EXH 8-1, Reactions—Criticism/Public, Box 1, A1 1054-C, OD/OWEO, RG 306, NA II.

60. Chernoff to Shakespeare, March 12, 1970; Hall, "America's Exhibit at the World's Fair," April 23, 1970; Schaefer to Shakespeare, July 28, 1970.

61. Don Shannon [Los Angeles Times Service], "America's Bag Is the Hit of Expo," *Honolulu Advertiser*, March 12, 1970, Folder: PR13, Public Opinion & Inquiries, Box 7, A1 1054-A, OD/OWEO, RG 306, NA II.

62. Judith B. Calhoun, "Disappointed with U.S. Pavilion," Letter to the Editor, *Japan Times*, June 18, 1970. The missive, and a number of responses taking issue with her criticism, are attached to Charles M. Magee to Howard E. Stingle, July 2, 1970, Folder: PR13, Public Opinion (Criticisms, commendations), Box 7, A1 1054-A, OD/OWEO, RG 306, NA II.

63. Barbara B. Triggs to Richard Nixon, October 22, 1970, Folder: EXH 8-1, Reactions—Criticism/Public, Box 1, A1 1054-C, OD/OWEO, RG 306, NA II.

64. Fred J. Haupt to Richard Nixon, May 19, 1970, Folder: EXH 8-1, Reactions—Criticism/Public, Box 1, A1 1054-C, OD/OWEO, RG 306, NA II. The three singers, according to the USIA, were a graduate engineer in electronics working for the U.S. Navy, a representative of a textbook company who makes his own guitars and lectures on American songs and folklore, and the Harvard-educated aerospace editor for *Science* magazine. Robert H. Leeper to Mrs. Robert G. Claney, August 13, 1970, Folder: EXH 8-1, Reactions—Criticism/Public, Box 1, A1 1054-C, OD/OWEO, RG 306, NA II.

65. Howard L. Chernoff to USIA [3 of 3], June 12, 1970, Folder: P2, GENERAL REPORTS (Reaction report—USPAV), Box 1, A1 1054-A, OD/OWEO, RG 306, NA II.

66. Chernoff to USIA [3 of 3], June 12, 1970.

67. Roderick, Associated Press dispatch, n.d.

68. Tamio Katori to Representative of the Government of the United States of America at Expo '70, June 25, 1970, Folder: Disposition: Agency Owned, Box 1, A1 1054-B, OD/OWEO, RG 306, NA II. On Katori's in-person request, see Patricia R. Ezell to Phil Rogers, August 13, 1970, Folder: Disposition: Agency Owned, Box 1, A1 1054-B, OD/OWEO, RG 306, NA II.

69. Naughton and Peterson published contemporaneous accounts of their ten-year journey in *Surfer* magazine. More recently they have been the subject of a documentary film; see *The Far Shore* (Soul Carvers Productions, 2003).

70. "It's Time to Reinvigorate the Spirit of Youth on the Run," Foreword, *Surfing* 46, no. 2 (February 2010): 8.

71. Bonnie Tsui, "Surfers Are Here! El Salvador Sheds Its Image," *New York Times*, September 13, 2009.

72. Joseph Heath and Andrew Potter, *Nation of Rebels: Why Counterculture Became Consumer Culture* (New York: HarperBusiness, 2004), 271.

73. Frank Hine, "Viet Nam Surfer," *Surfer* 7, no. 3 (July 1966): 21; "Viet Nam Surfing," *Surfer* 7, no. 3 (July 1966): 102, 104. One sailor, Terry Ogden, reported riding waves (on "three or four tapered bamboo strips" tied into a "spoon-shaped raft") near Danang in 1962. "Surf Spots," *Surfer Bi-Monthly* 3, no. 4 (October–November 1962): 30.

74. "Viet Contest," *Surfer* 8, no. 1 (March 1967): 74. *Surfer*, citing an Associated Press story, spelled the winner's name "Brinkley." A photograph of the surfer and others in the National Archives II spells the name "Binkley."

75. "Viet Competition," *Surfer* 8, no. 4 (September 1967): 85; "More Boards to Viet Nam," *Surfer* 7, no. 5 (November 1966): 79.

76. See, for example, the archival footage of military personnel surfing at Danang, Cam Ranh Bay, and Vung Tau in Film 111.LC.55979, RG 111, NA II; and Film 111.LC.56875, RG 111, NA II. See also *Between the Lines* (Pure Frustration Productions, 2008), as well as the satirical piece "A Little Slice of Surfing Paradise," *Surfer* 9, no. 3 (July 1968): 74–75. For more on surfing and other beach activities as a component of the military's war on boredom in Vietnam, see Meredith H. Lair, *Armed with Abundance: Consumerism and Soldiering in the Vietnam War* (Chapel Hill: University of North Carolina Press, 2011), 112–20, 193.

77. "Ding Repair and the War Effort," *Surfer* 10, no. 6 (January 1970): 99. On the military's guidebooks to Vietnam, see Laderman, *Tours of Vietnam*, 47–85.

78. James H. Maxon to COMUSMACV [Commander U.S. Military Assistance Command Vietnam], "VC Use of Surfboards," June 27, 1967, Folder 2164, Box 144, Vietnam Archive Collection, Vietnam Archive, Texas Tech University.

79. In addition to *Apocalypse Now*, Milius was the screenwriter for, among other projects, the first two Dirty Harry movies, and he directed *Conan the Barbarian* (1982) and half a dozen other films.

80. For more on *Big Wednesday*, see *Big Wednesday Redux* (TSJ [*The Surfer's Journal*] e-book, vol. 1.6, 2012).

81. Stephen G. Rabe, *The Killing Zone: The United States Wages Cold War in Latin America* (New York: Oxford University Press, 2012), 165.

82. "Gozzup," *Tracks* 82 (July 1977): 11.

83. "Pipeline: The Hawaiian Grapevine," *Surfer* 21, no. 8 (August 1980): 88.

CHAPTER THREE

1. The nature of the events of September 30 remains a matter of dispute. On problems with characterizing what transpired as a coup attempt, which is how it has often been characterized in the years since 1965, see Bradley R. Simpson, *Economists with Guns: Authoritarian Development and U.S.-Indonesian Relations, 1960–1968* (Stanford, CA: Stanford University Press, 2008), 173. Most of the details of my account draw from Simpson's invaluable study. An important earlier examination of U.S. complicity can be found in Geoffrey Robinson, *The Dark Side of Paradise: Political Violence in Bali* (Ithaca, NY: Cornell University Press, 1995), 282–86.

2. Simpson, *Economists with Guns*, 172. Simpson identifies "anti-Muslim organizations" as being among the perpetrators on page 172, but this appears to be a typo, as his work elsewhere in the book makes clear that it was Muslim, rather than anti-Muslim, organizations that sought to destroy the PKI; see, for example, page 187. Elements of the exterminationist campaign are explored in various essays in Robert Cribb, ed., *The Indonesian Killings of 1965–1966: Studies from Java and Bali*, Monash Papers on Southeast Asia, no. 21 (Clayton, Victoria, Australia: Centre of Southeast Asian Studies, Monash University, 1990).

3. "Indonesia: Vengeance with a Smile," *Time* 88, no. 3 (July 15, 1966): 22, 26. Indonesia, *Time* declared triumphantly on its cover, was "The Land the Communists Lost."

4. Amnesty International, *Political Killings by Governments* (London: Amnesty International Publications, 1983), 36; Robert Cribb, "Genocide in Indonesia, 1965–1966," *Journal of Genocide Research* 3, no. 2 (June 2001): 233.

5. Simpson, *Economists with Guns*, 191.

6. Amnesty International, *Political Killings by Governments*, 36.

7. Robert Cribb, "How Many Deaths? Problems in the Statistics of Massacre in Indonesia (1965–1966) and East Timor (1975–1980)," in *Violence in Indonesia*, ed. Ingrid Wessel and Georgia Wimhöfer (Hamburg: Abera, 2001), 91. See also Annie Pohlman, "Spectacular Atrocities: Making Enemies during the 1965–1966 Massacres in Indonesia," in *Theatres of Violence: Massacre, Mass Killing, and Atrocity Throughout History*, ed. Philip G. Dwyer and Lyndall Ryan (New York: Berghahn Books, 2012), 199–212.

8. Amnesty International, *Political Killings by Governments*, 36. See also Cribb, "Genocide in Indonesia," 236.

9. Geoffrey Robinson, *"If You Leave Us Here, We Will Die": How Genocide Was Stopped in East Timor* (Princeton, NJ: Princeton University Press, 2010), 6–7. The precise number of deaths and detentions remains unknown. Most scholars conservatively place the figure killed at approximately 500,000. Benedict Anderson suggested that it was "at least 600,000 and perhaps as many as two million." Benedict R. O'G. Anderson, introduction to *Violence and the State in Suharto's Indonesia*, ed. Benedict R. O'G. Anderson, Studies on Southeast Asia No. 30 (Ithaca, NY: Southeast Asia Program Publications, Cornell University, 2001), 9. Leslie Dwyer and Degung Santikarma believed the total to be higher than half a million given their research into "the important role that extramilitary killings played in Bali." Leslie Dwyer and Degung Santikarma, " 'When the World Turned to Chaos': 1965 and Its Aftermath in Bali, Indonesia," in *The Specter of Genocide: Mass Murder in Historical Perspective*, ed. Robert Gellately and Ben Kiernan (Cambridge: Cambridge University Press, 2003), 290–91 (note 2). Brad Simpson wrote that "[a]t least 1 million" were arrested. Simpson, *Economists with Guns*, 192.

10. Central Intelligence Agency, *Indonesia—1965: The Coup That Backfired*, Research Study, December 1968, 71, www.foia.cia.gov/sites/default/files/document_conversions/14/esau-40.pdf, accessed January 26, 2010. Amnesty International concluded that the atrocities "rank among the most massive violations of human rights since the Second World War." Amnesty International, *Political Killings by Governments*, 34.

11. Simpson, *Economists with Guns*, 189. Simpson added, "Washington did everything in its power to encourage and facilitate the army-led massacre of alleged PKI members, and U.S. officials worried only that the killing of the party's unarmed supporters might not go far enough, permitting Sukarno to return to power and frustrate the [Johnson] administration's emerging plans for a post-Sukarno Indonesia." Ibid., 193.

12. For an important introduction to the politics of the mass media, including which atrocities enjoy the close scrutiny of the American press, see Edward S. Herman and Noam Chomsky, *Manufacturing Consent: The Political Economy of the Mass Media* (New York: Pantheon Books, 1988).

13. Peter Arnett, "Indonesia: The Spice Islands Open Their Doors," in *Fodor's Guide to Japan and East Asia 1967*, ed. Eugene Fodor and Robert C. Fisher (New York: David McKay Company, 1967), 719.

14. Bill Dalton, *Indonesia Handbook* (Franklin Village, MI: Moon Publications, 1977), 11.

15. Ginny Bruce, Mary Covernton, and Alan Samagalski, *Indonesia: A Travel Survival Kit* (South Yarra, Victoria, Australia: Lonely Planet Publications, 1986), 27–29. The heading in the first edition was "The Abortive Coup and the Slaughter of the Communists"; in the second edition, it was simply "The Slaughter of the Communists." Joe Cummings, Susan Forsyth, John Noble, Alan Samagalski, and Tony Wheeler, *Indonesia: A Travel Survival Kit*, 2nd ed. (Hawthorn, Victoria, Australia:

Lonely Planet Publications, 1990), 27. Indonesia had earlier been covered in the publisher's guidebook to Southeast Asia, and in 1983 it produced a guidebook to Bali and Lombok. That 1983 volume's "Facts about Bali" section mentioned the "wholesale massacre of suspected communists throughout the archipelago, events which Bali was in the thick of." Mary Covernton and Tony Wheeler, *Bali & Lombok: A Travel Survival Kit* (South Yarra, Victoria, Australia: Lonely Planet Publications, 1983), 13.

16. Bruce, Covernton, and Samagalski, *Indonesia*, 563–65.

17. Dalton, *Indonesia Handbook*, 13. On the "pilfering" by Indonesia of East Timor, see ibid., 230. Lonely Planet wrote of the Indonesian government's "democratic veneer" and noted that "Suharto's government rests squarely on a foundation of military power," with opposition either already "eliminated" or currently "suppressed and muted." Bruce, Covernton, and Samagalski, *Indonesia*, 30–31.

18. See, for example, Noam Chomsky and Edward S. Herman, *The Political Economy of Human Rights*, vol. 1, *The Washington Connection and Third World Fascism* (Boston: South End Press, 1979), 129–217.

19. Leonard Lueras, *Surfing: The Ultimate Pleasure* (New York: Workman Publishing, 1984), 197. Those "rare occasion[s]," he wrote, were "when surfers have experienced incidents of unreasonable racism or 'this is my surf' territoriality." For the first edition (there have been several) of Lueras's guidebook to surfing in Indonesia, see Leonard Lueras and Lorca Lueras, *Fielding's Surfing Indonesia: A Guide to the World's Greatest Surfing* (Redondo Beach, CA: Periplus Editions/Fielding Worldwide, 1996). For biographical information on Lueras, see Lueras and Lueras, *Fielding's Surfing Indonesia*, 298; and Matt Warshaw, *The Encyclopedia of Surfing* (Orlando: Harcourt, 2003), 349.

20. For a collective statement published in the *Honolulu Star-Bulletin* by a number of well-known surfers protesting the "resumed bombings and continued war on Vietnam," see, for example, "Pipeline: Flashes and Freebies," *Surfer* 14, no. 1 (May 1973): 69.

21. Phil Jarratt, "The Wit and Wisdom of Surfers; or, The Complete Book of Bullshit," *Tracks* 96 (September 1978): 15.

22. Adrian Vickers, *Bali: A Paradise Created* (Berkeley: Periplus Editions, 1989), 2–3.

23. Ibid., 175. On the origins of the Suharto regime's tourism planning during the massacres of 1965 and 1966, see Adrian H. Vickers, "Selling the Experience of Bali, 1950–1971" (Wollongong, New South Wales: Centre for Asia Pacific Social Transformation Studies, University of Wollongong, 2001), 3, 18–19. I am grateful to Adrian Vickers for furnishing me with a copy of this paper.

24. Bradley R. Simpson, "Normalizing Suharto's Indonesia: Development, Tourism, and Crafts in Bali," paper presented at the annual meeting of the Society for Historians of American Foreign Relations, Hartford, Connecticut, June 29, 2012. I am indebted to Brad Simpson for providing me with a copy of this paper.

25. For more on this shift in Indonesian policy, see Simpson, *Economists with Guns*, 207–48.

26. U.S. Embassy in Jakarta to Secretary of State, January 23, 1969, Folder: TP INDON 1/1/67, Box 1472, Central Foreign Policy Files, 1967–1969, Economic, Record Group [hereafter RG] 59, National Archives II, College Park, Maryland [hereafter NA II]. On the heightened Indonesian-Singaporean tensions over the latter's execution of two Indonesian marines that led to Jones's invited intervention, see U.S. Embassy in Jakarta to Department of State, December 3, 1968, Airgram A-877, Folder: TP INDON 1/1/67, Box 1472, Central Foreign Policy Files, 1967–1969, Economic, RG 59, NA II. This latter document also mentions the Singaporean technical mission of April–May 1968.

27. Transcript of a radio speech by Dr. Goh Keng Swee, Minister of Finance of Singapore, April 16, 1968. The transcript is an attachment to a memorandum from the Director for Indonesia of Pan American Airways to its Vice President of International Affairs, August 6, 1968, Folder 16 (Singapore/Indonesia Cooperative Tourism Project, 1968), Box 427, Accession II (SC), Pan American World Airways, Inc. Records, Special Collections, Otto Richter Library, University of Miami.

28. U.S. Embassy in Jakarta to Department of State, November 9, 1968, Airgram A-846, Folder: TP INDON 1/1/67, Box 1472, Central Foreign Policy Files, 1967–1969, Economic, RG 59, NA II.

29. Vickers, *Bali*, 186.

30. Warshaw, *The Encyclopedia of Surfing*, 288. For a personal account of the experiences of Robert Koke and Louise Garrett (who would later marry Koke) as hoteliers in Bali, see Louise G. Koke, *Our Hotel in Bali: How Two Young Americans Made a Dream Come True: A Story of the 1930s* (Wellington: January Books, 1987).

31. David Elfick, "Paradise Found?" *Tracks* 35 (August 1973): 13. While not all of them were surfers—many were hippie travelers backpacking through Asia—the number of tourists frequenting Kuta increased "from less than a thousand in 1970 to nearly 15,000 in 1973," according to Michel Picard. Michel Picard, *Bali: Cultural Tourism and Touristic Culture*, trans. Diana Darling (Singapore: Archipelago Press, 1996), 78.

32. Lopez quoted in *Chasing the Lotus: The Lost Reels of Weaver and Wills* (2006).

33. Warshaw, *The Encyclopedia of Surfing*, 38, 289.

34. On the timing of the Indonesia trip, see Albert Falzon, "The Surfers," *Surfer* 13, no. 3 (September 1972): 68.

35. Alex Leonard has written that Uluwatu was first ridden by Australian and American surfers "in the early 1970s." Alex Leonard, "*Ombak Besar, Hati Besar, Orang Besar*: The Kuta Surfing Tradition and Its Heroes, 1969–2001" (PhD diss., Australian National University, 2006), 125, 131. Matt Warshaw, conversely, has suggested that the break was "almost certainly ridden in the late '60s by visiting American and Australian GIs." Warshaw, *The Encyclopedia of Surfing*, 659.

36. Neil Stebbins, "Uluwatu," *Surfer* 15, no. 6 (March 1975): 37. Some surfers would later declare, as did Stephen Spaulding in *Bali High* (1980), that Uluwatu was "often overrated."

37. On Bali as a "primitive Asian culture," see the advertisement for *Morning of the Earth* in *Surfer* 13, no. 4 (November 1972): 13. The name of the film borrows from Jawaharlal Nehru's reference to Bali as the "morning of the world."

38. Undoubtedly the most celebrated film is Bruce Brown's *The Endless Summer* (1966).

39. Duke Boyd, "Notes on Ulu," *Surfer* 15, no. 6 (March 1975): 42.

40. Robinson, *The Dark Side of Paradise*, xii.

41. Ibid., 1. Others have estimated the number killed on Bali to be closer to 100,000; see, for example, Dwyer and Santikarma, " 'When the World Turned to Chaos,' " 293.

42. Vickers, *Bali*, 9.

43. Robinson, *The Dark Side of Paradise*, 1. For Robinson's more detailed analysis of the atrocities in Bali, see ibid., 273–303.

44. Star Black, *Guide to Bali: Official Guide to the Island of Bali* (Sanur: Hotel Bali Beach Corporation, 1970), 2, 4, 12–13.

45. Robinson, *The Dark Side of Paradise*, 304.

46. "Timeless Land," *Tracks* 47 (August 1974): 14.

47. Neil Stebbins, "Uluwatu," *Surfer* 15, no. 6 (March 1975): 38, 40.

48. Ibid., 41.

49. Steve Shamison, "Maybe Someone's Trying to Tell Us Something," *Tracks* 50 (November 1974): 8.

50. Boyd, "Notes on Ulu," 43.

51. Advertisement for Qantas, *Tracks* 80 (May 1977): 12.

52. Boyd, "Notes on Ulu," 43.

53. Stebbins, "Uluwatu," 41.

54. Jeff Divine, "Uluwatu—Evil Waters," *Surfer* 17, no. 5 (January 1977): 65. Divine may have been referring to Grajagan, a now-fabled left in eastern Java; the "king," in this formulation, would presumably have been Suharto.

55. Bill Dalton, "Asia," *Tracks* 40 (January 1974): 17. Indonesia, proclaimed travel publisher Fielding, was "surfing's last frontier." Lueras and Lueras, *Fielding's Surfing Indonesia*, front cover.

56. Michael Fay, "Island Trips," *Tracks* 35 (August 1973): 13.

57. The spot was Lagundri Bay, a celebrated wave on the island of Nias off the west coast of Sumatra.

58. Erik Aeder, "Indonesia: Dream Wave Discoveries in the World's Largest Tropical Archipelago," *Surfer* 20, no. 3 (March 1979): 68.

59. Warshaw, *The Encyclopedia of Surfing*, 411. The film *ULU 32: 32 Years Surfing Indonesia* (2003) claims that the break was "first surfed" in 1974.

60. Aeder, "Indonesia," 77, 80, 82.

61. Ibid., 80–81.

62. While the Ford administration continued to provide Jakarta with considerable sums of military aid in the 1970s, support in the United States was not universal. A number of legislators grew frustrated with the human rights situation in Indonesia and the administration's failure, despite language adopted by Congress, to "sub-

stantially reduce or terminate security assistance to any country which engages in a consistent pattern of gross violations of human rights." Indonesia, witnesses testified, was among these gross violators. Representative Don Fraser, quoted in *Hearings before the Subcommittee on International Organizations of the House Committee on International Relations, Human Rights in Indonesia and the Philippines*, 94th Congress, December 18, 1975, and May 3, 1976 (Washington, DC: Government Printing Office, 1976), 1.

63. Aeder, "Indonesia," 77, 80; Amnesty International, *Indonesia: An Asian Gulag* (San Francisco: Amnesty International, Western Regional Office, 1976).

64. Amnesty International, *Indonesia: An Amnesty International Report* (London: Amnesty International Publications, 1977), 9. See also Amnesty International, Dutch Section, "Numbers! Numbers! Numbers!" *Indonesia Special* (Amsterdam: Amnesty International, Dutch Section, 1973), 13.

65. Amnesty International, *The Amnesty International Report 1975–1976* (London: Amnesty International Publications, 1976), 136–37.

66. Ibid., 136.

67. Hearings before the Subcommittee on International Organizations of the House Committee on International Relations, *Human Rights in Indonesia and the Philippines*, 9–10. The letter was introduced by Carmel Budiardjo, herself a former political prisoner and the founder of the human rights organization TAPOL. On the State Department's dismissive view of Budiardjo as a onetime British Communist married to an Indonesian Communist and as having past ties to "Communist front organization[s]" in Czechoslovakia and Indonesia, see Department of State, Report Submitted to the House Committee on International Relations, *Human Rights Practices in Countries Receiving U.S. Security Assistance*, 95th Congress, 1st sess., April 25, 1977 (Washington, DC: Government Printing Office, 1977), 9–10. Budiardjo's Communist affiliations led to her testimony being challenged in the House subcommittee hearing in 1975. Representative Wayne Hays, who was not a member of the subcommittee, explicitly questioned her honesty, noting that "the lady is a member of the Communist Party" and that he was familiar with "their reputation for veracity." Hearings before the Subcommittee on International Organizations of the House Committee on International Relations, *Human Rights in Indonesia and the Philippines*, 11. On criticism by Budiardjo and Benedict Anderson, then the associate director of the Cornell Modern Indonesia Project at Cornell University, of the State Department's reporting on human rights in Indonesia, see Hearings before the Subcommittee on International Organizations of the House Committee on International Relations, *Human Rights in Indonesia and the Philippines*, 5, 71.

68. Amnesty International, *Amnesty International Report 1978* (London: Amnesty International Publications, 1979), 162.

69. Dalton, "Asia," 17. Dalton authored numerous editions of the *Indonesia Handbook* first published in 1977 by Moon, the travel publishing company he founded that would over time produce dozens of guidebooks to destinations around the world. But even before then his *Indonesia: A Traveller's Notes*, a self-published

guide for "road freaks & the very very frugal" that first appeared in 1973, was selling hundreds of copies. Bill Dalton, *Indonesia: A Traveller's Notes* (Glebe, New South Wales: Tomato Press/Moon Publications, 1974), 2. For Dalton's recollection of his early publication history, see "Bill Dalton," *Rolf Potts' Vagabonding* (February 2003), www.rolfpotts.com/writers/dalton.html, accessed April 11, 2010.

70. Brad Simpson, " 'Illegally and Beautifully': The United States, the Indonesian Invasion of East Timor and the International Community, 1974–76," *Cold War History* 5, no. 3 (August 2005): 290.

71. Brad Simpson, ed., *A Quarter Century of U.S. Support for Occupation*, National Security Archive Electronic Briefing Book No. 174 (November 28, 2005), www.gwu.edu/%7Ensarchiv/NSAEBB/NSAEBB174/index.htm, accessed March 16, 2010. I am indebted to the work of Brad Simpson in bringing a number of important sources to my attention.

72. Monsignor Martinho da Costa Lopez, quoted in Adam Schwarz, *A Nation in Waiting: Indonesia's Search for Stability* (Boulder: Westview Press, 2000), 204.

73. Matthew Jardine, *East Timor: Genocide in Paradise* (Tucson: Odonian Press, 1995), 31. "Matthew Jardine" was the pen name of Joseph Nevins, the author of *A Not-So-Distant Horror: Mass Violence in East Timor* (Ithaca, NY: Cornell University Press, 2005).

74. Embassy in Jakarta to the Secretary of State, December 6, 1975, in William Burr and Michael L. Evans, eds., *East Timor Revisited: Ford, Kissinger and the Indonesian Invasion, 1975–76*, National Security Archive Electronic Briefing Book No. 62 (December 6, 2001), www.gwu.edu/~nsarchiv/NSAEBB/NSAEBB62/index.html, accessed March 15, 2010. On Kissinger's repeated denials that Washington gave Jakarta a "green light," see "Confronting Henry Kissinger," *Network News* [East Timor Action Network/U.S.] 12 (November 1995): 10; and the transcript of a WNYC radio interview with Kissinger, http://etan.org/news/kissinger/radio.htm, accessed March 16, 2010.

75. James Dunn, "The Timor Affair in International Perspective," in *East Timor at the Crossroads: The Forging of a Nation*, ed. Peter Carey and G. Carter Bentley (Honolulu: University of Hawai'i Press, 1995), 66.

76. Schwarz, *A Nation in Waiting*, 205.

77. Robinson, *"If You Leave Us Here, We Will Die,"* 2; Ben Kiernan, "The Demography of Genocide in Southeast Asia: The Death Tolls in Cambodia, 1975–79, and East Timor, 1975–80," *Critical Asian Studies* 35, no. 4 (December 2003): 594. Kiernan calculated the death toll from 1975 to 1980 to be approximately 150,000 people. Kiernan, "The Demography of Genocide in Southeast Asia," 593–94. Elsewhere, however, he offered that same figure for the period from 1975 to 1999; see Ben Kiernan, "War, Genocide, and Resistance in East Timor, 1975–99: Comparative Reflections on Cambodia," in *War and State Terrorism: The United States, Japan, and the Asia-Pacific in the Long Twentieth Century*, ed. Mark Selden and Alvin Y. So (Lanham, MD: Rowman & Littlefield Publishers, 2004), 200.

78. Amnesty International, *East Timor: Violations of Human Rights: Extrajudicial Executions, 'Disappearances,' Torture and Political Imprisonment, 1975–1984*

(London: Amnesty International Publications, 1985), 6. John G. Taylor concluded that "at least 200,000 East Timorese" died as a result of the Indonesian occupation. John G. Taylor, "'Encirclement and Annihilation': The Indonesian Occupation of East Timor," in *The Specter of Genocide*, ed. Gellately and Kiernan, 163.

79. Kiernan, "The Demography of Genocide in Southeast Asia," 585.

80. Arnold Kohen and John Taylor, *An Act of Genocide: Indonesia's Invasion of East Timor* (London: TAPOL, 1979).

81. See, for several examples, James Dunn, "Genocide in East Timor," in *Century of Genocide: Critical Essays and Eyewitness Accounts*, 2nd ed., ed. Samuel Totten, William S. Parsons, and Israel W. Charny (New York: Routledge, 2004), 263–93; Kiernan, "War, Genocide, and Resistance in East Timor, 1975–1999," 199–233; Robinson, *"If You Leave Us Here, We Will Die"*; Nina Silove, "Genocide in East Timor," in *Genocide Perspectives II: Essays on Holocaust and Genocide*, ed. Colin Tatz, Peter Arnold, and Sandra Tatz (Sydney: Brandl & Schlesinger/Australian Institute for Holocaust and Genocide Studies, 2003), 216–42; and Taylor, "'Encirclement and Annihilation,'" 163–85. For a dissenting view, at least in the context of extant international law, see Ben Saul, "Was the Conflict in East Timor 'Genocide' and Why Does It Matter?" *Melbourne Journal of International Law* 2, no. 2 (October 2001): 477–522. I am grateful to Robert Cribb, Craig Etcheson, Rowan Savage, Colin Tatz, and Sam Totten for bringing a number of sources on East Timor to my attention.

82. Henry Kissinger to Gerald Ford, ca. November 21, 1975, in Simpson, ed., *A Quarter Century of U.S. Support for Occupation*, www.gwu.edu/%7Ensarchiv /NSAEBB/NSAEBB174/index.htm, accessed March 16, 2010. For an excellent examination of how the West's position on East Timor was rooted not only in Cold War fears but also in concerns about regional instability and Timorese primitivism, see Simpson, "'Illegally and Beautifully,'" 281–315.

83. Daniel Patrick Moynihan (with Suzanne Weaver), *A Dangerous Place* (Boston: Little, Brown, 1978), 247; *Chega! Final Report of the Commission for Reception, Truth and Reconciliation in East Timor (CAVR)* (Commission for Reception, Truth and Reconciliation Timor-Leste, 2005), Part 8, Annex 1, 91–92, www.etan. org/news/2006/cavr.htm, accessed March 16, 2010.

84. *Chega!*, Part 8, Annex 1, 91.

85. Simpson, "'Illegally and Beautifully,'" 286.

86. *Chega!*, Part 8, Annex 1, 90.

87. Peter Neely, *Indo Surf and Lingo: Hardcore Surf Explorer's Guide to Indonesian Surf Spots and Indonesian Language*, 3rd ed. (Noosa Heads, Queensland: Indo Surf & Lingo, 1993), 35. Neely offered this counsel jointly of "Sumba, Timor & Irian Jaya." He did not distinguish between the islands (or the different parts of the islands), but it is likely that he was not particularly optimistic about the surf potential in East Timor; its limited exposure to decent swell did not suggest abundant possibilities. Nevertheless, it is worth acknowledging Neely's casual assumption—implied by his use of "Sumba, Timor & Irian Jaya"—that both East Timor and Irian Jaya (or West Papua) were legitimately part of Indonesia. For a

report in the *New York Times* listing East Timor as one of several destinations for more adventurous boat-tripping surfers, see Matt Higgins, "Surf's Up, and Upscale, as Sport Reverses Its Beach Bum Image," *New York Times*, February 11, 2007. At roughly the same time that Neely published the third edition of his surfing guidebook, Paul Ryan produced *Timor: A Traveller's Guide*. Ryan's book is not intended for surfers, but it is worth noting the salvific potential he saw in tourism for the Timorese people. "Even at the height of the war in 1976," he wrote in a preface, "less than one third of the island actually saw any fighting. Today, the guerilla force is spent, the leaders are in jail or overseas and life is desperately trying to get back to 'normal.' To try and trivialize the events of the past would be heartless but to ignore the benefits of peace and tourism would be criminal. Like most wars, the Timor question is more about economics than ideology and, in the long run, the interest of the people of Timor is in a secure and healthy lifestyle for themselves and their children rather than in the vagaries of political point scoring. I believe the tourist dollar and the impact of tourists will help the Timorese people more quickly achieve this goal than any amount of guns, politics or sympathetic leanings. A good comparison might be the present situation in Vietnam. There the previously anti-Western, Marxist government is inviting foreign tourists in to try and bolster a battered economy. The opening of East Timor to tourists in 1989 by the Indonesian government was with a similar intention. It may not be everyone's cup of tea but for those that do make the effort, I personally believe that the variety of Timorese life, the startling beauty of Timor's landscape and the warm friendliness of the Timorese people will be reward enough in itself. An added bonus is that you will actively help a land that is crying out for International assistance." Paul Ryan, *Timor: A Traveller's Guide* (Darwin, Northern Territory, Australia: Paul Ryan, 1993), 5. On East Timor contemporaneously remaining "a place where arbitrary detention and torture are routine and where basic freedoms of expression, association[,] and assembly are non-existent," see Human Rights Watch/Asia, *The Limits of Openness: Human Rights in Indonesia and East Timor* (New York: Human Rights Watch, 1994), 21–39; the quote is on page 21.

88. Bill Finnegan and Bryan Di Salvatore, "Notes from the Paradise Trail: Part 1," *Tracks* 109 (October 1979): 38.

89. Dick Hoole, "Indonesia: Sure to Please Ya," *Tracks* 106 (July 1979): 6–7. Hoole's comment about Indonesia as a "playground" was written as a specific reference to Australian surfers.

90. Phil Abraham, "Indonesia Needs You!" *Tracks* 119 (August 1980): 5.

91. Ibid.

92. Mário Carrascalão, "Interview with Mário Carrascalão," *Indonesia* 76 (October 2003): 5 (note 18).

93. For more on the Balibo Five—Gary Cunningham, Brian Peters, Malcolm Rennie, Greg Shackleton, and Tony Stewart—as well as Roger East, a sixth journalist killed by the Indonesians shortly afterward, see, among others, Desmond Ball and Hamish McDonald, *Death in Balibo, Lies in Canberra* (St. Leonards, New South Wales: Allen & Unwin, 2000); Jill Jolliffe, *Balibo* (Melbourne: Scribe Publi-

cations, 2009); Jolliffe, *Cover-Up: The Inside Story of the Balibo Five* (Melbourne: Scribe Publications, 2001); Tony Maniaty, *Shooting Balibo: Blood and Memory in East Timor* (Camberwell, Victoria: Viking/Penguin, 2009); Tom Sherman, *Report on the Deaths of Australian-Based Journalists in East Timor in 1975* (Canberra: Department of Foreign Affairs, June 1996); and Sherman, *Second Report on the Deaths of Australian-Based Journalists in East Timor in 1975* (Canberra: Department of Foreign Affairs and Trade, January 1999).

94. Abraham, "Indonesia Needs You!" 5; Phil Abraham, "1980 OM Bali Pro Am: Competing in Paradise," *Tracks* 119 (August 1980): 15.

95. "Big Jim Banks: Three Times Round the World with Cronulla's Powerful Stylist," *Australian Surfing World* 29, no. 5 [issue 179] (n.d.): 23. An illness shortly before the contest prevented Banks from competing in 1980, but he won the OM Bali Pro in 1981.

96. Kirk Willcox, "OM Bali Pro," *Tracks* 130 (July 1981): 7. On the 1981 contest, including the government's arrangement of a "formal reception" for the visiting surfers before a march along Kuta Beach, where "a large crowd gathered for more speeches," see also Gary Crear, "Bali: OM Bali Pro '81," *Australian Surfing World* 30, no. 2 [issue 184] (n.d.): 68–72. The quotes appear on page 72.

97. "Big Jim Banks," 23. While my research in surfing publications has by no means been exhaustive, *Australian Surfing World*'s brief mention of East Timor is the only reference to the Indonesian invasion and occupation I have ever seen in the surfing press.

98. Abraham, "Indonesia Needs You!" 5.

99. Picard, *Bali*, 70. "In spite of the undeniable size of this market," adds Picard, "the official position in Jakarta as well as in Denpasar continued to grant priority to deluxe tourism, which was clearly more prestigious, easier to standardize, and was considered more viable in terms of foreign exchange earnings." Ibid., 70.

100. Abraham, "Indonesia Needs You!" 5.

101. Ibid.

102. Ibid. For more on Ketut Menda, see Leonard, "*Ombak Besar, Hati Besar, Orang Besar*," 54–55, 159. Leonard's dissertation is a valuable anthropological examination of how numerous Balinese have embraced surfing since the 1970s. See also Alex Leonard, "Learning to Surf in Kuta, Bali," *Review of Indonesian and Malaysian Affairs* 41, no. 1 (2007): 3–32. I am grateful to Adrian Vickers for bringing Leonard's work to my attention and to Alex Leonard for providing me with a copy of his dissertation.

103. Alan Rich, "Project Lombok," *Tracks* (December 1981): 31.

104. Ibid.; Abraham, "Indonesia Needs You!" 5.

105. Rich, "Project Lombok," 32–33.

106. "Pipeline," *Surfer* 21, no. 11 (November 1980): 104.

107. Editor's comment following Ray Barber, "Secret Gripe," *Tracks* 125 (February 1981): 3.

108. Bruce Channon, "Inside Ride," *Australian Surfing World* 27, no. 5 [issue 167] (n.d.): 49. The magazine is undated but was probably published in 1979.

109. Warshaw, *The Encyclopedia of Surfing*, 38. On the involvement of the director general of tourism, see "Bali Surfing Club: Fifth Annual Contest," *Tracks* (January 1984): 81.

110. Channon, "Inside Ride," 49.

111. Tony Brinkworth, "Beyond Bali," *Surfer* 19, no. 1 (May 1978): 82, 85. See also Paul Holmes, "Java: In Place of Dreams," *Tracks* 84 (September 1977): 7.

112. Warshaw, *The Encyclopedia of Surfing*, 232, 610. For Bill Boyum's recollection of discovering the surf at Grajagan in 1972, see Bill Boyum and Gerry Lopez, "A Place of Challenge," *Surfer's Journal* 2, no. 1 (Spring 1993): 108–23. There is a discrepancy in Warshaw's encyclopedia. In the entry on "Grajagan," Warshaw indicates that the camp opened "two years" after G-land was first surfed in 1972. Ibid., 232. But in the "surfing resorts" entry, he lists its year of founding as 1978. Ibid., 610. The film *ULU 32* presents footage of Gerry Lopez at the camp—Lopez elsewhere says "we" called Grajagan "Surf Nigger Heaven"—in what it claims is 1976. And to further complicate matters, the same film says that Java (the island on which Grajagan is located) was "first surfed" in 1974. On Lopez and "Surf Nigger Heaven," see Boyum and Lopez, "A Place of Challenge," 113.

113. *Sea of Darkness* (Deco Entertainment / Instinctive Film, 2008); see also Mark Cherry, "Nothing Really Organized: From Newcastle to Indo with Peter McCabe," *Surfer's Journal* 19, no. 4 (Summer 2010): 94–95.

114. Advertisement for Garuda Indonesian Airways, *Tracks* 117 (June 1980): 14–15. Advertisements from Garuda appeared regularly in *Tracks* in subsequent months and years.

115. Advertisement for *Asian Paradise*, *Tracks* (December 1985): 68; advertisements for *Asian Paradise*, *Tracks* (January 1986): 17, 58. "Your last chance for a ticket to paradise is to experience Indonesia with Garuda Indonesian Airways," one of the latter advertisements stated, an apparent reference to the possibility of winning a "double return ticket" to Bali by attending one of the screenings. For a review of the film, including the alterations from the 1984 original, see John Elliss, "Review: *Asian Paradise*," *Tracks* (January 1986): 9.

116. Advertisement for Bali Surfing Tours, *Tracks* 103 (April 1979): 34.

117. See, for a couple of examples, the advertisements for That's Bali and Magic Carpet Tours, *Detours* 7 (Summer 1979/1980): 9, 18.

118. Advertisement for Bali: A Special Encounter, *Tracks* 106 (July 1979): 13. For commentary on the elevated level of service offered by Bali Special Encounter, see "Gozzup," *Tracks* 106 (July 1979): 27.

119. Phil Abraham, "Mondo Sumbawa: Discovering the Elusive Supersuck and Other Indonesian Pleasures," *Surfer* 29, no. 12 (December 1988): 50.

120. Bill Finnegan and Bryan Di Salvatore, "Notes from the Paradise Trail, Part 2: Skinny Boats in a Lost World," *Tracks* 110 (November 1979): 31.

121. Bill Finnegan and Bryan Di Salvatore, "Notes from the Paradise Trail, Part 3: Letters Home & Another Adios," *Tracks* 111 (December 1979): 55–57.

122. "Ex–La Gundhi Traveller," "The Nits Who Said Nias," *Tracks* 123 (December 1980): 5.

123. David (Mex) Sumpter, "More on Nias Etc.," *Tracks* 124 (January 1981): 3.

124. Ex–La Gundhi Traveller, "The Nits Who Said Nias," 5.

125. Lovett quoted in *The Golden Pig* (1996). For an account by Peter Troy, who accompanied Lovett and Geisel on that first trip, see Lueras and Lueras, *Fielding's Surfing Indonesia*, 172–74. Lovett's experience is also recounted in ibid., 174–75.

126. "Once Bitten Twice Shy," "Nias," *Tracks* (January 1984): 5. On professional surfer Thornton Fallander's malarial "brush with death" after surfing on Nias, see Tim Baker, "Paradise Lost," *Surfer* 30, no. 3 (March 1989): 80.

127. "Lagundi [*sic*] Wedge Team," "Nias," *Tracks* (June 1984): 5.

128. For a filmic look at how the arrival of foreign surfers at Lagundri drastically altered the lives of Niasans, see *The Golden Pig* (1996). By the early 2000s, the problems for tourists at Lagundri had gotten much more serious, with petty theft in particular having apparently reached "epidemic proportions," according to the Lonely Planet guidebook. There were also "frequent complaints of aggressive locals intimidating tourists and demanding cash or threatening a surfing 'accident.'" Some Niasans who rented surfboards were said to be demanding cash for damage that occurred before the rental, while "friendly 'guides'" were alleged to be selling nonexistent boat or airplane tickets. In addition, there were "some isolated but disturbing reports of locals tormenting turtles on the beach and asking tourists for cash in return for their release." By 2003, after "anxious losmen owners joined forces in an attempt to address Lagundri's deteriorating reputation," matters reportedly began to improve. Patrick Witton, Mark Elliott, Paul Greenway, Virginia Jealous, Etain O'Carroll, Nick Ray, Alan Tarbell, and Matt Warren, *Indonesia*, 7th ed. (Footscray, Victoria, Australia: Lonely Planet Publications, 2003), 465.

129. Warshaw, *The Encyclopedia of Surfing*, 411.

130. John McLean, *Island of the Gods* (Singapore: Winter Productions Limited, 1990), 213–14. McLean's other books include *Deep Inside: Surfing Stories* (Jersey, Channel Islands: Winter Productions, 1997); *Down the Line: More Surfing Stories* (London: Winter Productions, 2003); *The Golden Few* (London: Winter Productions, 2004); and *On the Edge: Surfing Stories* (London: Winter Productions, 2004).

131. McLean, *Island of the Gods*, 140–42. That the killers of Dayu's family were "communists" is clarified on pages 304–5.

132. Ibid., 236.

133. Ibid., 319, 321.

134. Ibid., 320. Or, as the East German assassin would have it, to "impos[e] communism on the rest of mankind." Ibid., 325.

135. Ibid., 301–2.

136. Ibid., 300. The Portuguese intelligence official, Manoel da Silva, is identified on page 313 as "the former chief of Military Intelligence for the Portuguese Territory of Timor."

137. Ibid., 302, 304. There was another reason for Australia's inaction, too. Its embassy in Jakarta was staffed by an agent for the Soviets who convinced the ambassador to dismiss the Portuguese intelligence. Ibid., 317.

138. Ibid., 302–4, 308.

139. Chase, "A Great Book, and a Rare Find," Amazon.com, July 9, 2008, www .amazon.com/Island-Gods-John-McLean/dp/1872970001, accessed February 27, 2011.

140. *Island of the Gods* only once broaches the issue of not traveling to Indonesia on moral grounds. The character who states that he "wouldn't go there on principle" because "[i]t's a dictatorship" that exercises "press censorship" is so obviously a hypocrite, however, that the novel cannot help but defuse whatever force such a principled argument may have had. McLean, *Island of the Gods*, 410–11.

141. Chris Ahrens, *The Surfer's Travel Guide: A Handbook to Surf Paradise* (Cardiff-by-the-Sea, CA: Chubasco Publishing Company, 1995), 179. "Bali is only the beginning," Ahrens wrote, "and with countless islands in the chain, Indonesia is an explorer's dream." Ibid., 189.

142. Rob Story, "Life Isn't Fair," *Outside* (June 2001): 47. "Such surf imperialism," wrote Story, "occurs wherever a developing nation butts up against prime oceanfront. It started in the sixties, when California surfers 'discovered' Baja. The Australians followed suit, laying claim to surf breaks in the South Seas. Now in both Mexico and much of Indonesia, the sight of white folks with surfboards elicits a Pavlovian response in local children, who run up begging for money and candy." Ibid., 47. See also Steve Barilotti, "Lost Horizons: Surf Colonialism in the 21st Century," *Surfer's Journal* 11, no. 3 (Summer 2002): 88–97.

143. Warshaw, *The Encyclopedia of Surfing*, 380–81.

144. On some of those realities, as well as surf-charter operators' failure to abide by sustainable tourism practices, see Jess Ponting, Matthew McDonald, and Stephen Wearing, "De-constructing Wonderland: Surfing Tourism in the Mentawai Islands, Indonesia," *Society and Leisure* 28, no. 1 (2005): 141–62.

145. Warshaw, *The Encyclopedia of Surfing*, 381. For a brief history of surf tourism in the Mentawais, see Jess Ponting, "Consuming Nirvana: An Exploration of Surfing Tourist Space" (PhD diss., University of Technology, Sydney, 2008), 123–38.

146. By the early 2000s, claimed Matt Warshaw, surf resorts had in fact become "the fastest-growing segment of the surf industry." Warshaw, *The Encyclopedia of Surfing*, 610–11.

147. Kevin Naughton, quoted in Warshaw, *The Encyclopedia of Surfing*, 610. Naughton and Craig Peterson became well-known surf travelers during the 1970s and 1980s when they wrote a series of articles from the road for *Surfer* magazine. For more on Naughton and Peterson, see *The Far Shore* (2003).

148. For a listing of just some of the camps and surf-tour companies available in 1990, see Ben Marcus, "Paradise in a Package: An Updated Guide to Surf Travel Options," *Surfer* 31, no. 7 (July 1990): 76–77.

CHAPTER FOUR

1. Nick Carroll, "South Africa: To Be or Not to Be?" *Tracks* (June 1985): 12. Nick Carroll, a well-known surf journalist and himself an accomplished competitive surfer, is Tom Carroll's older brother.

2. "World Champ Boycotts South African Tour," *Tracks* (May 1985): 8.

3. "Surfing," *Courier-Mail* (Brisbane), April 4, 1985.

4. The number of activist surfers was small, however. While some, such as Save Our Surf founder John Kelly, played significant roles in various campaigns, most surfers, according to Peter Westwick and Peter Neushul, remained politically apathetic when it came to the environment. Peter Westwick and Peter Neushul, *The World in the Curl: An Unconventional History of Surfing* (New York: Crown Publishers, 2013), 187–193.

5. R. DeBelle, "Top Surfie 'Ignores' Apartheid Boycott," *Herald* (Melbourne), July 10, 1987.

6. Interview with Martin Potter, Sorrento, Victoria, Australia, October 4, 2008.

7. Wendy Botha became an Australian permanent resident (and afterward a citizen) on the eve of her first world championship in order to get around restrictions she faced traveling on a South African passport. Steve Culbert, "ASP Round Up: Wendy's Story," *Zigzag* 12, no. 4 (July/August 1988): 38.

8. Alan Carter, "Don't Scorn Them," *Zigzag* 10, no. 5 (September/October 1986): 2.

9. Steve Lansing, "Segregated Beaches," *Surfer* 7, no. 5 (November 1966): 15.

10. Spike [Steve Pike], *Surfing South Africa* (Cape Town: Double Storey Books, 2007), 12. On South African surfing history, see Cornel Barnett, *Hitting the Lip: Surfing in South Africa* (Johannesburg: Macmillan South Africa, 1974), 70–93; Paul Botha, "A Brief History of South African Surfing," in *Surfing in South Africa*, ed. Steve Pike (Cape Town: Book, 2001), 10–18; Mark Jury, *Surfing in Southern Africa, Including Mauritius and Reunion* (Cape Town: Struik, 1989), 11–13; and Spike, *Surfing South Africa*, 10–29.

11. Interview with Dick Metz, Huntington Beach, California, July 26, 2007.

12. Dick Metz to Paul Botha, January 10, 2002, Folder: John Whitmore, Dick Metz Collection, Surfing Heritage Foundation, San Clemente, California [hereafter SHF].

13. "The Oom" is Dutch and Afrikaans for "the Uncle." On Whitmore as "the Oom" and the "father of South African surfing," see Henri du Plessis, "Fire in His Eyes, the Sea in His Heart," *Cape Argus* (Cape Town), July 31, 2001, Folder: John Whitmore, Dick Metz Collection, SHF. See also Paul Botha, "John Whitmore: The Doyen of South African Surfing, 1929–2001," *Zigzag* 26, no. 2 (March–April 2002): 20; Tony Heard, "Goodbye Oom," in Pike, *Surfing South Africa*, 21; Miles Masterson, "Well Connected: The Parallel Universe of South Africa's 'Godfather' of Surfing, John 'Oom' Whitmore," *Surfer's Journal* 20, no. 3 (June/July 2011): 74–87;

Melanie Peters, "The 'Oom' Catches His Last Wave," *Sunday Argus* (Cape Town), January 13, 2002, Folder: John Whitmore, Dick Metz Collection, SHF; and Matt Warshaw, *The Encyclopedia of Surfing* (Orlando: Harcourt, 2003), 696.

14. Interview with Dick Metz, July 26, 2007. See also Marcus Sanders and Kimball Taylor, *Jeffreys Bay: Down the Line at the World's Best Pointbreak* (St. Petersburg, FL: Airborne Media; Huntington Beach, CA: Surfline/Wavetrak, 2007), 42–46. For a slightly different account of their initial meeting, see Dick Metz to Paul Botha, January 10, 2002.

15. Ben Marcus, "Surf Like an Egyptian: The Surfing Heritage Foundation Unveils Its Collection," *Surfline*, n.d., www.surfline.com/surfnews/article.cfm?id=1404, accessed June 29, 2010; interview with Dick Metz, July 26, 2007. Metz was, noted the Surfing Heritage Foundation, "the driving force behind Surfline Hawaii and the Hobie Sports retail chain." "Dick Metz[,] Founder and Board Member," Surfing Heritage Foundation, n.d., http://files.surfingheritage.org/about/2009/08/dick-metz-founder-and-board-member.html, accessed June 29, 2010.

16. Botha, "John Whitmore," 21.

17. Interview with Dick Metz, July 26, 2007.

18. Warshaw, *The Encyclopedia of Surfing*, 107, 696.

19. See, for example, Warren McKinney to Harry Bold, March 3, 1965, Folder: Harry Bold, Dick Metz Collection, SHF. In addition to the film's revelation, Brown wrote about the break for *Surfer* magazine; see Bruce Brown, "Africa: The Perfect Wave," *Surfer* 5, no. 5 (November 1964): 48–55.

20. Bud Browne to Harry Bold, March 16, 1964, Folder: Harry Bold, Dick Metz Collection, SHF.

21. Bob Evans, "Jeffery's [*sic*] Bay," *Surfing World* 11, no. 3 (n.d.): 18. The magazine is undated but was probably published in 1968 or 1969.

22. Bruce Brown to Harry Bold, September 2, 1964, Folder: Harry Bold, Dick Metz Collection, SHF.

23. Brown quoted in *The Endless Summer Revisited* (2000). Brown revealed similar sentiments to me during an interview I conducted with him about *The Endless Summer II* (1994), the sequel to his original film, while I was interning at *Surfer* magazine in 1993. In that sequel, in which Pat O'Connell and Robert "Wingnut" Weaver visited Cape St. Francis, Brown noted that "[w]e were the first to surf here in the '60s, and when we asked local fishermen how often it broke like that, they said, 'All the time.' That's all the information we had. As it turned out, the place is fickle and doesn't get good all that often."

24. Sanders and Taylor, *Jeffreys Bay*, 47.

25. The closest the film came was during a segment on Durban's shark-netted beaches in which Brown, commenting that porpoises tend to keep sharks away, joked that "sharks and porpoises have yet to integrate in South Africa."

26. The rickshaw driver became suspended in the air when the surfers and their boards proved too heavy for him, and the young boy, a Zulu, was dubbed "Mr. Clean" by Brown in light of his dirty face and his raggedy clothes, the latter a presumed (but unacknowledged) marker of his poverty.

27. Bruce Brown to Harry Bold, April 7, 1965, Folder: Harry Bold, Dick Metz Collection, SHF. As noted earlier, Brown also joked during the film about sharks and porpoises having yet to integrate in South Africa.

28. "Travels with Hynson," *Bruce Brown Films*, n.d., Clippings File: Bruce Brown, Margaret Herrick Library, Academy of Motion Picture Arts and Sciences, Beverly Hills, California, 6. Not all Americans recognized Hynson's parallel. Dick Metz, who returned to South Africa periodically after his initial trip in the late 1950s, was, decades later, in fundamental disagreement with the historical narrative expressed by his compatriot (to whom, it should be noted, he was not consciously responding; he simply volunteered these historical ideas during our interview). "So many people think that . . . the English and the Dutch invaded South Africa and killed all the blacks," Metz said in 2007. But "[t]here were no blacks there," at least in the Cape Town, Durban, and East London areas. "They didn't run 'em out—you know, do what we did to the Indians," he asserted. Rather, South Africa was, until the arrival of the Dutch and the British, essentially a virgin land. "Nobody lived there," he claimed. Blacks only came to what is today South Africa following white settlement, according to Metz, and they came in search of jobs. "They couldn't survive where they lived, so they crossed the border, came to South Africa, and then they became the Bantus of South Africa." Metz claimed that the lack of inhabitants was true of most of what is today South Africa, though not perhaps of the country's border areas. Interview with Dick Metz, July 26, 2007. While his history may have been mistaken—at a minimum, he overlooked the Khoikhoi and San presence prior to European contact (on contact with the indigenous peoples of the Cape of Good Hope, see, for example, Brian M. Fagan, *Clash of Cultures*, 2nd ed. [Walnut Creek, CA: AltaMira Press, 1998], 35–56; and Mohamed Adhikari, *The Anatomy of a South African Genocide: The Extermination of the Cape San Peoples* [Athens: Ohio University Press, 2011 (2010)])—Metz at least recognized apartheid's existence during his visits; he recalled the segregated beaches, for example. Still, he believed the system was gradually breaking down and did not see himself, as a foreign tourist, having a role to play in expediting the process.

29. Ron Perrott, "'Crocodiles,' Zulus, and Surf Suid Afrika," *Surfer* 7, no. 2 (May 1966): 65. For a photograph of three black surfers on a South African beach that, judging from the boards and style of fashion, appears to be roughly contemporaneous with Perrott's article, see Brian Gillogly, "Politics of Surfing," *Surfer* 25, no. 10 (October 1984): 88.

30. Perrott, "'Crocodiles,' Zulus, and Surf Suid Afrika," 62.

31. Patrick McNulty, "Editorial: Black and White Photography," *Surfer* 8, no. 1 (March 1967): 25.

32. John Miller, "Suid Afrika Surf" (letter to the editor), *Surfer* 7, no. 3 (July 1966): 21.

33. Traci Sommers, "Suid Afrika Surf" (letter to the editor), *Surfer* 7, no. 3 (July 1966): 21.

34. W. Kalama, "Black and White" (letter to the editor), *Surfer* 8, no. 2 (May 1967): 11.

35. McNulty, "Black and White Photography," 25. The magazine also added this practical, if unusual, opposition to apartheid: "[A] good tan has always been a status symbol in the sunny world of surfing. So a dark skin pigment is perhaps the weakest reason for limiting a surfer's activity in the water." Ibid., 25.

36. Tom Ghent, "Black and White" (letter to the editor), *Surfer* 8, no. 2 (May 1967): 11.

37. Jackson Lanhart, "Segregated Beaches" (letter to the editor), *Surfer* 7, no. 5 (November 1966): 15.

38. Douglas Booth, *The Race Game: Sport and Politics in South Africa* (London: Frank Cass, 1998), xix.

39. Charles Lewis, "Segregated Surfing (cont.)" (letter to the editor), *Surfer* 7, no. 6 (January 1967): 17.

40. Pete Wendland, "African Beaches" (letter to the editor), *Surfer* 7, no. 4 (September 1966): 9, 11.

41. Daniel R. Bomberry, "Segregated Surfing (cont.)" (letter to the editor), *Surfer* 7, no. 6 (January 1967): 16–17. Ironically, twenty years later several young South Africans would take to the pages of *Surfer* to spotlight youthful opposition to apartheid and/or chastise young foreign professionals who competed in their country while claiming, as did Australian surfer Mark Occhilupo, that they were simply too young to worry about "that stuff." "What about the hundreds of kids (under 16) that are being baton-charged, tear-gassed[,] and even shot?" asked the secretary of the non-racial Isipingo Surfing Club in Durban. "Aren't they too young to worry about politics as well?" Secretary of Isipingo Surfing Club, "Out of Africa" (letter to the editor), *Surfer* 27, no. 10 (October 1986): 20. See also Donavan Shaw, "Black and White Issue" (letter to the editor), *Surfer* 28, no. 12 (December 1987): 11. On Occhilupo's Spur TV interview in which he claimed he was "too young to think about that stuff," see John Elliss, "South Africa: Surfing in the Emergency Zone," *Tracks* (September 1985): 26. For Australian responses to Occhilupo's statement, see the letters by Chris Curtis and "R.U. Apathetic" in *Tracks* (November 1985): 5.

42. Steve Lansing, "Segregated Beaches" (letter to the editor), *Surfer* 7, no. 5 (November 1966): 15.

43. Jay Thornton, "African Beaches" (letter to the editor), *Surfer* 7, no. 4 (September 1966): 9.

44. Jim Kenworthy, "Black and White" (letter to the editor), *Surfer* 8, no. 2 (May 1967): 11.

45. Ballard T. Edwards IV, "Hot Potatoes" (letter to the editor), *Surfer* 8, no. 1 (March 1967): 15. For a reader ruing the "very bad stereotype" of "[t]he surfer . . . as a 'beach bum' who doesn't care what is going on in the world," and thus "fully disagree[ing]" that the segregation issue should be dropped by the magazine, see Pete Cohen, "More Involvement" (letter to the editor), *Surfer* 8, no. 3 (July 1967): 18.

46. On the editors' agreement that the "segregation issue" should be dropped "like a hot potato," see the editorial comment in response to Eugene Wilson, "Segregated Surfing (cont.)" (letter to the editor), *Surfer* 7, no. 6 (January 1967): 17.

47. Duke Boyd, "Pipeline: Robert August's World Tour," *Surfer* 5, no. 3 (July 1964): 81; McNulty, "Black and White Photography," 25.

48. Sanders and Taylor, *Jeffreys Bay*, 81, 100.

49. Keith Hosking, "Segregated Beaches" (letter to the editor), *Surfer* 7, no. 5 (November 1966): 13.

50. Chris Currie, "Segregated Beaches" (letter to the editor), *Surfer* 7, no. 5 (November 1966): 13, 15.

51. G. A. Krause, "Segregated Beaches" (letter to the editor), *Surfer* 7, no. 5 (November 1966): 15.

52. Eddie Nilson, "Segregated Surfing (cont.)" (letter to the editor), *Surfer* 7, no. 6 (January 1967): 17.

53. Bobby Ludlow, "Segregated Beaches" (letter to the editor), *Surfer* 7, no. 5 (November 1966): 15. In 1975, Peter Drouyn, a leading Australian surfer who had traveled to South Africa under the partial sponsorship of the Pretoria regime, told the *Australian* newspaper that the "coloured people" in South Africa do not surf because they "are afraid of the water" and they "consider the surf a voodoo area." They thus do not "develop surfing talent," he said. Drouyn quoted in Glen Thompson, "California Dreaming: Surfing Culture, the Sixties, and the Displacement of Identity in South Africa," paper presented at the 23rd Biennial Conference of the Southern African Historical Society, University of KwaZulu-Natal, Howard College Campus, Durban, South Africa, June 27–29, 2011, 16. I am grateful to Glen Thompson for providing me with a copy of his unpublished manuscript.

54. Loma Cuine, "Segregated Beaches" (letter to the editor), *Surfer* 7, no. 5 (November 1966): 15. Though often merely inferred, there were times when whites' claims about blacks' alleged disinterest in aquatic pursuits were framed in explicitly physiological terms. "Some sports the African is not suited for," maintained Frank Braun of the South African white Olympic committee in 1968. "In swimming the water closes their pores and they cannot get rid of carbon dioxide, so they tire quickly." Braun quoted in Joan Brickhill, *Race Against Race: South Africa's "Multinational" Sport Fraud* (London: International Defence and Aid Fund for Southern Africa, 1976), 44.

55. On the Balinese surf culture, see Alex Leonard, "Learning to Surf in Kuta, Bali," *Review of Indonesian and Malaysian Affairs* 41, no. 1 (2007): 3–32; and Leonard, "*Ombak Besar, Hati Besar, Orang Besar*: The Kuta Surfing Tradition and Its Heroes, 1969–2001" (PhD diss., Australian National University, 2006).

56. Kevin Dawson, "Swimming, Surfing, and Underwater Diving in Early Modern Atlantic Africa and the African Diaspora," in *Navigating African Maritime History*, ed. Carina E. Ray and Jeremy Rich, Research in Maritime History, no. 41 (St. John's, Newfoundland: International Maritime Economic History Association, 2009), 82. See also Kevin Dawson, "Enslaved Swimmers and Divers in the Atlantic World," *Journal of American History* 92, no. 4 (March 2006): 1327–55.

57. Dawson, "Swimming, Surfing, and Underwater Diving in Early Modern Atlantic Africa and the African Diaspora," 99–104.

58. Currie, "Segregated Beaches," 15.

59. Ballard T. Edwards IV, "Segregated Surfing (cont.)" (letter to the editor), *Surfer* 7, no. 6 (January 1967): 17. See also Darryl K. Morse, "Integrated" (letter to the editor), *Surfer* 8, no. 3 (July 1967): 17–18. On African American surfers more broadly, see especially Ted Woods's documentary *White Wash* (Trespass Productions, 2011).

60. *South African Surfer* was edited by Harry Bold, the same correspondent to whom Bruce Brown had earlier joked about blacks running an "independent African nation." Brown to Bold, April 7, 1965.

61. Rodger Ashe, "Interview with Ant van den Heuvel," *South African Surfer* 3, no. 1 (1966): 11. In his comment about "most people," it is unclear whether van den Heuvel was referring to South Africans or Americans (or both).

62. G. Klug, "To the Editor," *South African Surfer* 3, no. 3 (n.d.): 3.

63. Jack McCoy, "Short Snorts: 'Durban 500,'" *Tracks* 36 (September 1973): 25; Johnathon Barnes, "Tracks Interview: Peter Drouyn," *Tracks* 26 (November 1972): 9. According to Peter Drouyn, the South Africans "wanted an Australian, a Californian[,] and a Hawaiian." As the Australian, his costs were covered by the government and a couple of corporate sponsors. Barnes, "Tracks Interview," 9. These may be the surfers who had "all their expenses paid" that were addressed by the longtime anti-apartheid activist Sam Ramsamy; see Sam Ramsamy, *Apartheid, the Real Hurdle: Sport in South Africa & the International Boycott* (London: International Defence and Aid Fund for Southern Africa, 1982), 87. Unfortunately, however, Ramsamy did not specifically identify them. Such expense-paid trips of athletes were explicitly condemned in 1976 by the International Seminar on the Eradication of Apartheid and in Support of the Struggle for Liberation in South Africa, a meeting organized by the United Nations Special Committee Against Apartheid in consultation with the Organization of African Unity. The seminar also encouraged a convention, such as that proposed by Michael Manley of Jamaica, that "would involve an obligation on States to impose sanctions against sporting teams and organizations whose members collectively or individually participate in sports activities in South Africa or against teams from South Africa." United Nations Centre Against Apartheid, "International Seminar on the Eradication of Apartheid and in Support of the Struggle for Liberation in South Africa (Havana, Republic of Cuba, 24–28 May 1976)," Notes and Documents Sem/1 (New York: United Nations Centre Against Apartheid, Department of Political and Security Council Affairs, June 1976), 9–10. Similar sentiments were expressed the following year. See United Nations Centre Against Apartheid, "World Conference for Action Against Apartheid (Lagos, Nigeria, 22–26 August 1977)," Notes and Documents Conf. 1/Part I (New York: United Nations Centre Against Apartheid, Department of Political and Security Council Affairs, September 1977), 6, 11–12.

64. This was because, he said, "we and the world have too many screwed ideas on what's happening in Africa. Find out for yourself, as I did." Midget Farrelly, "My South African Happening," *Surfing World* 12, no. 6 (n.d.): 43. For a critical response, see Lesley Miles, "Letters," *Surfing World* 13, no. 1 (n.d.): 8. For a critical response to Lesley Miles, see Reginald C. Blunt, "Letters," *Surfing World* 13, no. 5

(n.d.): 6. Blunt had previously written about South Africa for the Australian publication *Surfabout*; see Reg Blunt, "It's All on Board in Springbok Land," *Surfabout* 2, no. 6 (n.d.): 26–27. The magazine is undated but was probably published in 1964.

65. Bob Evans, "Bob Evans Writes on His All New '68 Movie Production 'The Way We Like It,'" *Surfing World* 11, no. 3 (n.d.): 29. The magazine is undated but was probably published in 1968 or 1969. Evans wrote of Durban: "Durban is a pretty groovy place—and after all the tales we had heard about apartheid and its problems, it was refreshing to note that the predominantly dark population seem like a pretty happy group. Certainly they are not walking the streets with a big chip on their shoulders. You get the impression that the South African [g]overnment have [*sic*] a pretty strong grip on the situation, and that the majority of the population[,] regardless of color or creed[,] are prepared to let things stand as they are." Evans's nonchalance prompted an impassioned response from photographer and writer Rennie Ellis; see Rennie Ellis, "Forum," *Surfing World* 12, no. 4 (n.d.): 8; and Ellis, "It's Not the Way I Like It," *Surfing World* 12, no. 4 (n.d.): 37–39. Ellis's response in turn prompted a couple of readers to weigh in; see Reg Blunt, "Letters," *Surfing World* 13, no. 2 (n.d.): 8; and P. M. Rogers, "Letters," *Surfing World* 13, no. 3 (n.d.): 6.

66. Richie Strell, "Human Rights," *Surfer* 27, no. 2 (February 1986): 11.

67. "Advocate Praised for Exposing Surfers," *Barbados Advocate*, February 24, 1989.

68. "Black Africa," *Tracks* 12 (September 1971): 4. On the South African team last competing in the amateur world titles in 1978, see Robin De Kock, "Title Fight," *Zigzag* 8, no. 3 (May 1984): 12. Nick Carroll reported in *Tracks*, in what may have perhaps been a distinction between world title contests and other international events, that South African teams had competed in the United States and Peru into the 1980s. Carroll, "South Africa: To Be or Not to Be?" 12. On the contest in Peru, which featured teams from Australia, South Africa, Peru, Brazil, and Puerto Rico, see Alan Atkins, "Aussies in Peru: ASA Team Gets Done Up," *Tracks* (June 1985): 12, 48.

69. On sport and apartheid politics in South Africa, see Robert Archer and Antoine Bouillon, *The South African Game: Sport and Racism* (London: Zed Press, 1982); Douglas Booth, "Hitting Apartheid for Six? The Politics of the South African Sports Boycott," *Journal of Contemporary History* 38, no. 3 (July 2003): 477–93; Booth, *The Race Game*; Mihir Bose, *Sporting Colours: Sport and Politics in South Africa* (London: Robson Books, 1994); Richard E. Lapchick, *The Politics of Race and International Sport: The Case of South Africa* (Westport, CT: Greenwood Press, 1975); Lapchick, "South Africa: Sport and Apartheid Politics," *Annals of the American Academy of Political and Social Science* 445 (September 1979): 155–65; Eric J. Morgan, "Black and White at Center Court: Arthur Ashe and the Confrontation of Apartheid in South Africa," *Diplomatic History* 36, no. 5 (November 2012): 815–41; John Nauright, *Sport, Cultures, and Identities in South Africa* (London: Leicester University Press, 1997), 124–56; Rob Nixon, "Apartheid on the Run: The South African Sports Boycott," *Transition* 58 (1992): 68–88; "Sport and Apart-

heid," *Comment* 44 (London: Catholic Institute for International Relations, 1982); and Cornelius Thomas, ed., *Sport and Liberation in South Africa: Reflections and Suggestions* (Alice, Eastern Cape, SA: National Heritage and Cultural Studies Centre, University of Fort Hare; Pretoria: Department of Sport and Recreation, 2006).

70. For one instance of the regime's international propaganda, see *Sport in South Africa: A Political Backgrounder* (London: Director of Information, South African Embassy, 1978). On surfing, see ibid., 21, 23.

71. Booth, "Hitting Apartheid for Six?" 484.

72. The Minister of Coloured Relations of the South African government reported in February 1980 that, "excluding schoolchildren," the number of "Coloureds" who "actively participated" in "surf-riding" was 39. Statistics were "not available" for "Indians," according to the Minister of Indian Affairs, while, for "Africans," official figures—again excluding schoolchildren—either were not reported or totaled zero; how to interpret the data on "Africans" is unclear. Ramsamy, *Apartheid, the Real Hurdle*, 100, 102.

73. "Lawrence, Mike, and Ken," "Re: Point of Controversy" (letter to the editor), *Surfer* 17, no. 2 (July 1976): 24. Another South African wrote, "As regards surfing, there is no rule which prevents non-whites from participating in the sport. These people all have beautiful large beaches next to ours where they can do exactly as they please. Non-whites have as yet not developed an interest in the sport; many of them fear going too deep into the sea—this being part of their (African) ancient beliefs that the sea is an evil spirit. Africans are quite content to paddle on the edges, and few are found going beyond the breakers. The Asiatics are more inclined toward fishing, and very good they are too!" Lisa Tmegaardt, "Re: Point of Controversy" (letter to the editor), *Surfer* 17, no. 2 (July 1976): 24. Both letters were in response to an earlier letter on surfing and apartheid; see Larry Felker, "Point of Controversy" (letter to the editor), *Surfer* 16, no. 4 (November 1975): 13.

74. Booth, "Hitting Apartheid for Six?" 483.

75. "The best beaches are reserved for whites," the anti-apartheid movement noted in the mid-1970s, "while the most remote and least attractive beaches are allocated to blacks." Brickhill, *Race Against Apartheid*, 69. These differences have more recently drawn the attention of historian Glen Thompson, who wrote that the beaches reserved for blacks in Cape Town, Durban, and Port Elizabeth were farther from urban transport routes and were considered more dangerous swimming beaches than those reserved for whites. The black beaches also often suffered from a lack of surf lifesavers on duty, according to Thompson. Thompson, "California Dreaming," 16. While beach apartheid did not necessarily translate into disparities in wave quality (though it generally did), it did mean that beach attendance was more difficult and less attractive for nonwhites. For a scholarly analysis of South Africa's segregated beaches, see Kevin Durrheim and John Dixon, "The Role of Place and Metaphor in Racial Exclusion: South Africa's Beaches as Sites of Shifting Racialization," *Ethnic and Racial Studies* 24, no. 3 (May 2001): 433–50. Thompson has also noted that a number of local surf clubs, which governed competitive

surfing throughout South Africa, were racially exclusive, barring blacks from membership. Glen Thompson, "Judging Surf Culture: The Making of a White Exemplar Masculinity during the 1966 Natal and South African Surfriding Championships Held in Durban," *Journal of Natal and Zulu History* 26 (2008): 96–97. I am grateful to Glen Thompson for providing me with a copy of this article.

76. Tmegaardt, "Re: Point of Controversy" (letter to the editor), 24. "Believe me," she wrote, "if a non-white came onto our beach, no one would be likely to interfere with him. He is there as part of our heritage, and we'll accept him as anyone else on the beach."

77. David Macgregor, "Competition Sparks Racial 'Surf War,'" *Natal Mercury* (Durban), October 2, 1989. For an editorial response to the "racial 'surf war,'" including regret that such incidents can "be used as ammo" to further criticize South Africa's international reputation, see Craig Sims and Dave Macgregor, "Editorial," *Zigzag* 13, no. 6 (November/December 1989): 10. At the same time that the surfers of color were being harassed in Durban, antiracism activists were protesting beach segregation in Cape Town and Port Elizabeth, with many of those in Cape Town wearing visors that said "Free the Beaches" while being verbally attacked by local residents. "1000 at Beach Protest 'Picnic,'" *Natal Mercury* (Durban), October 2, 1989.

78. Darryl Brandreth, "The Other Side of the Coin," in Spike, *Surfing South Africa*, 26. In the 1980s, wrote Steve Pike, black surfers were "chased from whites-only beaches." Spike, *Surfing South Africa*, 22, 73. While South African journalist (and surfer) Tony Heard commented on their increasing visibility "around the time of Steve Biko"—"historically concentrated on certain remote beaches by South Africa's idiotic race laws," these "[b]lack surfers" began "to break out and to be seen prominently hanging ten, locked in[,] and hitting the lip all over the place, including the pristine, safer, once whites-only beaches"—he did not mention their harassment. Tony Heard, "Sepia Moments from South Beach," in Pike, *Surfing in South Africa*, 159.

79. Spike, *Surfing South Africa*, 22–23.

80. Rafiq Bagus, quoted in *Taking Back the Waves* (Uhuru Productions/SABC2, 2005).

81. Warshaw, *The Encyclopedia of Surfing*, 554; Ahmed Collier, his wife, Fawzia, and son Cass all discuss his arrest in *Taking Back the Waves*. Cass Collier's eviction from the Cape Town beach must have come after the first months of 1990, as he told *Surfer* in an interview that year that he himself had never been "thrown off a beach" but that his father and "a lot of my friends" had. "Testing 1-2-3: Cass Collier," *Surfer* 31, no. 6 (June 1990): 66.

82. Hoffmeyr quoted in *Taking Back the Waves*. While Collier did not surf on the regular South African circuit, he did compete in the country with the small but nonracial South African Surfing Union (SASU). "Testing 1-2-3: Cass Collier," 66.

83. Steve Morton, "No Guts, No Glory: Collier Comes of Age," *Zigzag* 14, no. 5 (September/October 1990): 33.

84. On Aikau hosting Collier, see *Taking Back the Waves*. For more on the Smirnoff Pro-Am, see Richard W. Johnston, "You Can Always Surf on It," *Sports Illustrated* 35, no. 23 (December 6, 1971): 102–3.

85. Phil Jarratt, *Mr. Sunset: The Jeff Hakman Story* (London: Gen X Publishing in association with General Publishing Group, 1997), 106.

86. Fifteen years later, *Surfer* noted, tongue-in-cheek, that Jeffreys Bay, South Africa's fabled right-hand pointbreak, represented the sport's "best reason to toss away all moral beliefs to satisfy cheap, carnal surf lust." Matt Warshaw, "The Best Surf Article in the History of Mankind," *Surfer* 28, no. 8 (August 1987): 142.

87. Stuart Holmes Coleman, *Eddie Would Go: The Story of Eddie Aikau, Hawaiian Hero and Pioneer of Big Wave Surfing* (New York: St. Martin's Griffin, 2001), 109. See also Jarratt, *Mr. Sunset*, 106–8; and Warshaw, *The Encyclopedia of Surfing*, 7–8. Coleman cited Shaun Tomson in raising the possibility that Aikau was not denied entry to the hotel but instead "just felt unwelcome there." According to Coleman, Tomson said, "My impression was that he wasn't comfortable staying in the hotel where Jeff and Billy were staying. So my dad invited him to come stay at the Eden Rock, where we were." Coleman, *Eddie Would Go*, 109. Tomson told me, however, that Aikau was "refused admittance at [the] hotel," which is consistent with other published accounts. Interview with Shaun Tomson, Los Angeles, California, August 4, 2007.

88. David M. Abshire to Ronald V. Dellums, November 4, 1971, Folder: TRV—Travel 1970 General, Box 280, Subject Numeric Files, 1970–73, Administration, Record Group 59, National Archives II, College Park, Maryland. Abshire was responding to a query about whether the State Department had considered negotiating with the South African government over having "visiting blacks declared 'white' while on South African soil."

89. "South Africa Is a Wipe Out," *Drum* (August 22, 1972), 14. "Not all the Whites have been like that," Aikau added. "Amongst friends, I feel relaxed. But I can sense the racial discrimination. There is this colour problem all over the world. But here in South Africa, man, it's real heavy." Ibid., 14.

90. Jarratt, *Mr. Sunset*, 107.

91. Interview with Shaun Tomson, August 4, 2007. While touting South Africa as an international destination, Cornel Barnett, in the first book to appear on South African surfing (it was published in 1974), mentioned Aikau's visit yet failed to acknowledge the Hawaiian's troubling reception. Barnett, *Hitting the Lip*, 177. The book as a whole ignores the issue of apartheid and is premised on the assumption that surfers are (and will continue to be) white.

92. Hamilton quoted in Jarratt, *Mr. Sunset*, 108. The basis for Hamilton's conclusion is unclear, but it is worth noting the comments of antiapartheid activist Dennis Brutus in discussing foreign athletes in South Africa. "The only non-whites they are likely to make contact with are the bedroom girls who make their beds, the men who clean up in the hotel," he said in a 1969 interview. "I am always amazed when I hear that they have asked these people whether they like apartheid and whether they are happy. I do not see what else these people can say but yes, otherwise they are out of a job within the next few hours. And losing a job in South Africa is very serious if you are black, because you also lose your home, you lose the right to be in the town at all and you are liable to go to prison, simply for being in the town

if you are out of a job. These people are very vulnerable." " 'If You Play Sport with South Africa, You Are Condoning Apartheid': Dennis Brutus Interviewed," *Outlook* (Sydney) (April 1969): 5.

93. Jarratt, *Mr. Sunset*, 108.

94. Coleman, *Eddie Would Go*, 110. Jarratt attributes the comment to an interview with a reporter for the *Honolulu Advertiser*; see Jarratt, *Mr. Sunset*, 108.

95. "Flash," *Surfer* 13, no. 4 (November 1972): 71. On South African blacks being barred from competition, see "South Africa Is a Wipe Out," 14; and Coleman, *Eddie Would Go*, 109.

96. Thompson, "California Dreaming," 18. The other "dark nation" was Puerto Rico.

97. Gillogly, "Politics of Surfing," 87; interview with Shaun Tomson, August 4, 2007.

98. Phil Jarratt, "Coming Out on Apartheid: A Conversation with Tom Carroll and Martin Potter," *Surfer* 26, no. 11 (November 1985): 31.

99. DeBelle, "Top Surfie 'Ignores' Apartheid Boycott."

100. Reno Abellira, "The Jeffrey's Experience," *Surfer* 18, no. 5 (January 1978): 40.

101. Anonymous member, quoted in Muhammad Shafique, "Black Surfing in South Africa: A Look at Wynberg Surf Club," *Tracks* (August 1986): 47.

102. R. W. J. Opperman of the South African Olympic and National Games Association dismissed the agreement as a "prime example of misinformed prejudice." South African Olympic and National Games Association, "Questions and Answers on South African Sport," in *Sport in South Africa: Report of the Sports Council's Fact-Finding Delegation* (London: Sports Council, 1980), 154. The Gleneagles Agreement, known officially as the Commonwealth Statement on Apartheid in Sport, is reproduced in Ramsamy, *Apartheid, the Real Hurdle*, 68–69.

103. The United Nations General Assembly noted shortly after the Gleneagles Agreement was adopted that "[s]urf riding" remained a sport in which South Africa was still able to "participate internationally." "The campaign against apartheid sports continues," its Centre Against Apartheid wrote, "as some international sports federations have not taken the necessary action." United Nations Centre Against Apartheid, "South Africa's Standing in International Sport," Notes and Documents 20/78 (New York: United Nations Centre Against Apartheid, Department of Political and Security Council Affairs, July 1978), 1, 4.

104. Mike Tomson, "Africa: The South African Circuit," *Tracks* 82 (July 1977): 15.

105. Bruce Raymond, "A Few Views," *Tracks* 83 (August 1977): 10. Jim Banks would later echo this view. While noting that before he ever went to South Africa he was "really *really* down on apartheid," after he visited he "still thought apartheid was bad" but "could see why it had happened" and "how it was a lot easier to run the whole country that way." Given that "blacks have to be educated a lot more before they can run the country," if they "took over it would revert back to [its] tribal" state, he claimed. "Big Jim Banks: Three Times Round the World with Cronulla's Powerful Stylist," *Australian Surfing World* 29, no. 5 [issue 179] (n.d.): 23, 27.

106. Fitzgerald quoted in Phil Jarratt, "The Wit & Wisdom of Surfers; or, The Complete Book of Bullshit," *Tracks* 96 (September 1978): 15.

107. Terry Fitzgerald, "A Few Views," *Tracks* 83 (August 1977): 10.

108. Simon Anderson, "A Few Views," *Tracks* 83 (August 1977): 10.

109. Raymond, "A Few Views," 10.

110. Peter Townend, "A Few Views," *Tracks* 83 (August 1977): 10.

111. Brian Cregan, "A Few Views," *Tracks* 83 (August 1977): 10.

112. Phil Jarratt, "To Go or Not to Go? Aussies in Africa," *Tracks* 83 (August 1977): 9. Other surfers did not advocate a boycott but spoke out against apartheid while in the country, such as a group of Australians in a "Steve Biko Lives" rally at the Beach Hotel, a local pub in Jeffreys Bay, in 1980. Derek Hynd, "South African Pro-Tour '84: In the Shadow of Giant Jeffrey's," *Surfer* 25, no. 12 (December 1984): 50. According to a later report, the Afrikaaner owner of the local hotel "threatened violent retribution" when the report's author and others scrawled a "Steve Biko freedom slogan" on the establishment's pool table. Derek Hynd, "The Most Beautiful Country on Earth," *Tracks* (September 1987): 50.

113. Jarratt, "To Go or Not to Go?" 9.

114. Paul Naude, "The Return of the World: A Major Step Forward for Amateur Surfing," *Surfer* 19, no. 7 (November 1978): 62. For a valuable analysis of the effects of apartheid on competitive surfing in South Africa, including its amateur ranks, see Glen Thompson, "'Certain Political Considerations': South African Competitive Surfing during the International Sports Boycott," *International Journal of the History of Sport* 28, no. 1 (January 2011): 32–46.

115. Elliss, "South Africa: Surfing in the Emergency Zone," 45.

116. United Nations Centre Against Apartheid, "Register of Sports Contacts with South Africa: 1 January–30 June 1982," Notes and Documents 11/83 (New York: United Nations Centre Against Apartheid, May 1983), 10. The participation of foreign surfers in South African contests, as well as the participation of South Africans in foreign contests, was tracked by the United Nations. For a sampling of its reports, see United Nations Centre Against Apartheid, "Register of Sports Contacts with South Africa: 1 April–31 December 1981," Notes and Documents 7/82 (New York: United Nations Centre Against Apartheid, February 1982), 39, 51, 60; United Nations Centre Against Apartheid, "Register of Sports Contacts with South Africa: 1 January–30 June 1982," 10, 17, 24; and United Nations Centre Against Apartheid, "Register of Sports Contacts with South Africa: 1 July–31 December 1984," Notes and Documents 7/85 (New York: United Nations Centre Against Apartheid, May 1983), 28.

117. Interview with Tom Carroll, Newport, New South Wales, October 8, 2008.

118. Tom Carroll and Kirk Willcox, *The Wave Within* (Sydney: Ironbark, 1994), 84.

119. Carroll, for personal reasons, wished not to identify his friend. Interview with Tom Carroll, October 8, 2008. Peter Simons, an Australian surfer and photographer, experienced a similar episode of what his white South African acquain-

tances called "coon hunting" along a shantytown's disused airfield on which young local children played soccer. "[M]y eyes and mind still remember," he wrote. E-mail correspondence with Peter Simons, May 21 and 22, 2013.

120. For a contemporaneous brochure arguing that "normal sports" were not possible in an "abnormal society," see *Apartheid Sport: Change but No Improvement* (Continental Sports, 1984). The quote is attributed broadly to "the discriminated South African" by journalist Fekrou Kidane on page 5 of the brochure. On South African surfers of color embracing the sentiment, see Shafique, "Black Surfing in South Africa," 46.

121. Interview with Tom Carroll, October 8, 2008.

122. Carroll and Willcox, *The Wave Within*, 83.

123. Phil Jarratt, "Apartheid: The Cries Won't Die" (letter to the editor), *Surfer* 27, no. 4 (April 1986): 11. Jarratt cited the case of Glen Ella but may have meant his brother Mark. Glen Ella competed in South Africa in 1985; Mark Ella publicly stated that, while he would be assured of significant financial rewards if he did so, he could not play in South Africa "until the apartheid system is disbanded." S. O'Connor (Queensland Newspapers), "Aussies High in SA Links," *Telegraph*, December 17, 1985.

124. Queensland Newspapers, "I'm Disappointed in Cash: Hawke," *Courier-Mail* (Brisbane), November 18, 1987. See also Helen Pitt, "Cash's South Africa Trip Disappoints PM," *Sydney Morning Herald*, November 18, 1987.

125. In a mark of surfing's mainstream appeal, in the mid-1980s Carroll was twice nominated the "ABC [Australian Broadcasting Corporation] Sportstar of the Year" as well as the "Young Australian of the Year." "Buzzzzzzz," *Tracks* (February 1986): 7.

126. Jocko McRoberts, "Applauded Stand" (letter to the editor) *Surfer* 27, no. 1 (January 1986): 19. McRoberts was congratulating not only Tom Carroll but also Tom Curren and Martin Potter. For immediate expressions of support from several Australians, as well as one note of opposition, see the letters under "TC and South Africa," *Tracks* (June 1985): 3.

127. "Carroll's Boycott Call," *Zigzag* 9, no. 3 (May/June 1985): 8. References to the "Boycott Bombshell" also appear on the magazine's cover and in the table of contents on page 1.

128. Nick Williams, "Shaun Tomson," *Zigzag* 9, no. 4 (July/August 1985): 7. Williams's rant spurred a letter from the associate editor of the Australian magazine *Tracks*, who questioned whether it was "blind patriotism or deep resentment" that prompted the "cynicism with which [Williams] wrote off Tom Carroll"; see John Elliss, "Why Isn't Shaun World Champ?" *Zigzag* 9, no. 5 (September/October 1985): 4. On the alleged response of Carroll's manager to the piece by Williams, see "Splab Splab: Hear This," *Zigzag* 9, no. 5 (September/October 1985): 28. For a response to Carroll's manager, see Jean-Pierre Botha, "Tell Him Off," *Zigzag* 9, no. 6 (November/December 1985): 4.

129. Carroll and Willcox, *The Wave Within*, 83; interview with Tom Carroll, October 8, 2008.

130. Interview with Tom Carroll, October 8, 2008. See also Jarratt, "Coming Out on Apartheid," 31–32.

131. Carroll, "South Africa: To Be or Not to Be?" 12; John Elliss, "Interview: Tom Carroll," *Tracks* (October 1985): 51; Queensland Newspapers, "Legal Aid to Surfer 'Entirely Unjustified,'" *Courier-Mail* (Brisbane), May 23, 1985.

132. Greg Kelton, "Hawke Strengthens Trade Policy Against S. Africa," *Courier-Mail* (Brisbane), May 22, 1985.

133. Queensland Newspapers, "Legal Aid to Surfer 'Entirely Unjustified.'" *Tracks* attributed the decision to Shaun Tomson. "Buzzzzzzz," *Tracks* (July 1985): 7.

134. "Buzzzzzzz," *Tracks* (August 1985): 7. Instinct also signed on Greg Anderson.

135. On broad treatments of sport and foreign policy, see Gerald R. Gems, *The Athletic Crusade: Sport and American Cultural Imperialism* (Lincoln: University of Nebraska Press, 2006); Steven J. Jackson and Stephen Haigh, eds., *Sport and Foreign Policy in a Globalizing World* (London: Routledge, 2009); and Andrew Johns and Heather Dichter, eds., *Diplomatic Games: Sport, Statecraft, and International Relations since 1945* (Lexington: University Press of Kentucky, forthcoming).

136. C. William Walldorf Jr., *Just Politics: Human Rights and the Foreign Policy of Great Powers* (Ithaca, NY: Cornell University Press, 2008), 112.

137. "Conversation between President Nixon and the President's Assistant for National Security Affairs (Kissinger)," September 28, 1971, *Foreign Relations of the United States, 1969–1976, Volume XXVIII: Southern Africa* (Washington, DC: Government Printing Office, 2011), 144–45.

138. Thomas Borstelmann, *The Cold War and the Color Line: American Race Relations in the Global Arena* (Cambridge, MA: Harvard University Press, 2001), 255.

139. Simon Stevens, "'From the Viewpoint of a Southern Governor': The Carter Administration and Apartheid, 1977–81," *Diplomatic History* 36, no. 5 (November 2012): 846.

140. Borstelmann, *The Cold War and the Color Line*, 255.

141. Reagan quoted in Gerald M. Boyd, "President Opposes Additional Steps on South Africa," *New York Times*, July 23, 1986. See also Robert Pear, "U.S. Report Stirs Furor in South Africa," *New York Times*, January 14, 1989. On the Reagan administration and South Africa, see Borstelmann, *The Cold War and the Color Line*, 259–63.

142. Interview with Tom Curren, Santa Barbara, California, August 5, 2007. Despite missing the South African leg of the world tour, Curren performed well enough elsewhere to claim the 1985 world championship, an accomplishment he attributed to the additional training he undertook while avoiding the South African contests.

143. Interview with Martin Potter, October 4, 2008. On Potter's childhood, see also Nick Carroll, "Killers: Martin Potter," *Tracks* (December 1985): 38–39. *Tracks* reported in 1985 that Potter had "recently moved from South Africa to England to avoid compulsory national service." "World Champ Boycotts South African

Tour," 8. For Potter's explanation, see Matt Warshaw, "A Prodigy Meets Reality: It's Not Always Easy Being Martin Potter," *Surfer* 28, no. 6 (June 1987): 75; and "Sweet Rivals," *Surfer's Journal* 22, no. 2 (April/May 2013): 124.

144. Interview with Martin Potter, October 4, 2008. "His highly publicized move to England in 1984 (for family and military reasons)," wrote Steve Morton, "caused much uproar in his Durban home town. 'Traitor!' bellowed his former friends as they saw him evading Magnus Malan [the South African defense minister] and joining Aussie world champ Tom Carroll's anti-apartheid boycott." Steve Morton, "The South African Surfing Scene," in Jury, *Surfing in Southern Africa*, 143.

145. Interview with Martin Potter, October 4, 2008.

146. Jarratt, "Coming Out on Apartheid," 31.

147. Interview with Martin Potter, October 4, 2008.

148. Graham Cassidy, "ASP General Meeting: No Story for the Media," *Tracks* (June 1985): 14. Carroll and Potter both believed that the ASP was violating its constitution in sanctioning events on segregated beaches that "might preclude ASP members." Jarratt, "Coming Out on Apartheid," 31.

149. Elliss, "South Africa: Surfing in the Emergency Zone," 45; "World Derby: Was This Trip Really Necessary?" *Surfer* 27, no. 11 (November 1986): 127. When one considers the organization's refusal to "sanction events in Hawaii because they were not worth enough money and didn't fully comply with ASP rules," John Elliss wrote in 1985, "it makes you wonder why they are so determined to prop up the lagging South African leg." Elliss, "South Africa: Surfing in the Emergency Zone," 45. In response to Elliss's report on the 1985 contests, the ASP noted that they fell below the required purse because of "the rand's unforseen [*sic*] plummet on the financial market" at a time when it was "too late to re-evaluate the situation." "Buzzzzzzz," *Tracks* (October 1985): 17. This was not the case in 1986, however, when the ASP sanctioned the South African contests despite the prize money falling "well below" the tour minimum. Graham Cassidy and Editor, "ASP Meets Again," *Tracks* (March 1986): 10; see also "World Derby: Was This Trip Really Necessary?" When a motion was brought before the organization to curb the South African tour, it was rejected by the ASP executives. C. Ryan, "Sth. Africa a Problem for Aussie Surf Pros," *Sunday Mail* (Brisbane), January 19, 1986.

150. Phil Jarratt, "Point of View: The ASP Returns to South Africa," *Surfer* 27, no. 11 (November 1986): 36.

151. Elliss, "South Africa: Surfing in the Emergency Zone," 22. The reticence of some publications to offend South Africans was made clear when a competing publication, *Australian Surfing World*, published a lengthy article whose author, a medical doctor, forcefully denounced apartheid and the South African regime. Unusually, the editors included a disclaimer at the end of the piece stating that the "opinions expressed" were those of the author and "not necessarily" those of the publishers. "And if you think that's a cop out," they continued, "any correspondence concerning the aforementioned will be promptly ignored." The article is

Rodney Kirsop, "Doctor at Large: Exploring the World with Rodney Kirsop," *Australian Surfing World* 199 (n.d.), 50–69. Kirsop's comments on apartheid appear on page 59; the editorial disclaimer appears on page 68. The magazine is undated but was probably published in 1984 or 1985.

152. Matt Warshaw, "'No Policy': The ASP Responds," *Surfer* 26, no. 12 (December 1985): 31.

153. On surfers protesting this view, see, for example, Thom Panunzio, "No Neutral Ground" (letter to the editor), *Surfer* 27, no. 3 (March 1986): 11. Panunzio's missive, the editor of *Surfer* noted, was one of "many letters" the magazine received on the subject, "all of which echoed Mr. Panunzio's sentiments."

154. Chris Warshaw, "Black and White," *Surfer* 27, no. 11 (November 1986): 12.

155. Tomson became an American citizen in 1984. Shaun Tomson with Patrick Moser, *Surfer's Code: 12 Simple Lessons for Riding Through Life* (Salt Lake City: Gibbs Smith, 2006), 29.

156. See, for example, John Elliss, "Shaun Tomson," *Tracks* (December 1986): 51, 82.

157. On the government's sponsorship of South Africans' travels, see Gillogly, "Politics of Surfing," 87; and "Michael Tomson: 'The African Attitude,'" *Surfer* 17, no. 6 (March 1977): 30. On government funding of the South African Surfriders Association, see Shafique, "Black Surfing in South Africa," 46; and Thompson, "California Dreaming," 18. Shaun Tomson also surfed as a representative of the South African Defense Force in the Gunston 500 in 1973. There is a photograph of him in uniform, surfboard in hand, at "Independent Newspapers 2," Surfing Heritage South Africa, http://surfingheritage.co.za/site/independent_newspapers/35, accessed September 17, 2010. Michael Tomson, Shaun Tomson's cousin, wrote matter-of-factly in 1977 that "government sponsorship of surfing has been a reality for years." Mike Tomson, "South Africa," *Tracks* 79 (April 1977): 15.

158. Michael Tomson, "South Africa on the Ropes," Op-Ed, *New York Times*, January 13, 1979. For a recent profile of Tomson, who cofounded the surfwear brand Gotcha, see Phil Jarratt, "Top to Bottom, Inside Out: The Multifaceted Surfing Career of Michael Tomson," *Surfer's Journal* 15, no. 5 (Fall 2006): 26–37.

159. "Michael Tomson: 'The African Attitude,'" 30, 33.

160. *Sport in South Africa: A Political Backgrounder*, 23.

161. Interview with Shaun Tomson, August 4, 2007; Elliss, "Shaun Tomson," 51. Tomson noted, for instance, that he opposed U.S. support for the Contras in Nicaragua in the 1980s, as well as the Reagan administration's Strategic Defense Initiative, but that that would not preclude him from competing in the United States. "The Year in Review," *Surfer* 30, no. 2 (February 1989): 79. Perhaps more than any other writer, Dave Zirin has effectively sought to demolish the argument that sport is apolitical; see, for example, Dave Zirin, *A People's History of Sports in the United States: 250 Years of Politics, Protest, People, and Play* (New York: New Press, 2008). Also excellent is his film *Not Just a Game: Power, Politics, and American Sports* (Media Education Foundation, 2010).

162. Tomson with Moser, *Surfer's Code*, 29.

163. Ibid., 28.

164. Interview with Shaun Tomson, August 4, 2007.

165. "World Champ Boycotts South African Tour," 8.

166. Matt Warshaw, *The History of Surfing* (San Francisco: Chronicle Books, 2010), 397; Matt Warshaw, "And Then There Were Three: A Conversation with Tom Curren," *Surfer* 26, no. 11 (November 1985): 32. "I stand here not in defence of South Africa," he told the assembled guests, "but in defence of pro surfing." Carroll, "South Africa: To Be or Not to Be?" 12.

167. On Cheyne Horan's 1985 boycott, see Paul Holmes, "The Year in Review: People, Spots, and Spectacular Swells That Kept Surfing Very Much Alive during Nineteen Hundred and Eighty Five," *Surfer* 27, no. 2 (February 1986): 35; and Derek Hynd, "South Africa '85: Power and Action Despite Politics," *Surfer* 26, no. 12 (December 1985): 28–35. On "Free Mandela" on his board, see Warshaw, *The History of Surfing*, 398; see also Paul Holmes, "Barbados Political Pepper Sauce: Apartheid Is Hot Issue on Caribbean TV Shoot," *Surfer* 30, no. 7 (July 1989): 61. To four-time world champion Mark Richards, Horan was the "real hero." He "dared to surf in South African events with a Free Mandela sticker on his board," he said. Conversely, Carroll's "public stance . . . was over the top," Richards told the *Sydney Morning Herald*. Graham Cassidy, "At 30, Tommy Gun Still Fires a Bullet," *Sydney Morning Herald*, April 17, 1992. On Richards's early opposition to an ASP boycott, see John Elliss, "South African Tour: ASP Goes for 'Gratitude,'" *Tracks* (April 1986): 13.

168. Tim Williams, "Who Is Boycotting?" *Zigzag* 10, no. 4 (July/August 1986): 1. Williams was not, to be sure, an apologist for apartheid, denouncing it as an "ugly system" while stating that, in reference to the boycotting professionals, "having the courage of one's convictions is a truly noble virtue."

169. Carter, "Don't Scorn Them," 2.

170. See, for example, Donovan Shaw, "Ramifications . . ." (letter to the editor), *Zigzag* 11, no. 5 (September/October 1987): 4.

171. *Tracks* reported that "the Ho brothers didn't go for personal reasons, Barton Lynch stayed home so he could train, Damien Hardman was injured[,] and Gary Elkerton gave it a miss for safety reasons," as did Chris Frohoff and Mike Lambresi. John Elliss, "South Africa Survives a Shaking," *Tracks* (August 1986): 54. Whether the politics of traveling to South Africa influenced any of these decisions is unclear. Almost certainly that was not the case with Barton Lynch, however, who was a vocal opponent of the boycott movement. For Lynch's contemporary views of the boycott, which he opposed because "as a professional surfer" he was "a businessman," and one should not take into consideration the politics of one's "business partners" (although he did find apartheid "conceptually very disturbing," he added), see Barton Lynch, "Barton's View," *Tracks* (September 1985): 26. For a brief nod to Lynch's politics—deeply concerned about the Communist threat, his "favourite human being" was Ronald Reagan—see "Buzzzzzzz," *Tracks* (March 1986): 7.

172. "Buzzzzzzz," *Tracks* (July 1986): 7; Elliss, "South Africa Survives a Shaking," 54. A bomb did in fact go off during the surfers' visit, but in Cape Town, "not

far from the Woodstock Holiday Inn" where the competitors were staying for the first of South Africa's two contests, rather than in Durban, which was the site of the second contest, the Gunston. Robin De Kock, "S.A. Pro Season: The Surfabout Diaries or the Stories Behind the Stories," *Zigzag* 10, no. 5 (September/October 1986): 8.

173. "World Derby: Was This Trip Really Necessary?" 127.

174. Elliss, "Shaun Tomson," 51. The final tally was five to three, with Tomson joining ASP vice president Graham Cassidy and Australian representative Wayne "Rabbit" Bartholomew in the minority. For details of the voting process, see Elliss, "South Africa Survives a Shaking," 54. For Tomson's assertion that only safety considerations would ever cause him to vote against staging local contests in South Africa, see Doug Macdonald, "Shaun Sez . . . ," *Zigzag* 10, no. 5 (September/October 1986): 12.

175. Elliss, "South African Tour: ASP Goes for 'Gratitude,'" 13. On ASP tour director Al Hunt's 1986 warning that South Africa would have to ensure the "correct" prize money for its contests to be sanctioned by the ASP in 1987, see Paul Naude, "SA Leg's Future?" *Zigzag* 10, no. 5 (September/October 1986): 14.

176. Jarratt, "Point of View: The ASP Returns to South Africa," 38.

177. "World Derby: Out of the Gate, It's Tom Curren and the X Factor!" *Surfer* 28, no. 10 (October 1987): 119; Paul Holmes, "Testing 1-2-3: Vetea 'Poto' David," *Surfer* 28, no. 10 (October 1987): 46. Those who chose not to compete in South Africa were—in addition to Carroll, Curren, and Potter—Mark Occhilupo, Gary Elkerton, Derek Ho, Michael Ho, Greg Day, Mark Richards, and Wayne Bartholomew. Elkerton and the Ho brothers were among those who stayed away in 1986. It is unclear whether Vetea David did not make the trip for political reasons, as he did compete in South Africa in 1988, where he placed seventeenth in the Sea Harvest International. "World Derby: Out of Africa," *Surfer* 29, no. 11 (November 1988): 153.

178. "Buzz," *Tracks* (September 1987): 7. Garcia was the 2000 world champion. While in South Africa he was questioned about what *Tracks* called "the situation." "'But I got my own rights,' [Garcia] answered indignantly. In reply to whether he got hassled because of his skin colour, he said: 'I only get hassled when I don't wear my shirt in the hotel.'" "South Africa: Young Aussies Seize Their Chance," *Tracks* (September 1987): 49.

179. "Buzz," *Tracks* (September 1987): 7.

180. "World Derby: Out of the Gate, It's Tom Curren and the X Factor!" 119.

181. "World Derby: Free-for-All!" *Surfer* 29, no. 10 (October 1988): 127. In addition to Carroll, Curren, and Potter, those who stayed away from South Africa were Sunny Garcia, Charlie Kuhn, Michael Ho, and Brad Gerlach. In "putting human rights before money, standings[,] and ego," the absent professionals were "the real winners" of the two contests, one surfer opined. Scott Gangel, "The Real Winners" (letter to the editor), *Surfer* 30, no. 1 (January 1989): 14.

182. Robin De Kock, "ASP Update," *Zigzag* 12, no. 5 (September–October 1988): 10.

183. "World Derby: Californians Dominate Op and Gunston 500," *Surfer* 30, no. 11 (November 1989): 173.

184. Peter Brewer, "New Wave of Enthusiasm for South African Meet," *Sunday Tasmanian* (Hobart), June 24, 1990.

185. T. Bartholomew, "Surfing Champ to Boycott Gunston," *Sunday Mail* (Brisbane), July 2, 1989.

186. "A Decade of Deliverance," *Zigzag* 14, no. 1 (January/February 1990): 15.

187. Paul Holmes, "Shaun Banned from Brazil: Surfing in Political Imbroglio," *Tracks* 96 (September 1978): 7. South African surfers were also barred from entering Indonesia; see Carroll, "South Africa: To Be or Not to Be?" 12. In what *Tracks* called "politics . . . rear[ing] its ugly head in the ranks of professional surfing," the IPS [International Professional Surfers, the predecessor to the ASP] tour, at "the request of South Africa" and "with the support of delegates representing pro surfers," inserted into its rule book in December 1980 a clause that could remove a contest from the professional circuit if the host country were to bar a competitor from another country. Graham Cassidy, "Political Move Mars Meeting," *Tracks* 125 (February 1981): 5.

188. Moira Hodgson, "SA's Image Improving," *Zigzag* 11, no. 3 (May/June 1987): 7; "Interviews: Mike Burness," *Zigzag* 10, no. 5 (September/October 1986): 10; Craig Sims, "Backwash: ASP Update," *Zigzag* 11, no. 4 (July/August 1987): 54; Craig Sims, "Backwash: ASP Update," *Zigzag* 11, no. 6 (November/December 1987): 11; and Archer and Bouillon, *The South African Game*, 295.

189. Craig Sims, "ASP Round Up," *Zigzag* 12, no. 3 (May/June 1988): 34, 36.

190. Sims, "ASP Round Up," 34; Lawrence Atkinson, "Burn: Michael Burness Speaks Out!" *Zigzag* 12, no. 4 (July/August 1988): 39.

191. Robin De Kock, "Backwash: The I.S.A.," *Zigzag* 11, no. 1 (January/February 1987): 28. In 1986, moreover, a seventeen-member Springbok team had its visas withdrawn by the American government two days before leaving for what was to be its biggest tour ever in the United States. The squad still managed to make the trip, however, when the surfers traveled as "individuals." "A Decade of Deliverance," 16.

192. Following his visit to the newspaper's offices, the *Barbados Advocate* paraphrased *Surfer* editor Paul Holmes as reporting that "a number of countries, including Japan and Indonesia, had refused entry to a number of professional surfers whose names had appeared" on United Nations lists of athletes who had competed in South Africa. "Advocate Praised for Exposing Surfers."

193. On the contest being the first Caribbean event sanctioned by the ASP East, see Holmes, "Barbados Political Pepper Sauce," 56.

194. Roger Baxter, "Look at Surfing Before It's Too Late" (letter to the editor), *Barbados Advocate*, February 11, 1989.

195. Hayden Coppin, "Surfers with S.A. Links," *Barbados Advocate*, February 16, 1989. On a cheery profile of Rudolph and Kuhn a day earlier, see "Surfers Get Set: Two Test Waves," *Barbados Advocate*, February 15, 1989.

196. Coppin, "Surfers with S.A. Links."

197. Hayden Coppin, "2 Surfers Banned," *Barbados Advocate*, February 18, 1989.

198. On the withdrawal of the advertisements, see Robert Best, "We Have to Laugh to Cry," *Barbados Advocate*, February 18, 1989; and "BSA Officials Shun Advocate Sports Team," *Barbados Advocate*, February 18, 1989.

199. "BSA Officials Shun Advocate Sports Team"; "BAJ Takes Up Surfing Issue," *Barbados Advocate*, February 24, 1989.

200. Coppin, "Surfers with S.A. Links."

201. "Immigration Dept. Under Fire," *Barbados Advocate*, February 19, 1989; Holmes, "Barbados Political Pepper Sauce," 61.

202. Holmes, "Barbados Political Pepper Sauce," 61.

203. Warshaw, *The Encyclopedia of Surfing*, 331; Warshaw, *The History of Surfing*, 398.

204. Ibid.

205. Holmes, "Barbados Political Pepper Sauce," 61.

206. "World Derby: Tour Regroups; Hardman and Potter Are Ready," *Surfer* 31, no. 11 (November 1990): 140.

207. Those boycotting the 1989 contest were—in addition to Carroll, Curren, and Potter—Derek Ho, Richie Collins, Todd Holland, Sunny Garcia, Glen Winton, Jeff Booth, Hans Hedemann, and Mike Parsons. Mitch Thorson missed the contest because he traveled to the United States for medical treatment, while Mark Occhilupo missed it due to the death of his father. Brewer, "New Wave of Enthusiasm for South African Meet."

208. Undoubtedly contributing to the large crowds was the beachside Ocean Africa festival that accompanied the contest. Lance Slabbert, "ASP World Championship Tour: Power Surge: Elkerton Wins in South Africa, Takes the Lead," *Surfer* 34, no. 12 (December 1993): 78–79. A year earlier, Potter had incurred a $5,000 fine for apparently failing to notify the ASP that he would not be competing in South Africa. Derek Hynd, "Sunny Side Up," *Surfer* 33, no. 12 (December 1992): 32. (The ASP had reportedly revised its rules to allow for fines to be levied for nonattendance in contests. Kalinga Seneviratne, "Pressure to Boycott South Africa Sports," Inter Press Service, June 29, 1992.) On further figures for the Ocean Africa festival, which had seen its attendance increase to an estimated 700,000 people by 1997, see Thompson, "Judging Surf Culture," 83 (note 5).

209. Graham Cassidy, "Carroll May End S. Africa Boycott," *Sydney Morning Herald*, July 12, 1991; David Knox, "Surf Champ Sticks with His Boycott," *Sunday Mail* (Brisbane), February 10, 1991. On Carroll's contemplation of a return to South Africa in 1992, see Cassidy, "At 30, Tommy Gun Still Fires a Bullet."

210. According to the Australian press, Steve Tshwete, the South African minister of sport, planned to be there to greet him, though I have been unable to confirm this meeting through other print sources, and I learned of it only after my 2008 interview with Carroll. T. Kavanagh, "Carroll Will End Boycott," *Sunday Mail* (Brisbane), June 30, 1996.

211. Stu Nettle, "Bob and Tom . . . and Nelson Mandela," *Swellnet*, July 16, 2010, www.swellnet.com.au/news/698-bob-and-tom-and-nelson-mandela, accessed February 14, 2011; interview with Tom Carroll, October 8, 2008; Carroll and Willcox, *The Wave Within*, 85–87.

CHAPTER FIVE

1. "Box Office/Business for *North Shore* (1987)," IMDb.com, n.d., www.imdb .com/title/tt0093648/business, accessed December 10, 2012.

2. E-mail announcement from the California Surf Museum, "North Shore at La Paloma," November 5, 2012; CSF, "25 Year Anniversary of Iconic Surf Movie 'North Shore,'" California Surf Museum, November 2, 2012, http://surfmuseum. org/csf12/25-year-anniversary-of-iconic-surf-movie-north-shore/, accessed December 7, 2012.

3. For more on the professionalization of the sport, see, for example, the Edward Norton–narrated documentary *Bustin' Down the Door* (Screen Media Films/ Fresh & Smoked, 2008).

4. Peter Westwick and Peter Neushul are particularly effective in puncturing the myth of surfing's environmental purity. Peter Westwick and Peter Neushul, *The World in the Curl: An Unconventional History of Surfing* (New York: Crown Publishers, 2013), 218–41.

5. Zach Weisberg, "The Surf Biz Is Growing Up," *Inertia*, November 25, 2010, http://www.theinertia.com/business-media/surf-business-surf-industry-is-growing-up-target-nike/, accessed September 13, 2012.

6. See, for example, Jess Ponting, "Liberalizing Nirvana: An Analysis of the Consequences of Common Pool Resource Deregulation for the Sustainability of Fiji's Surf Tourism Industry," *Journal of Sustainable Tourism* (forthcoming). I am grateful to Jess Ponting for sharing with me an early version of his research on this issue. See also "San Diego's Surfing Culture Catches an Academic Wave," KPBS, October 31, 2011, www.youtube.com/watch?v=ZqCuPVVwuig, accessed July 25, 2012.

7. Weisberg, "The Surf Biz Is Growing Up."

8. *Non-endemic* is the term used by the organic surf industry to refer to those corporations without roots in the community who have sought to penetrate the market.

9. Tanzina Vega, "Nike Tries to Enter the Niche Sports It Has Missed," *New York Times*, June 2, 2011.

10. Mike Sciacca, "Simpson Advances in U.S. Open Heats," *Huntington Beach Independent*, August 2, 2012, www.hbindependent.com/sports/tn-hbi-0802-uso-pen-20120801,0,6002797.story, accessed September 20, 2012. The year before, in 2008, Nike took over another long-standing contest, this one at Lower Trestles in San Clemente; it became the Nike Lowers Pro. And the Nike subsidiary Hurley sponsored the Hurley Pro, one of ten World Championship Tour contests worldwide, at the same Orange County break.

11. Vega, "Nike Tries to Enter the Niche Sports It Has Missed."

12. Target Corporation, "Target Signs Women's Professional Surfer Carissa Moore," Press Release, July 23, 2009, http://pressroom.target.com/news/target -signs-professional-surfer-carissa-moore, accessed September 20, 2012. On the rise

of women's surfing, see Krista Comer, *Surfer Girls in the New World Order* (Durham, NC: Duke University Press, 2010).

13. Target Corporation, "Target Signs Professional Surfer Kolohe Andino," Press Release, January 20, 2010, http://pressroom.target.com/news/target-signs -professional-surfer-152120, accessed September 20, 2012.

14. Samantha Critchell (Associated Press), "Surfer Style Is Cool and Carefree," *Houston Chronicle*, July 9, 2006.

15. Matt Warshaw, *The Encyclopedia of Surfing* (Orlando: Harcourt, 2003), 641.

16. Westwick and Neushul, *The World in the Curl*, 110. Mark Richards, the four-time world champion from 1979 to 1982, sold beer, Ford cars, and Kentucky Fried Chicken on Australian TV. Ibid., 292.

17. Rarick, Noll, and Hamilton quoted in *Riding Giants* (Forever Films, Studio-Canal, and Setsuna LLC, 2004).

18. Peralta quoted in *Riding Giants*.

19. "In the countercultural analysis," write philosophers Joseph Heath and Andrew Potter, "simply having fun comes to be seen as the ultimate subversive act. Hedonism is transformed into a revolutionary act." But "[h]aving fun is not subversive, and it doesn't undermine any system. In fact, widespread hedonism makes it more difficult to organize social movements, and much more difficult to persuade anyone to make a sacrifice in the name of social justice." Joseph Heath and Andrew Potter, *Nation of Rebels: Why Counterculture Became Consumer Culture* (New York: HarperBusiness, 2004), 9.

20. For more on the politics of branding, see Naomi Klein, *No Logo* (New York: Picador, 1999); and Alissa Quart, *Branded: The Buying and Selling of Teenagers* (New York: Basic Books, 2003).

21. Robert Gardner, "Editorial," *Surfer Bi-Monthly* 3, no. 4 (October–November 1962): 7; "Editorial," *Surfer Quarterly* 2, no. 2 (Summer 1961): 1. On "hodaddies" and "gremlins," see "What Is a Gremlin?" and "What Is a Ho-Daddy?" in *Surfer Quarterly* 2, no. 3 (Fall 1961): 1.

22. Gardner, "Editorial," 7.

23. "Editorial," *Surfer Quarterly* 2, no. 4 (Winter 1961): 3. See also "Editorial: An Active Interest," *Surfer Bi-Monthly* 4, no. 1 (February–March 1963): 9.

24. Warshaw, *The Encyclopedia of Surfing*, 660.

25. "Surf Spots," *Surfer Bi-Monthly* 4, no. 3 (June–July 1963): 39.

26. "Doctor/Lawyer/Indian Chief," *Surfer* 6, no. 2 (May 1965): 61.

27. See, for example, Westwick and Neushul, *The World in the Curl*, 107–108. On Orange County's economic reliance on the Cold War, see also Lisa McGirr, *Suburban Warriors: The Origins of the New American Right* (Princeton, NJ: Princeton University Press, 2001).

28. Lizabeth Cohen, *A Consumer's Republic: The Politics of Mass Consumption in Postwar America* (New York: Vintage Books, 2003).

29. Alan Green, "How We Got Started," in Phil Jarratt, *The Mountain and the Wave: The Quiksilver Story* (Huntington Beach, CA: Quiksilver Entertainment, Inc., 2006), 22; Warshaw, *The Encyclopedia of Surfing*, 374–75, 487.

30. Warshaw, *The Encyclopedia of Surfing*, 374. McKnight stepped down as CEO in January 2013.

31. Thomas Frank, *The Conquest of Cool: Business Culture, Counterculture, and the Rise of Hip Consumerism* (Chicago: University of Chicago Press, 1997), 224.

32. Warshaw, *The Encyclopedia of Surfing*, 375.

33. Fred Pawle, "A Perfect Corporate Storm," *Weekend Australian*, September 29, 2012.

34. Jim Rutenberg, "New York's Big Break: Surfing Sees Opportunity," *New York Times*, September 4, 2011.

35. Matt Higgins, "Neptune on a Shortboard," *New York Times*, November 14, 2010. The *Times* followed Slater's lead in suggesting that comparing athletes from different sports was a pointless exercise. On the opposite coast, the *Los Angeles Times* called the argument that Slater is the "greatest athlete ever" an "argument that holds water." Baxter Holmes, "Slater's Wave as High as Ever," *Los Angeles Times*, August 3, 2012.

36. Jonah Bloom, "Marketers Should Jump on Quiksilver's Creative Wave," *Advertising Age* 75, no. 29 (July 19, 2004): 17; Jennifer Pendleton, "Matt Jacobson," *Advertising Age* 75, no. 39 (September 27, 2004): S30; "Boost Mobile and Quiksilver Continue Brand Alliance with Second Roxy-Branded Wireless Phone," *Business Wire*, September 1, 2004.

37. "Box Office/Business for *Riding Giants* (2004)," IMDb.com, n.d., www.imdb.com/title/tt0389326/business, accessed December 10, 2012.

38. Bloom, "Marketers Should Jump on Quiksilver's Creative Wave," 17.

39. "Boost Mobile and Quiksilver Continue Brand Alliance with Second Roxy-Branded Wireless Phone."

40. Joseph Kahn, "When Chinese Workers Unite, the Bosses Often Run the Union," *New York Times*, December 29, 2003. Two years later, Chinese authoritarianism became the butt of a Quiksilver marketing joke. When the company commissioned skateboarder Danny Way to jump over the Great Wall of China in 2005 in a promotion for its DC Shoes brand, advertisements on MTV and ESPN featured a fictitious "Chinese Minister of Extreme Sports" announcing that "mandatory support of Danny Way is greatly encouraged." Alice Z. Cuneo, "Quiksilver Enters China with Extreme Stunt," *Advertising Age* 76, no. 27 (July 4, 2005): 11.

41. China Labor Watch, "Textile Sweatshops; Adidas, Bali Intimates, Hanesbrands Inc., Piege Co (Felina Lingerie), Quiksilver, Regina Miracle Speedo, Walcoal America Inc., and Wal-Mart Made in China," Press Release, November 19, 2007, http://digitalcommons.ilr.cornell.edu/globaldocs/305/, accessed December 4, 2012.

42. David Laskin, "Where a Tycoon Made It Just to Give It Away," *New York Times*, October 21, 2007.

43. Anna Edwards, "Design with Green Twist," *Courier Mail* (Brisbane), November 16, 2006.

44. "Environmental Grants Program," n.d., www.patagonia.com/us/patagonia.go?assetid=2927, accessed September 20, 2012.

45. On "Patagonia Reef," see Warshaw, *The Encyclopedia of Surfing*, 122; and Westwick and Neushul, *The World in the Curl*, 190, 219.

46. On the atypical nature of its corporate activism, see Andrea Adelson, "Wedded to Its Moral Imperatives," *New York Times*, May 16, 1999.

47. "Malloy Brothers Move to Patagonia," *Surfer*, July 22, 2010, www.surfermag .com/features/malloys_patagonia/, accessed September 20, 2012.

48. "Chris Malloy," n.d., www.patagonia.com/us/ambassadors/surfing/chris -malloy/71243, accessed September 20, 2012.

49. "Dan Ross," n.d., www.patagonia.com/us/ambassadors/surfing/dan-ross /71103, accessed September 20, 2012.

50. On the company's generous flextime and leave policies, see, for example, Steven Greenhouse, "Working Life (High and Low)," *New York Times*, April 20, 2008. Greenhouse's article was adapted from his book *The Big Squeeze: Tough Times for the American Worker* (New York: Alfred A. Knopf, 2008).

51. Yvon Chouinard, *Let My People Go Surfing: The Education of a Reluctant Businessman* (New York: Penguin Press, 2005).

52. On the wages of workers in the garment industry, see *Global Wage Trends for Apparel Workers, 2001–2011* (Worker Rights Consortium, July 2013), www.amer icanprogress.org/wp-content/uploads/2013/07/RealWageStudy-3.pdf, accessed July 12, 2013.

53. Institute for Global Labour and Human Rights, "Another CAFTA Failure 2008: Salvadoran Women Sewing $165 Jackets for the North Face and $54 Shirts for Eddie Bauer Cannot Afford Milk for Their Children," May 22, 2008, www. globallabourrights.org/reports?id=0501, accessed December 7, 2012.

54. "Fair Labor Association (FLA)," n.d., www.patagonia.com/us/patagonia. go?assetid=68405, accessed July 1, 2013. For some of the problems with most global factory monitoring, see Stephanie Clifford and Steven Greenhouse, "Fast and Flawed Inspections of Factories Abroad," *New York Times*, September 2, 2013. Clifford and Greenhouse note that Patagonia has sought more rigorous (even while more costly) audits.

55. See, for example, the response to "Do workers in factories making Patagonia clothes earn a living wage?" in "FAQs," n.d., www.patagonia.com/us/patagonia.go ?assetid=67517, accessed July 12, 2013.

56. Guy Trebay, "Back to the Beach," *New York Times*, June 1, 2006.

57. Warshaw, *The Encyclopedia of Surfing*, 375.

58. On Machado as "the world's most famous soul surfer," see the written introduction by "MclitoOF" for "Rob Machado the Drifter (Full Movie)," *YouTube*, April 10, 2012, www.youtube.com/watch?v=56yxJlMiwoU, accessed October 10, 2012.

59. "Biography," n.d., www.robmachado.com/bio/, accessed October 9, 2012.

60. *The Drifter* (Rob Machado, 2009).

61. Josh Hunter, "Caught on Tape: O'Neill Talks about Signing Jordy Smith," *TransWorld Business*, November 8, 2007, http://business.transworld.net/49/fea tures/caught-on-tape-steve-ward-talk-about-signing-jordy-smith/, accessed October 11, 2012.

62. Shawn Price, "Smith Sets Off Buzz in Surfing World about Endorsement," *Orange County Register*, August 15, 2007.

63. Will Swanton, "Meet the Man Whose 'No' Ticked Off Nike," *Sun Herald* (Sydney), March 2, 2008.

64. Ibid.

65. "Julian Heads for Ballito," *Daily News* (Durban), April 11, 2011.

66. Fred Pawle, "It's a Balancing Act as Aussie Surf Brands Hang On," *Australian*, December 29, 2011.

67. "Nike 6.0 Women's Surf Movie: *Leave a Message*," Press Release, April 11, 2011, http://nikeinc.com/news/nike-60-women<#213>s-surf-movie-leave-a-message, accessed December 11, 2012.

68. Zach Weisberg, "Nike Transitions Surf Focus to Hurley," *Inertia*, November 27, 2012, www.theinertia.com/business-media/nike-transitions-surf-focus-to-hurley/, accessed February 15, 2013; Jeff Mull, "Nike Pulls Back," *Surfer* (November 27, 2012), www.surfermag.com/features/nike-pulls-back/, accessed July 2, 2013.

69. "Jimmy the Saint," November 27, 2012, 1:19 p.m., and "Rob," November 27, 2012, 2:15 p.m., at Mull, "Nike Pulls Back."

70. Pawle, "A Perfect Corporate Storm."

71. Matthew Smith, "Not Waving, Drowning," *BRW* (November 1, 2012): 16.

72. International Labor Rights Forum, "2010 Sweatshop Hall of Shame," November 17, 2009, www.laborrights.org/creating-a-sweatfree-world/sweatshops/resources/12211, accessed December 11, 2012.

73. On the flight-related eccentricities of Jeffries, see Julie Creswell, "Suit Exposes Strict Manual for Abercrombie Flight Crew," *New York Times*, October 20, 2012. On Abercrombie & Fitch's racist, sexist, and otherwise offensive marketing and employment practices, see, among many others, Eric Platt, "11 Reasons Why People Hate Abercrombie & Fitch," *Business Insider*, August 15, 2012, www.businessinsider.com/hate-abercrombie-and-fitch-2012-8?op=1, accessed December 11, 2012.

74. Hollister is "the coolest destination for genuine SoCal style clothes for guys and girls," its website summary pronounces, imploring consumers to "[c]heck out the hottest new looks to hit the pier." Google Search descriptor for Hollister Co., n.d., https://www.google.com/#hl=en&sugexp=les%3B&gs_nf=3&gs_rn=0&gs_ri=hp&tok=6KjM9N_7T5Whie16Wjgifg&cp=8&gs_id=00r&xhr=t&q=hollister&pf=p&tbo=d&output=search&sclient=psy-ab&oq=holliste&gs_l=&pbx=1&bav=on.2,or.r_gc.r_pw.r_qf.&fp=c0acdbc8739c055c&bpcl=39650382&biw=1348&bih=688, accessed December 11, 2012.

75. Abercrombie and Fitch, "Brand History," n.d., https://associate.anfcorp.com/anf/webdav/site/extranet/shared/docs/New Store Associate/Brand History.pdf, accessed December 13, 2012.

76. Kevin Kemper, "Round Two over '22,'" *Columbus Business First*, August 25, 2003, www.bizjournals.com/columbus/stories/2003/08/25/story2.html?page=all, accessed December 14, 2012.

77. Josh Hunter, "How Hollister Co. Stole Surf: Eight Years After Abercrombie & Fitch Invaded the Surf Market, What Can Be Done to Defend Against

Them?" *TransWorld Business*, August 7, 2008, http://business.transworld.net/8642/features/how-hollister-co-stole-surf-eight-years-after-abercrombie-fitch-invaded-the-surf-market-what-can-be-done-to-defend-against-them/, accessed on December 13, 2012.

78. Ibid.

79. "HOLLISTER Now Open," n.d., www.westfield.com.au/bondijunction/news-and-events/2013/events/03/hollister, accessed July 2, 2013.

80. "Hollister Brand 'Fictitious,'" *BBC News*, November 10, 2009, http://news.bbc.co.uk/2/hi/business/8340453.stm, accessed December 13, 2012.

81. Piper Jaffray, "Teen Fashion Spending Declines 24 Percent according to the 14th Biannual Piper Jaffray 'Taking Stock with Teens' National Study," Press Release, October 10, 2007, www.piperjaffray.com/2col.aspx?id=287&releaseid=106 1006, accessed January 16, 2013.

82. Piper Jaffray, "16th Semi-Annual Piper Jaffray 'Taking Stock with Teens' Study Indicates Bottom May Be Nearing for 'Discretionary Recession,'" Press Release, October 9, 2008, www.piperjaffray.com/2col.aspx?id=287&releaseid=1207 428, accessed December 11, 2012.

83. Pawle, "It's a Balancing Act as Aussie Surf Brands Hang On."

84. See, among others, Anjali Athavaley, "Web Surfers Think It's a Swell Idea to Talk Business in Wetsuits," *Wall Street Journal*, October 8, 2012, http://online.wsj.com/article/SB10000872396390444223104578034713717683392.html, accessed July 7, 2013; Marissa Brassfield, "Is Surfing the New Golfing? Executives Swap Golf Bags for Surfboards," *PayScale*, July 18, 2012, www.payscale.com/career-news/2012/07/is-surfing-the-new-golfing, accessed July 7, 2013; Shah Gilani, "Want to Climb the Corporate Ladder or Jump Off: Learn to Surf," *Forbes* (July 18, 2012), www.forbes.com/sites/shahgilani/2012/07/18/want-to-climb-the-corporate-ladder-or-jump-off-learn-to-surf/, accessed July 7, 2013; Matt Higgins, "Surf's Up, and Upscale, as Sport Reverses Its Beach Bum Image," *New York Times*, February 11, 2007; and Evan Pondel, "Exec Downtime: Squash, Golf, and . . . Surfing?" *Christian Science Monitor*, May 24, 2007.

EPILOGUE

1. For Luce's original reference to an "American century," see Henry R. Luce, "The American Century," *Life* (February 17, 1941): 61–65.

2. Justin Housman, "Surf City, China?" *Surfer* (April 24, 2013), www.surfermag.com/features/surf-city-china/, accessed June 24, 2013.

3. On the transition from skating to surfing, see Jeff Mull, "Will China Become Surfing's Next Frontier?" *Surfer* (October 4, 2012), www.surfermag.com/features/will-china-become-surfing%E2%80%99s-next-frontier/, accessed June 21, 2013.

4. "Surfing China's 'Silver Dragon,'" *CNN*, June 5, 2013, www.cnn.com/video/data/2.0/video/sports/2013/06/05/china-surfing-silver-dragon-river.red-bull.html, accessed June 13, 2013; "Red Bull Qiantang: Surfing Shootout," *Surfline*, n.d., www

.surfline.com/video/contests/red-bull-qiantang-surfing-shootout_95487, accessed June 17, 2013; "Surfers Ride Silver Dragon Tidal Bore in China," *BBC*, October 1, 2012, www.bbc.co.uk/news/world-asia-19792563, accessed June 17, 2013.

5. "Curren in China," YouTube.com, September 30, 2011, www.youtube.com/watch?v=ppiP8YMVCgE, accessed June 24, 2013; "Kick Flips and Cutbacks with Curren in China," YouTube.com, October 11, 2013, www.youtube.com/watch?v=-Qh_2UTPpys, accessed June 24, 2013; "Curren in China," Hurley.com, September 16, 2011, www.hurley.com/blog/blog.cfm/aid/48090/CURREN-IN-CHINA, accessed June 24, 2013.

6. Mull, "Will China Become Surfing's Next Frontier?"

7. Terrence Ogden and Thomas Ling reported surfing in Hong Kong in 1963; see "Surf Spots," *Surfer Bi-Monthly* 4, no. 2 (April–May 1963): 36; and "Surf Spots," *Surfer Bi-Monthly* 4, no. 6 (December 1963–January 1964): 62. On Rod Payne's 1979 effort to surf at Hong Kong's Big Wave Bay—he was removed from the water by the police—see Matt Warshaw, *The Encyclopedia of Surfing* (Orlando: Harcourt, 2003), 120. On Peter Drouyn in China, see "Peter Drouyn: Back from China," *Tracks* (January 1986): 11; "Peter Drouyn Bails to China! More Than a Surf Trip," *Surfer* 27, no. 3 (March 1986): 21; and Mike Perry, "Drouyn's Foray," *Surfer* 28, no. 6 (June 1987): 108, 160, 163.

8. On the Americans' trip to China, see "*Surfer* Stages China Surf Expedition: Historic Journey in Sports' Diplomacy," *Surfer* 28, no. 4 (April 1987): 21; Paul Holmes, "The China Exchange: A Surfari with a Difference," *Surfer* 28, no. 6 (June 1987): 54; and Matt George, "Beyond the Great Wall: The First Surfers in China," *Surfer* 28, no. 6 (June 1987): 100–109.

9. On the fledgling Chinese surf culture, see Martin Patience, "Chinese Island of Hainan Prepares to Host Surfing Event," *BBC*, January 29, 2013, www.bbc.co.uk/news/world-asia-21256187, accessed June 26, 2013.

10. *Mon Ran* is Japanese for "Dream Wave." Brandon Zatt, "Treasure Island," *Enterprise China* (May 2008), http://enterprisechina.net/node/402, accessed June 19, 2013.

11. "About Us," Surfing China, n.d., www.surfingchina.org/english/contact.asp, accessed June 19, 2013.

12. Housman, "Surf City, China?"; Zatt, "Treasure Island."

13. Mull, "Will China Become Surfing's Next Frontier?"

14. Zach Weisberg, "A Champion for Surfers and for Causes," *New York Times*, March 27, 2011. On the Chinese policies to which Schumacher objected, see her comment published on March 4, 2011, at 12:26 a.m. in Jeff Mull, "Defending Longboard Champ Boycotts World Title Events: ASP Set to Debut First-Ever Sanctioned Surf Contest in China Amid Controversy," *Surfer* (March 3, 2011), www.surfermag.com/features/defending-longboard-champ-boycotts-world-title-events/, accessed June 21, 2013; and Cori Schumacher, "Why I'm Boycotting," *Inertia*, April 5, 2011, www.theinertia.com/politics/why-im-boycotting-cori-schumacher-longboarding-china/, accessed July 10, 2013.

15. Mull, "Defending Longboard Champ Boycotts World Title Events."

16. See, for example, Chris Grant, "Backbone in a Tilted World: The Cori Schumacher Interview," *JettyGirl Online Surf Magazine*, July 28, 2011, www.jettygirl .com/blog/2011/07/28/backbone-in-a-tilted-world-the-cori-schumacher-interview/, accessed July 10, 2013. See also Schumacher's comment published on March 6, 2011, at 9:52 p.m. in Mull, "Defending Longboard Champ Boycotts World Title Events."

17. For more on women and surfing, see Krista Comer, *Surfer Girls in the New World Order* (Durham, NC: Duke University Press, 2010).

18. Janna Irons, "All Sexy, No Surfing," *Surfer*, July 2, 2013, www.surfermag. com/blogs/opinion/all-sexy-no-surfing/, accessed July 9, 2013.

19. Weisberg, "A Champion for Surfers and for Causes"; Zach Weisberg, "World Champion Boycotts 2011 ASP Tour," *Inertia*, February 27, 2011, www. theinertia.com/politics/cori-schumacher-world-longboard-champion-boycotts -2011-asp-tour-china/, accessed January 23, 2013. On Schumacher's participation in civil rights issues, see her published comment beneath the article in *The Inertia*.

20. Slater, according to *Wait Wait . . . Don't Tell Me!* host Peter Sagal, "may be the coolest person ever to appear on our show"; the program can be downloaded at "Champion Surfer Kelly Slater Plays 'Not My Job,' " *Wait, Wait . . . Don't Tell Me!*, September 19, 2009, www.npr.org/templates/story/story.php?storyId=112978885, accessed June 26, 2013.

21. Ian Rogers, "The Politics of Surfing," *Fistfulayen*, January 5, 2007, www. fistfulayen.com/blog/2007/01/the-politics-of-surfing/, accessed January 28, 2013; Kelly Slater, "Board Politics: Kelly Slater Explains the Abu Ghraib Images on His Board," *Surfline*, June 27, 2007, www.surfline.com/community/whoknows/who knows_bamp.cfm?id=9875, accessed January 21, 2013. For both positive and negative reactions to Slater's board, see Calvin Sloan, "A Letter of Gratitude to Kelly Slater for His Politics," August 12, 2012, http://concarlitos.com/2012/08/12/lettertoslater /, accessed January 21, 2013; and the blog entry and accompanying comments in Rogers, "The Politics of Surfing."

22. Kelly Slater with Phil Jarratt, *For the Love* (San Francisco: Chronicle Books, 2008), 8.

23. Ibid., 14.

24. Ibid., 141.

25. Ibid., 143–46.

26. "Real Talk with Kelly Slater," *Stab*, September 26, 2012, http://stabmag. com/real-talk-with-kelly-slater/, accessed January 22, 2013.

27. Slater with Jarratt, *For the Love*, 142.

28. "Welcome," Surfing 4 Peace, n.d., www.surfing4peace.org/s4pindex/Wel come.html, accessed January 21, 2013.

29. Louise Roug, "In Gaza, Surfers Find Peace and Freedom Riding the Deep Blue," *Los Angeles Times*, July 29, 2007, http://articles.latimes.com/2007/jul/29/world /fg-gazasurf29, accessed January 22, 2013.

30. Warshaw, *The Encyclopedia of Surfing*, 296, 450; see also Dorian Paskowitz, "In the Beginning: A Dr. Dorian Paskowitz Tale," *Surfer's Journal* 22, no. 3 (June/ July 2013): 126–27.

31. "Welcome," Surfing 4 Peace.

32. "History," Surfing 4 Peace, n.d., www.surfing4peace.org/s4pindex/History
.html, accessed January 22, 2013.

33. Editors, "Surfing for Peace: Kelly Slater in True Championship Form,"
Surfer (October 20, 2007), www.surfermag.com/features/slater-surfforpeace/, accessed January 22, 2013.

34. "Gaza Surf Relief," Explore Corps, n.d., www.explorecorps.org/Projects
/Entries/2007/11/14_Gaza_Surf_Relief.html, accessed January 22, 2013; "Gaza Surf
Club," Explore Corps, n.d., at www.explorecorps.org/Projects/Entries/2008/1/15_
Surf_Corps_%26_The_Gaza_Surf_Club.html, accessed January 22, 2013; "Gaza
Surfer Girl Project," May 26, 2011, www.surfing4peace.org/s4pindex/NewsAnd
Events/Entries/2011/5/26_the_GAZA_SURFER_GIRL_project.html, accessed
June 26, 2013.

35. Stephen Boyd, "Surfing a Postnationalist Wave: The Role of Surfing in Irish
Popular Culture," paper presented at L'Irlande et la Culture Populaire/Ireland and
Popular Culture, University of Reims Champagne-Ardenne, October 20, 2012.
I am grateful to Stephen Boyd for providing me with a copy of his paper.

36. So far had surfing come that, in 2000, surfers even created a charitable organization to provide community health and development assistance to a number of
Indonesians; for more on SurfAid International, see www.surfaidinternational.org,
accessed February 6, 2013.

INDEX

Page references in italics indicate illustrations.

11–12, 14–15; population of, 10, 166–67n11; as surfing mecca, 44, 56. *See also* Americanization of Hawaiian surfing

Hawaiian Organic Act (1900), 21

Hawaii Five-O, 169n44

Hawaii Promotion Committee, 33–34, 36, *37*

Hawai'i Tourist Bureau, 23, 38

Hawk, Steve, 181n36

Hawke, Bob, *117*, 117–18, 125, 130

Hays, Wayne, 191n67

Heard, Tony, 108, 207n78

Heath, Joseph, 56, 220n19

Hedemann, Hans, 218n207

Herbert, A. S., 172n76

History of the Hawaiian Islands and Hints to Travelers Visiting the Hawaiian Islands, 29

Ho, Coco, 148

Ho, Derek, 92, 111, 123, 215n171, 216n177, 218n207

Ho, Don, 169n44

Ho, Michael, 92, 111, 123, 215n171, 216nn177,181

Hofmeyr, Nicolaas, 108

Holland, Todd, 218n207

Hollister, 6, 150–53, 223n74

Holman, Lucia Ruggles, 12–13

Holman, Thomas, 12–13

Holmes, Paul, 105, 217n192

Hoole, Dick, 76; *Storm Riders*, 84

Hooper, Paul, 173n86

Horan, Cheyne, 123, 215n167

Houston, James D., 166n9

Hughes, Chip, 86

Hui Nalu, 25

Hui Nalu club, 170nn52,55

Hunter, Genevive, 138

Huntington, Henry, 34

Hurley, 135, 145, 147, 148–49, 154–55

Hurley, Bob, 148–49

Hurley Pro, 219n10

Hustace, Harold, 24

Hynson, Mike, 48–49, 95–97, 201n28

Indonesia: Amnesty International on atrocities in, 72–73, 74; Bali, 64–69, 83, 89, 189n31, 190n41, 198n141; construction as tourist paradise, 62–72, *71*, 89; coup in, 5, 61; East Timor, atrocities in, 62, 73–80, 192n77, 193n78, 194n87; Java, 70, 196n112; Mentawais, 89–90; Nike in, 147; outer-island development of, 77–85, *78*; peacefulness of Indonesians, 71–72; repression/atrocities in, 5, 61–63, 67, 71–72, 85–86, 89, 186n2, 187nn9,10,11, 188n17, 191n67; and Singapore, 65; surfing contests in, 77, 78–81, 195nn95,96; surfing in, 4–5, 62, 64, 70, 76, 190n55 (*see also* Bali; Kuta Beach; Lagundri Bay; Uluwatu); U.S. aid to, 190–91n62

Instinct Clothing, 91, 116–18

Institute for Global Labour and Human Rights, 144

International and World Surfing Championships (Makaha), 45

International Labor Rights Forum, 150

International Professional Surfers Association (IPSA), 110–11

International Seminar on the Eradication of Apartheid, 204n63

International Surf Life Saving Carnival, 41

Iraq War, 160

Irons, Janna, 158

Israeli surfers, 161

Jacobson, Matt, 141

Jarratt, Phil, 109, 110, 113–14, 116, 121, 124, 160, 211n123

Java, 70, 196n112

Jeffreys Bay (South Africa), 93, 129–30, 208n86

Jeffries, Mike, 150

Jerusalem's American Colony, 20–21

Joint Struggle to Crush Expo and the Japan-U.S. Security Treaty, 54

Jones, Howard, 65

Jordan, Michael, 148

Juda, Mohammed, 161

Kahanamoku, Duke, 3, 25–26, *30*, 31–36, 166n9, 174n96, 176–77nn121,122,123

Kame'eleihiwa, Lilikala, 12

Kamehameha I, 9